LUFTWAFFE
HANDBOOK
1935–1945

LUFTWAFFE HANDBOOK
1935–1945

GORDON WILLIAMSON

SUTTON PUBLISHING

First published in the United Kingdom in 2006 by
Sutton Publishing Limited · Phoenix Mill
Thrupp · Stroud · Gloucestershire · GL5 2BU

British Library Cataloguing in Publication Data
A catalogue record for this book is available from the British Library.

ISBN 0-7509- 4119-7

Endpapers, front: A Heinkel He 162 Salamander; *rear:* An early Junkers Ju 87.

Typeset in 10/13pt New Baskerville.
Typesetting and origination by
Sutton Publishing Limited.
Printed and bound in England by
J.H. Haynes & Co. Ltd, Sparkford.

CONTENTS

INTRODUCTION AND ACKNOWLEDGEMENTS

From its creation in 1935 to Germany's final defeat in May 1945, the Luftwaffe grew from a disguised air sports club to a massive organisation in which nearly 3.5 million German soldiers served, not only in flying units and the normal accompanying ground support arms, but dozens of field divisions, paratroop divisions and even the bizarrely titled 'Parachute Panzer Corps' bearing Hermann Göring's name.

The Luftwaffe was the youngest branch of the armed forces. Unlike the Army and Navy, whose histories stretched back for centuries, it was a creation of the Third Reich. Hitler is quoted as saying, 'I have a Christian Navy, a reactionary Army and a National Socialist Luftwaffe.' It is doubtful, nevertheless, whether the bulk of the Luftwaffe's manpower were in reality convinced national socialists, especially as vast numbers of them were conscripts with no choice other than to serve in the branch of the armed forces into which they were assigned. Even in the early days of the service, most of those who joined were simply those with a passion for flying. Certainly, young Germans who developed their interest in flying through uniformed organisations such as the DLV (Deutsche Luftsportverband), NSFK (National Sozialistisches Flieger Korps) and the Hitler Youth (membership of which was compulsory) would have come under considerable Nazi influence, but the main driver for most was the urge to fly, whether in gliders or powered aircraft. There can be no doubt that many who served in the Luftwaffe would indeed have been dedicated Nazis. But this branch, however, also drew men like Werner Mölders, a devout Catholic who spoke out against the regime, and Adolf Galland, who made no bones about the fact that he would refuse orders that required him to act unchivalrously to his adversaries.

In the end, the average soldier serving in the Luftwaffe, whether he was a fighter ace or a foot-slogger in one of the field divisions, was little different from his equivalent in the forces of the other combatant nations, with the same fears and facing the same dangers. After Stalingrad, when the tide of war could be seen by all to have turned irrevocably against Germany, the Luftwaffe soldier must have realised that his sacrifices on the battlefield were merely prolonging the agony of a final and total defeat.

Faced with inadequate training and shortages of fuel, and aircraft which, though they were some of the finest in existence at the start of the war, were now rapidly being surpassed by those of their enemies, the

Luftwaffe's fighter pilots continued to take to the skies, hopelessly outnumbered and knowing that their chances of survival were desperately slim.

In reality, the Luftwaffe was doomed to failure from the start. Superbly equipped for tactical operations in support of the rapidly advancing ground forces of the Blitzkrieg, it was totally unable to mount the type of strategic operations needed to strike deep into the enemy's heartland and destroy the industrial capacity needed to maintain its war effort.

Given the vast size and complexity of the Luftwaffe, a single volume cannot hope to cover every aspect of the organisation. It would require a multi-volume work to do justice to the subject of its uniforms and insignia alone, to say nothing of the aircraft themselves, and the operational histories of its squadrons, field and paratroop divisions, and so on.

This volume aims therefore to give a simple overview of the Luftwaffe. A list of recommended reading for those wishing to study specific areas in greater depth is provided in the Bibliography.

I should particularly like to thank Belgian historian Josef Charita for his kind assistance in providing photographic material for this work. My good friend and keen Luftwaffe collector François Saez also provided many rare photographs from original wartime Luftwaffe fliers' photograph albums in his collection. Thomas Huss of German-Historika (www.german-historica.de) provided a number of excellent photographs. Other wartime photographs and photographs of original militaria were sourced from Jacques Calero, Detlev Niemann (www.detlev-niemann.de), US National Archives and from the author's collection.

CHRONOLOGY

28 June 1919
Treaty of Versailles prohibits Germany from possessing aircraft.

15 April 1925
Agreement signed with Soviet Union permitting German use of Soviet air base near Moscow.

21 May 1926
Paris Aviation Agreement permits German civil aviation.

2 February 1933
Hermann Göring appointed as Reichskommissar für Luftfahrt (Commissioner for Aviation).

25 March 1933 Creation of the Deutsche Luftsportverband (DLV)

9 March 1935
Official announcement of the creation of the Luftwaffe as the third branch of the Wehrmacht.

8 August 1935
Hermann Göring officially appointed as Reichsminister der Luftfahrt und Oberbefehlshaber der Luftwaffe (Minister of Aviation and Commander-in-Chief of the Air Force).

1 September 1939
Outbreak of war.

27 September 1939
Warsaw surrenders after heavy air bombardment by the Luftwaffe.

17 July 1940
The Luftwaffe's night-fighter arm officially formed.

8 August 1940
Start of Luftwaffe's bombing campaign against British radar stations.

10 August 1940
The so-called 'Adlertag', pinnacle of the daylight offensive against Great Britain.

23 August 1940
Commencement of the night bombing offensive against Great Britain (the 'Blitz').

15 September 1940
Largest airborne attack yet on Britain. The Luftwaffe loses fifty-six aircraft.

20 May 1941
Luftwaffe paratroopers begin assault on Crete.

22 June 1941
Commencement of Operation Barbarossa.

21 July 1941
Luftwaffe bombs Moscow.

22 January 1943
Luftwaffe bombers launch Fritz-X radio-guided bombs against British ships, sinking the cruiser HMS *Spartan* and the destroyer HMS *Janus*.

19 February 1944
Heaviest Luftwaffe bombing raid on Great Britain since 1940.

30 March 1944
Luftwaffe inflicts heaviest-ever losses in a single raid on the RAF during an attack on Nuremberg when ninety-six bombers are shot down.

13 June 1944
First V1 flying bomb launched against Great Britain.

8 September 1944
First V2 rockets hit Great Britain.

1 January 1945
Operation Bodenplatte launched, the last major Luftwaffe operation of the Second World War, involving over 700 aircraft.

15 October 1946
Hermann Göring cheats the Nuremberg hangman, committing suicide by taking poison.

CHAPTER ONE

THE INTERWAR YEARS AND THE CREATION OF THE NEW LUFTWAFFE

Following the collapse of the last great offensive on the Western Front in 1918 and the subsequent German surrender, the terms of the Treaty of Versailles saw Germany forbidden to own any military aircraft. The Germans, however, though prohibited from manufacturing military aircraft, continued to study progress in other nations, analysed the lessons learned in the First World War, and began secret experimentation in new technologies. German expertise in aircraft design therefore never faltered.

Aircraft design and manufacture of civilian aircraft was permitted again in limited

As a decorated First World War flying ace and member of the Nazi inner circle, Hermann Wilhelm Göring, shown here in SA brownshirt uniform from the early days of the movement, was a logical choice for appointment by Hitler to the post of commander-in-chief of the new Luftwaffe.

fashion after 1922 and those who would emerge as the great figures in military aircraft design in the not so distant future, names like Hugo Junkers, Ernst Heinkel, Willy Messerschmitt and others, continued to work in the industry. In reality, design and development work never really stopped. Germany entered into secret agreements with a number of other nations to establish research and development sites outside Germany. The most significant of these was the establishment set up near Moscow by the Junkers firm. These sites were also used for the training of future aircrew and technicians. In order to conceal the true nature of their activities, volunteers from the armed forces were required to resign, so that their training would technically be as civilians. Of course, when they were recalled to service once the Luftwaffe was formed, they were quickly reinstated.

In May 1926, all restrictions on the development and production of civil aircraft were lifted. Many of the designs which were produced, though ostensibly civilian in nature, were deliberately planned as being suitable for military use with very little amendment to the basic design. Thus Lufthansa found itself using Junkers 52 trimotors which would become the transport workhorse of the Luftwaffe, and Focke Wulf Fw 200 passenger planes which would become, as the Condor maritime bomber, the scourge of the Allied convoys; and even the Heinkel 111, mainstay of the Luftwaffe bomber squadrons in the Second World War, would see pre-war service with Lufthansa as a mail plane.

Almost as soon as civil flying was legalised once again, the Reichswehr began to plan for the re-creation of a German air force, initially of fifteen squadrons, but in 1931, extended to thirty. The Ministry of Defence (Reichswehr Ministerium) secretly supported and funded the training of future military pilots in

agreement with the civil aviation industry through the Reich's Transport Ministry (Reichs Verkehrsministerium) and in the encouragement and support of 'sport' flying. Future military pilots were even trained under the clever guise of 'advertising' companies, flying aircraft that would tow advertising banners in flights over populated areas. One wonders how many people watching a light aircraft flying over their city towing a banner advertising the local brewery would have realised that they were watching future fighter pilots in the making.

Training of pilots continued throughout the interwar years, with many of those who would become Luftwaffe personnel trained as civilian pilots. One extremely important source of future military pilots was the very popular sport flying culture in Germany. Glider flying had always been a popular pastime and was fostered by a number of youth organisations. This was something that, after the advent of the Nazis, received continuing encouragement through organisations such as the NSFK (National Sozialistisches Flieger Korps) and the DLV (Deutsche Luftsportverband), created in 1933 and which provided training in both glider and powered aircraft under the guise of sporting activities. The NSFK had been created in 1931 by the High Command of the Sturmabteilung (SA), as back-up to the already extant Flieger-SA. Only a few months later, however, control of the NSFK passed to Hermann Göring. When the DLV was created on 25 March 1933, the NSFK and virtually all other flying organisations within Germany were absorbed into it.

Within the DLV was a section known as the Fliegerschaft, who were effectively the DLV aircrew and it was this element which would form the initial cadre of pilots and aircrew for the future Luftwaffe. When the existence of the Luftwaffe was formally announced in 1935, the Fliegerschaft was

Although it is probably the Messerschmitt Me 109 fighter that, to most, epitomises the image of the Luftwaffe, in its early days it was armed predominantly with biplanes, such as the Heinkel He 51, which equipped the majority of the Jagdgeschwadern. (*François Saez*)

absorbed into it, and two years later the DLV was effectively disbanded and those personnel not required for military service channelled into a new, re-created NSFK.

With the coming to power of Hitler in 1933, the build-up of Germany's armed forces had begun in earnest. Hitler insisted on the creation of a new air force as soon as possible and appointed his trusted follower and former fighter pilot Hermann Göring as Minister of Aviation (Reichsminister der Luftfahrt). Through 1933 and 1934 the basic structures were rapidly set in place, the training of pilots accelerated, and the command structure established, with Germany divided into 'air districts' or Luftkreise, analogous to the 'military districts' or Wehrkreise of the Army. Finally, in February 1935, all attempts at secrecy

ceased, and by this time over twenty new military airfields had been completed, with over a dozen more under construction. Hundreds of pilots had been secretly trained, providing a nucleus of skilled personnel who could now begin to pass on their skills and knowledge to a whole new generation of willing volunteers.

On 26 February Hitler had promulgated an order declaring the existence of the new Reichsluftwaffe, which was formally established as the third branch of the German armed forces with Göring, as Minister of Aviation, its commander-in-chief. On 16 March 1935 Hitler reintroduced conscription, and at the same time altered the title of the armed forces from Reichswehr to Wehrmacht. Similarly, the Army changed from Reichsheer to Heer, the Navy from

Reichsmarine to Kriegsmarine and the Air Force from Reichsluftwaffe to Luftwaffe. In August 1935 Göring's status was further clarified when he was officially appointed Minister of Aviation and commander-in-chief of the Air Force (Reichsminister der Luftfahrt und Oberbefehlshaber der Luftwaffe).

Although the secrecy surrounding the existence of a German air force was now gone (in reality the Allied powers were not unaware that Germany was secretly rearming but had done nothing to interfere), efforts were still made to conceal just how fast it was being built up. Over the next few years, production was ordered of large numbers of fighter planes such as the Messerschmitt Bf 109 and Bf 110, the Junkers Ju 87 Stuka and the Heinkel He 111 and Dornier Do 17 light bombers. By 1938 Germany was producing aircraft at the rate of 1,100 per year and by the outbreak of war in 1939 the Luftwaffe possessed over 4,000 aircraft, including over 1,100 bombers, more than 770 single-engine fighters and over 330 dive-bombers.

One major omission in the development of German air power in the interwar years was the complete lack of a naval air arm. Major warships of course carried the usual spotter planes, but these were crewed by Luftwaffe, not naval, pilots. Eventual interservice cooperation, such as that which would occur during the war years between maritime reconnaissance aircraft and U-boats, was always problematic because of poor coordination. There was never any real enthusiasm for the development of a genuine naval air doctrine and aircraft carriers were thought of as unnecessary. The one such vessel that was eventually launched, the *Graf Zeppelin*, was never completed.

By the time of the attack on Poland in September 1939, the Luftwaffe's strength was in the region of 370,000 men, but of this number only around 20,000 were actually aircrew, indicative of the huge number of support personnel required to maintain an effective air arm. The Luftwaffe was able to field 2,000 combat aircraft divided almost equally between bombers and fighters. It was, however, woefully short of stocks of bombs and even those that were available were relatively light, none being over 500kg. The Luftwaffe, in fact, depended on the success of the Blitzkrieg philosophy, as a long-drawn-out campaign would have seen Göring's bombers run out of bombs in little more than three weeks of concentrated operations.

Germany continued to increase production of aircraft throughout the war. Amazingly, despite the continued Allied air assault on Germany, which grew in ferocity with each passing year, German aircraft production increased rather than declined. Production under the control of Albert Speer as Armaments Minister in the second half of the war was phenomenal. From a base figure of 10,800 aircraft built in 1940, the first full year of war, a further 12,400 were built in 1941, 15,400 in 1942, 24,800 in 1943 and 40,600 in 1944. Unfortunately, by this point in time, although there was no shortage of aircraft, there was precious little fuel with which to power them and a desperate shortage of trained pilots to fly them.

As well as the flying units, the Luftwaffe consisted of paratroops and other field formations, anti-aircraft units, communications units, engineers and numerous smaller elements. In all, it is estimated that somewhere around 3.4 million personnel served in the various elements of the Luftwaffe, increasing from 400,000 in 1939, through a peak of 1.7 million in 1942 and reducing to around 1 million in 1945. Of these, around 165,000 were killed in action, with around 155,000 missing, believed killed, and over 190,000 wounded. Throughout the entire war, only 120 Luftwaffe personnel were charged with desertion. The Knight's Cross of the Iron Cross was awarded to 1,785 Luftwaffe soldiers,

Germany's biplane fighters, though of relatively good standard for their day and impressive enough when seen in the massed flying displays with which Hitler loved to demonstrate the power of his armed forces, were to prove wanting when they encountered more modern Curtiss and Polikarpov monoplanes of the Republican forces during the Spanish Civil War. They were quickly relegated to a ground support role once the Messerschmitt Me 109 became available. (*François Saez*)

representing around one-quarter of the total number of these medals awarded.

There can be no doubt that, of the most successful fighter aces ever, the majority are those who flew for the Luftwaffe in the Second World War. Even after taking into account the possibilities of over-optimistic 'kill' claims (which were rare, in fact, as the Luftwaffe had a fairly rigid system for recording successes, which required claims to be witnessed or verified from wreckage, etc.), the scores achieved by most German aces were far in excess of those achieved by their Allied counterparts. It is also true that the majority of Luftwaffe personnel fought as clean a war as circumstances

allowed (as did the Allies, though there were instances of less-chivalrous behaviour by pilots of all the combatant nations in the Second World War).

Many of the night-fighter aces were also spectacularly successful, far more so than those of any other nation. The dive-bombers also had their 'Experten' in pilots such as Hans-Ulrich Rudel, probably the most decorated military personality in history, and many less-well-known, but equally successful, bomber pilots.

As the war progressed and combat attrition saw many of the great aces lost in battle, the percentage of new and inexperienced fliers increased, as did the quality of

The pre-war Luftwaffe did possess a number of excellent trainer aircraft, one of the more interesting of which was the Focke Wulf Fw 56 Stösser, a distinctive, high-wing parasol monoplane with fixed undercarriage. This was a single-seat trainer for advanced flying training once the new pilot was skilled enough to fly solo. (*Josef Charita*)

the opposition they faced. Luftwaffe losses grew apace and as their machines (with a few notable exceptions) began to compare less favourably with new Allied developments, the Germans found themselves changing from hunters to hunted. Ground troops, accustomed to first-class close support from their Air Force colleagues, began wondering where the Luftwaffe had disappeared to. As German ground forces in Normandy in the summer of 1944 were being torn apart by overwhelmingly superior Allied air power, they could be forgiven for feeling that the Luftwaffe had deserted them. German fliers, however, fought with great tenacity and courage to the very last days of the war, suffering in-

creasingly crippling losses against a numerically vastly superior enemy that was far more capable than they were of making good combat losses.

In conclusion, Germany was not failed by the Luftwaffe, but by those who refused to grasp the need for a strategic bomber arm capable of delivering sustained damage to the enemy's industrial capabilities, or the need for a strategic fighter force capable of doing more than simply escorting bombers, until it was too late. Political interference ensured that, although technically superior aircraft such as the Me 262 jet did see combat, opportunities were wasted by insisting on their use in a totally inappropriate role.

CHAPTER TWO

ORGANISATION AND COMMAND STRUCTURE

The supreme commander of all of the armed forces (Oberste Befehlshaber der Wehrmacht) was, from 1938 when he decided to take direct control of them, Adolf Hitler. Under Hitler in the chain of command sat a supreme commander for each of the three branches of the armed forces, the Oberbefehlshaber der Marine (Ob.d.M.), Oberbefehlshaber der Luftwaffe (Ob.d.L.) and the Oberbefehlshaber des Heeres (Ob.d.H.).

Hermann Göring held the post of Oberbefehlshaber der Luftwaffe until the closing days of the war, and at the same time

Hermann Göring as Generalfeldmarschall, holding the post of Reichsminister der Luftfahrt und Oberbefehlshaber der Luftwaffe. This photograph was taken just before the outbreak of war, as evidenced by the lack of Second World War decorations.

was Minister of Aviation (Reichsminister der Luftfahrt) and sat at the Air Ministry (Reichsluftfahrtministerium, or RLM) in Berlin. On his final fall from grace in the closing days of the war, on 25 April 1945 Göring was sacked and replaced as commander-in-chief of the Luftwaffe by Generalfeldmarschall Robert Ritter von Greim. Greim then held the post for a mere thirteen days, until the surrender on 8 May 1945.

With Göring at its head, Luftwaffe High Command, the Oberkommando der Luftwaffe, or OKL, was divided into two branches. The forward element, bearing the code-name 'Robinson', was headed by the Chief of the Luftwaffe General Staff and included the Operations Staff, the Commander of Signals, the Commander of Training and elements of the Luftwaffe Intelligence. This section of the Luftwaffe High Command was located in proximity to the C-in-C Armed Forces. A second, rear element, code-named 'Kurfürst', was made up of all of the other departments of the Luftwaffe High Command and was based in Berlin. The two were kept in very close touch by a number of liaison officers, assisted by a first-class communications network.

Directly responsible to Göring was the Luftwaffe General Staff (Generalstabes der Luftwaffe), a post held by the following officers:

General Walther Wever	1 Mar 1935–3 Jun 1936
Generalfeldmarschall Albert Kesselring	5 Jun 1936–31 May 1937
Generaloberst Hans-Jürgen Stumpff	1 Jun 1937–31 Jan 1939
Generaloberst Hans Jeschonnek	1 Feb 1939–19 Aug 1943
Generaloberst Günther Korten	25 Aug 1943–22 Jul 1944
General der Flieger Werner Kreipe	1 Aug 1944–Oct 1944
General der Flieger Karl Koller	12 Nov 1944–8 May 1945

Sitting below the General Staff was the Leadership Staff of the Air Force, (Luftwaffenführungsstabes) headed by its own 'Chef' or chief. The following officers held the post of Chef der Luftwaffenführungsstabes:

General der Flieger Bernhard Kühl	1934–Spring 1936
General der Flieger Wilhelm Mayer	Spring 1936–Apr 1937
General der Flieger Paul Deichmann	Apr 1937–Sep 1937
General der Flieger Bernhard Kühl	Sep 1937–28 Feb 1939
General der Flieger Otto Hoffmann von Waldau	1 Sep 1939–10 Apr 1942
Generaloberst Hans Jeschonnek	10 Apr 1942–mid-Mar 1943
General der Flieger Rudolf Meister	mid-Mar 1943–mid-Oct 1943
General der Flieger Karl Koller	mid-Oct 1943–mid-Aug 1944
General der Flieger Eckhardt Christian	mid-Aug 1944–12 Apr 1945
General der Flieger Karl Heinz Schulz	12 Apr 1945–8 May 1945

Matters relating to the Luftwaffe were the subject of two daily conferences, the principal of which was the afternoon meeting at the Führerhauptquartier, attended by the chiefs of staff of all three services and presided over by Hitler himself. In the course of these meetings the general progress of the war was discussed and strategic decisions at the highest level were made. Operational instructions in the furtherance of these decisions were sent directly to individual Luftflotte commanders from the 'Robinson' element of the General Staff.

LUFTGAUE

Within Germany, and later in the occupied territories, the basic organisational unit of the Air Force was the Luftgau, or air district, which was responsible for administration, supply, training, maintenance, etc. The location of the Luftgau could be variable. The following Luftgaue were formed:

LUFTGAU I

Formed Aug 1938

Location: Königsberg (1938–45), Schloppe (1945)

Known Commanding Officers

Generalleutnant Johannes Lentzsch	Aug 1938–Jan 1939
Generalmajor Max Mohr	Jan 1939–May 1939
General der Flieger Walter Musshoff	Jun 1939–Feb 1940
Generalleutnant Wilhelm Wimmer	Feb 1940–May 1940
Generalleutnant Wilhelm Süssmann	May 1940–Jan 1941
General der Flieger Richard Putzier	Jan 1941–Aug 1943
General der Flieger Hellmuth Bieneck	Aug 1943–Aug 1944
General der Flieger Albert Vierling	Aug 1944–Feb 1945

Disbanded Feb 1945

LUFTGAU II

Formed Oct 1937, disbanded Apr 1938, re-formed Sep 1939

Location: Stettin (1937–8), Posen (1938–43)

Known Commanding Officers

Oberst Wolfgang Wiegand	Oct 1937–Apr 1938
Generalmajor Kamillo Ruggera	Sep 1939–Feb 1941
Generalleutnant Hellmuth Bieneck	Feb 1941–Jan 1943

Absorbed into Luftgau I, Jan 1943

LUFTGAU III

Formed Apr 1937

Location: Hamburg (1937), Berlin (1937–45)

Known Commanding Officers

Generalleutnant Max Mohr	Apr 1937–June 1937
General der Flieger Albert Kesselring	Jun 1947–Oct 1937
Generalmajor Graf von Sponeck	Oct 1937–Mar 1938
Generaloberst Hubert Weise	Mar 1938–Oct 1939
Generalmajor Gerhard Hoffmann	Oct 1939–Jun 1940
General der Flakartillerie Alfred Haubold	Jul 1940–Mar 1943
Generalleutnant Walter Friedensberg	Mar 1943–Aug 1943
General der Flakartillerie Gerhard Hoffmann	Aug 1943–Feb 1945
General der Flieger Walter Boenicke	Feb 1945–Apr 1945

LUFTGAU IV

Formed Apr 1936

Location: Berlin (1936–7), Dresden (1937– 41)

Known Commanding Officers

Generalmajor Graf von Sponeck	Apr 1936–Oct 1937
General der Flieger Wilhelm Mayer	Oct 1937–Dec 1941

Redesignated Luftgau Moskau in Dec 1941

Generalmajor Emil Zenetti commanded Luftgau V from October 1937 to June 1938. Zenetti reached the rank of General der Flakartillerie and was decorated with the Knight's Cross of the War Merit Cross with Swords for his services to the war effort on 26 March 1945. (*Josef Charita*)

LUFTGAU V

Formed Oct 1937, disbanded Jun 1938, re-formed Sep 1944

Location: Stuttgart (1937–45)

Known Commanding Officers
Generalmajor Emil Zenetti	Oct 1937–Jun 1938
Generalleutnant Karl Drum	Sep 1944
Generalleutnant Herbert Rieckhoff	Sep 1944–Apr 1945

Disbanded Apr 1945

LUFTGAU VI

Formed Apr 1936

Location: Breslau (1936–7), Münster (1937– 45)

Known Commanding Officers
Generalmajor Rudolf Bogatsch	Apr 1936–Nov 1937
General der Flieger August Schmidt	Nov 1937–Jan 1944
Generalleutnant Ernst Dörffler	Jan 1944–Apr 1945

Disbanded Apr 1945

Rudolf Bogatsch, shown here as a General der Flieger, commanded Luftgau VI from April 1936 to November 1937, and Luftgau IX from March to August 1944. He subsequently served as liaison with the Oberbefehlshaber des Heeres and was decorated with the Knight's Cross of the Iron Cross on 20 March 1942.

LUFTGAU VII

Formed Oct 1937

Location: Bavaria
Munich (1937–44), Kloster Scheyern (1944–5), Markt Schwaben (1945)

Known Commanding Officers
General der Flakartillerie Emil Zenetti   Jul 1938–Sep 1944
Generalleutnant Wolfgang Vorwald   Sep 1944–Apr 1945

LUFTGAU VIII

Formed Oct 1937

Location: Breslau (1937–43), Kracow (1943–4), Breslau (1945), Prague (1945)

Known Commanding Officers
General der Flieger Bernhard Waber   May 1939–Oct 1941
General der Flieger Walter Somme   Nov 1941–Aug 1944
General der Flieger Veit Fischer   Aug 1944–May 1945

LUFTGAU IX

Location: Hannover (1936), Weimar (1937–8)

Known Commanding Officers
General der Flieger Rudolf Bogatsch   Mar 1944–Aug 1944

Disbanded Aug 1944

LUFTGAU XI

Formed Oct 1937

Location: Hannover (1937–40), Hamburg (1940–5)

Known Commanding Officers
General der Flieger Ludwig Wolff   Oct 1937–May 1945

LUFTGAU XII

Formed Oct 1937

Location: Giessen (1937–8), Wiesbaden (1938–44)

Known Commanding Officers

General der Flakartillerie Friedrich Heilingbrunner	Mar 1938–Mar 1944

Disbanded Apr 1944

LUFTGAU XIII

Formed Oct 1937, disbanded 1941, re-formed Jan 1943, disbanded May 1943

Location: Nuremberg

Known Commanding Officers

General der Flakartillerie Dr Eugen Weissmann	Sep 1939–Jun 1940
General der Flakartillerie Friedrich Heilingbrunner	Jan 1943–May 1943

LUFTGAU XIV

Formed Sep 1944

Location: Wiesbaden (1944–5)

Known Commanding Officers

Generalleutnant Martin Harlinghausen	Sep 1944–Apr 1945

Disbanded Mar 1945

LUFTGAU XV

Formed 1944

Location: Prague (1944–5)

Known Commanding Officers

General der Flieger Kuno-Heribert Fütterer	Dec 1944–Jan 1945
General der Flieger Alfred Bülowius	Jan 1945–Feb 1945
General der Flieger Kuno-Heribert Fütterer	Feb 1945–Apr 1945

Disbanded Apr 1945

LUFTGAU XVI

Formed Dec 1944

Location: Dresden

Known Commanding Officers

General der Flieger Alfred Bülowius	Oct 1944–Dec 1944
General der Flieger Willi Harmjanz	Dec 1944–Jan 1945
General der Flieger Alfred Bülowius	Jan 1945

Disbanded Jan 1945

LUFTGAU XVII

Location: Vienna (1939–45)

Known Commanding Officers

General der Flakartillerie Friedrich Hirschauer	Sep 1939–Jul 1942
General der Flieger Rudolf Bogatsa	Jul 1942–Sep 1943
General der Flieger Stefan Frölich	Sep 1943–Feb 1944
General der Flieger Egon Doerstling	Feb 1944–May 1945

LUFTGAU XXV

Location: Russia

Known Commanding Officers

General der Flieger Albert Vierling	Jun 1943–Aug 1944

Disbanded Aug 1944

LUFTGAU XXVI

Location: Riga (1943–4)

Known Commanding Officers

General der Flieger Richard Putzier	Aug 1943–Aug 1944

Disbanded Aug 1944

LUFTGAU XXVII

Location: Smolensk (1943–4)

Known Commanding Officers
General der Flieger Veit Fischer   Apr 1943–Aug 1944

Disbanded Aug 1944

LUFTGAU XXVIII

Location: Milan (1943–4)

Known Commanding Officers
General der Flieger Alfred Mahnke   Jul 1943–Aug 1944

Disbanded Sep 1944

LUFTGAU XXX

Location: Belgrade (1943–4)

Known Commanding Officers
General Bernhard Waber   Jul 1943–Aug 1944

Disbanded August 1944

LUFTGAU BALKAN

Location: Greece

Known Commanding Officers
General der Flieger Alexander Andrae   Apr 1941–Jul 1941

Disbanded Jul 1941

LUFTGAU BELGIEN-NORDFRANKREICH

Formed Jun 1940

Location: Brussels

Known Commanding Officers
Generalmajor Fritz Löb   Jun 1940
General der Flieger Kurt Pflugbeil   Jun 1940–Aug 1940
General der Flieger Alexander Andrae   Aug 1940–Sep 1944

Disbanded Sep 1944

LUFTGAU CHARKOW

Location: Charkow

Known Commanding Officers
General der Flieger Bernhard Waber   Sep 1942–Mar 1943

Absorbed into Luftgau XXV, Jun 1943

LUFTGAU FINNLAND

Location: Finland

Known Commanding Officers
General der Flieger Julius Schulz   Aug 1941–Nov 1943

Absorbed into Kommandierender General der Deutschen Luftwaffe in Finnland, Nov 1943

LUFTGAU HOLLAND

Location: Amsterdam

Known Commanding Officers
General der Flakartillerie Alfred Haubold   May 1940–Jul 1940
General der Flieger Hans Siburg   Jul 1940–Aug 1943
General der Flieger Egon Doerstling   Aug 1943–Jan 1944

Disbanded Jan 1944

LUFTGAU KIEW

Location: Kiev

Known Commanding Officers
General der Flieger Bernhard Waber   Oct 1941–Sep 1942

Absorbed into Luftgau Charkow, Sep 1942

LUFTGAU MOSKAU

Location: Minsk

Known Commanding Officers
General der Flieger Veit Fischer   Oct 1941–Mar 1943

Redesignated Luftgau XXVII, Apr 1943

LUFTGAU NORWEGEN

Location: Oslo (1940–4)

Known Commanding Officers

General der Flieger Karl Kitzinger	Apr 1940–Jun 1941
General der Flieger Willi Harmjanz	Jun 1941–Jan 1944
Generalleutnant Eduard Ritter von Schleich	Jan 1944–Oct 1944

Redesignated Kommandierender General der Deutschen Luftwaffe in Norwegen, Oct 1944

LUFTGAU PETERSBURG

Location: Riga

Known Commanding Officers

Generalmajor Hans Prockl	1942–3

Redesignated Luftgau XXVI, Apr 1943

LUFTGAU ROSTOW

Location: Rostov

Known Commanding Officers

General der Flieger Albert Vierling	Oct 1941–Jun 1943

Redesignated Luftgau XXV, Jun 1943

LUFTGAU SÜD

Location: Munich

Known Commanding Officers

General der Flieger Alfred Mahnke	Jun 1943–Jul 1943

Disbanded Jul 1943

LUFTGAU SÜDOST

Location: Greece

Known Commanding Officers

General der Flieger Wilhelm Mayer	Oct 1941–Jun 1943

Disbanded Jul 1943

LUFTGAU TUNIS

Location: Tunis

Known Commanding Officers

General der Flieger Gottlob Müller　　　　　　Mar 1943–Jul 1943

Disbanded Jul 1943

LUFTGAU WARSCHAU

Location: Warsaw

Known Commanding Officers

General der Flieger Friedrich Cranz　　　　　　May 1940–Sep 1940

Disbanded Sep 1940

LUFTGAU WESTFRANKREICH

Location: Paris (1940–4)

Known Commanding Officers

General der Flakartillerie Eugen Weissmann　　　Jun 1940–Jul 1940
General Eugen Weissmann　　　　　　　　　　Aug 1940–Jun 1944
General der Flieger Karl Drum　　　　　　　　Jul 1944–Sep 1944

Redesignated Luftgau V, Sep 1944

LUFTFLOTTEN

Operationally, the air force was organised into Luftflotten, or Air Fleets. The Luftflottenkommando, or Air Fleet Commands were also established on a district or regional basis, each being commanded by a very senior officer, often of the rank of Generaloberst or even Generalfeldmarschall, who was responsible for the formations under him in their operational role. Under the control of each Luftflotte would be a number of subsidiary commands: the Fliegerkorps, the Fliegerdivision, the Jagdkorps, the Jagddivision, and the Jagdfliegerführer.

Further, there were local commands known as Fliegerführer, or Air Commander, e.g. Fliegerführer Atlantik, Fliegerführer Afrika, etc. Thus, for instance, a fighter unit could be under the control of a Jagdfliegerführer (Jafü), or Fighter Commander for its tactical employment, which was in turn subordinated to a Fliegerkorps or Fliegerdivision under the final control of the Luftflotte. At the outbreak of war, four Luftflotten existed, with more being created as the situated merited. The following Luftflotten were formed:

LUFTFLOTTE 1

Known Commanding Officers

Generalfeldmarschall Albert Kesselring	Sep 1939–Jan 1940
Generaloberst Hans-Jürgen Stumpff	Jan 1940–May 1940
General der Flieger Wilhelm Wimmer	May 1940–Aug 1940
Generaloberst Alfred Keller	Aug 1940–Jun 1943
Generaloberst Günther Korten	Jun 1943–Aug 1943
General der Flieger Kurt Pflugbeil	Aug 1943–Apr 1945

Areas of Operation

1939 – Germany
1942 – Central Sector Eastern Front
1943 – Baltic
1945 – Lithuania

Constituent Units 1939

Aufklärungsgruppe 10	Aufklärungsgruppe 120
Aufklärungsgruppe 11	Aufklärungsgruppe 121
Aufklärungsgruppe 21	Jagdgeschwader 1
Aufklärungsgruppe 41	Jagdgeschwader 2
	Jagdgeschwader 3

Albert Kesselring, seen here as a Generalfeldmarschall, was one of Germany's better field marshals and a holder of the Knight's Cross with Oakleaves, Swords and Diamonds. Kesselring was the first commander of the first air fleet to be formed, Luftflotte 1. (*Josef Charita*)

Jagdgeschwader 20
Jagdgeschwader 21
Kampfgeschwader 1
Kampfgeschwader 2
Kampfgeschwader 3
Kampfgeschwader 4
Kampfgeschwader 25
Kampfgeschwader 152
Lehrgeschwader 2
Sturzkampfgeschwader 1
Sturzkampfgeschwader 2
Zerstörergeschwader 1
Zerstörergeschwader 2

Constituent Units 1943
Aufklärungsgruppe 22
Aufklärungsgruppe 122
Jagdgeschwader 54
Kampfgeschwader 53
Nachtaufklärungsgruppe
Nahaufklärungsgruppe 8
Nahaufklärungsgruppe 11
Seeaufklärungsgruppe 127
Störkampfstaffeln Luftflotte 1
Sturzkampfgeschwader 5

LUFTFLOTTE 2

Known Commanding Officers

General der Flieger Hellmuth Felmy	Sep 1939–Jan 1940
Generalfeldmarschall Albert Kesselring	Jan 1940–Jun 1943
Generalfeldmarschall Wolfram Freiherr von Richthofen	Jun 1943–Sep 1944

Areas of Operation
1939 – Germany
1942 – North Africa, Greece, Italy
1944 – Italy

Disbanded Sep 1944

Constituent Units 1939
Aufklärungsgruppe 12
Aufklärungsgruppe 122
Jagdgeschwader 26
Kampfgeschwader 26
Kampfgeschwader 27
Kampfgeschwader 28
Zerstörergeschwader 26

Constituent Units 1943
Aufklärungsgruppe 12
Aufklärungsgruppe 122
Jagdgeschwader 27
Jagdgeschwader 51

Jagdgeschwader 53
Jagdgeschwader 77
Ju 90 Staffel
Kampfgeschwader 1
Kampfgeschwader 26
Kampfgeschwader 30
Kampfgeschwader 54
Kampfgeschwader 76
Kampfgeschwader 77
Korps Transport Staffel
Lehrgeschwader 1
Nachtjagdgeschwader 2
Savoy Staffel
Schlachtgeschwader 2

Schnellkampfgeschwader 10	Transportgeschwader 5
Seeaufklärungsgruppe 126	Transportgruppe 30
Seetransport Staffel	Zerstörergeschwader 1
Transportgeschwader 1	Zerstörergeschwader 26

LUFTFLOTTE 3

Known Commanding Officers

Generalfeldmarschall Hugo Sperrle	Sep 1939–Aug 1944
Generaloberst Otto Dessloch	Aug 1944–Sep 1944
Generalleutnant Alexander Holle	Sep 1944

Areas of Operation

1939 – Germany
1942 – France, Holland, Belgium
1944 – France, Holland, Belgium
1945 – Holland, Germany

Redesignated Luftwaffen-Kommando West in Sep 1944

Affecting his trademark monocle, the typically unsmiling Generalfeldmarschall Hugo Sperrle was commander of Luftflotte 3 from the outbreak of war until August 1944. He was decorated with the Knight's Cross of the Iron Cross on 17 May 1940 for the part played by his forces in the Polish campaign and the campaign in the west. (*Josef Charita*)

Constituent Units 1939

Aufklärungsgruppe 13
Aufklärungsgruppe 22
Aufklärungsgruppe 23
Aufklärungsgruppe 123
Jagdgeschwader 51
Jagdgeschwader 52
Jagdgeschwader 53
Jagdgeschwader 70
Jagdgeschwader 71
Jagdgeschwader 72
Kampfgeschwader 51
Kampfgeschwader 53
Kampfgeschwader 54
Kampfgeschwader 55
Sturzkampfgeschwader 51
Zerstörergeschwader 52

Constituent Units 1943

Aufklärungsfliegerstaffel 222
Aufklärungsgruppe 33
Aufklärungsgruppe 122
Aufklärungsgruppe 123
Jagdgeschwader 2
Jagdgeschwader 26
Jagdgeschwader 54
Kampfgeschwader 2
Kampfgeschwader 40
Kampfgeschwader 66
Korpstransport Staffel
Küstenfliegergruppe 196
Nahaufklärungsgruppe 13
Schnellkampfgeschwader 10

LUFTFLOTTE 4

Known Commanding Officers

Generaloberst Alexander Löhr	Sep 1939–Jul 1942
Generalfeldmarschall Wolfram Freiherr von Richthofen	Jul 1942–Sep 1943
Generaloberst Otto Dessloch	Sep 1943–Aug 1944
Generalleutnant Alexander Holle	Aug 1944–Sep 1944
General Otto Dessloch	Sep 1944–Apr 1945

Areas of Operation

1939 – Germany
1942 – Southern Sector, Russian Front
1944 – Hungary, Yugoslavia, Romania, Bulgaria
1945 – Hungary, Yugoslavia

Redesignated Luftwaffen-Kommando 4 in Apr 1945

Constituent Units 1939

Aufklärungsgruppe 14
Aufklärungsgruppe 31
Aufklärungsgruppe 124
Jagdgeschwader 76
Jagdgeschwader 77
Kampfgeschwader 76
Kampfgeschwader 77

Sturzkampfgeschwader 76
Sturzkampfgeschwader 77
Zerstörergeschwader 76

Constituent Units 1943

Aufklärungsgruppe 22
Aufklärungsgruppe 23
Aufklärungsgruppe 100

Aufklärungsgruppe 121
Aufklärungsgruppe 122
Jagdgeschwader 3
Jagdgeschwader 51
Jagdgeschwader 52
Kampfgeschwader 3
Kampfgeschwader 27
Kampfgeschwader 51
Kampfgeschwader 55
Kampfgeschwader 100
Korps Transport Staffeln
Nachtaufklärungsgruppe
Nahaufklärungsgruppe 1

Nahaufklärungsgruppe 6
Nahaufklärungsgruppe 9
Nahaufklärungsgruppe 14
Schlachtgeschwader 1
Schlachtgeschwader 2
Seeaufklärungsgruppe 125
Störkampfstaffeln Luftflotte 4
Sturzkampfgeschwader 2
Sturzkampfgeschwader 3
Sturzkampfgeschwader 77
Transportgeschwader 3
Zerstörergeschwader 1

LUFTFLOTTE 5

Known Commanding Officers

Generalfeldmarschall Erhard Milch	Apr 1940–May 1940
Generaloberst Hans-Jürgen Stumpff	May 1940–Nov 1943
General der Flieger Josef Kammhuber	Nov 1943–Sep 1944

Areas of Operation
1942–4 Norway, Finland

Disbanded Sep 1944

Generalleutnant Josef Kammhuber was best known for his role as commander of Germany's night-fighter defences, a role he first assumed in July 1940. Promoted to General der Flieger, he was appointed commander of Luftflotte 5 in November 1943 and held the post until September 1944.

Constituent Units 1940
Aufklärungsgruppe 22
Aufklärungsgruppe 121
Aufklärungsgruppe 124
Jagdgeschwader 77
Kampfgeschwader 26
Kampfgeschwader 30
Küstenfliegergruppe 506
Zerstörergeschwader 76

Constituent Units 1943
Aufklärungsgruppe 22
Aufklärungsgruppe 32

Aufklärungsgruppe 120
Aufklärungsgruppe 124
Jagdgeschwader 5
Kampfgeschwader 30
Korps Transport Staffel
Küstenfliegergruppe 196
Küstenfliegergruppe 406
Küstenfliegergruppe 706
Küstenfliegergruppe 906
Seeaufklärungsgruppe 125
Transportgruppe 20
Versuchsverband des Oberkommando der
Luftwaffe

LUFTFLOTTE 6

Known Commanding Officers

Generalfeldmarschall Robert Ritter von Greim	May 1943–Apr 1945
Generaloberst Otto Dessloch	Apr 1945–May 1945

Areas of Operation
1944 – Central Sector, Russian Front
1945 – East Prussia

General der Flieger Otto Dessloch was, at various points, commander of Luftflotten 3, 4 and 6. A highly respected figure, he was decorated with the Knight's Cross of the Iron Cross on 24 June 1940 for his command of II Flak Korps during the Polish and western campaigns. He later received the Oakleaves on 10 May 1944 for his command of Luftflotte 4. Dessloch survived the war.

Constituent Units 1943

Aufklärungsgruppe 11	Korps Transport Staffel
Aufklärungsgruppe 14	Nachtaufklärungsgruppe
Aufklärungsgruppe 100	Nahaufklärungsgruppe 3
Aufklärungsgruppe 121	Nahaufklärungsgruppe 4
Jagdgeschwader 26	Nahaufklärungsgruppe 5
Jagdgeschwader 51	Nahaufklärungsgruppe 10
Kampfgeschwader 1	Nahaufklärungsgruppe 15
Kampfgeschwader 4	Störkampfstaffeln Luftflotte 6
Kampfgeschwader 51	Sturzkampfgeschwader 1
	Zerstörergeschwader 1

LUFTFLOTTE 10

Known Commanding Officers

General der Flieger Hans-Georg von Seidel	Jul 1944–Feb 1945
General der Flieger Stefan Frölich	Feb 1945–Apr 1945

LUFTFLOTTE REICH

Known Commanding Officers

Generaloberst Hans-Jürgen Stumpff	Feb 1944–May 1945

Areas of Operation
1944–5 – Germany

On a tactical level, the largest formation was the Geschwader, roughly equivalent to the Wing in the RAF. This would have on strength anything between 80 and 90 aircraft for bomber units to 120 for fighters (the latter increased to around 160 later in the war). The Geschwader was commanded by a Kommodore, with a minimum rank of Major but more often an Oberstleutnant or Oberst. The Geschwader was designated by its type, thus Jagdgeschwader for a Fighter Wing, Kampfgeschwader for a Bomber Wing, etc.

Answering to the Geschwaderkommodore was a staff consisting of a 'Ia' (Operations Officer), an Adjutant, a 'IIa' (Assistant Adjutant with commissioned rank), a 'IIb' (Assistant Adjutant with senior non-commissioned rank), a Staff Major, a 'Ic' (Intelligence Officer), as well as a Nachrichten Offizier (Intelligence/Signals Officer), a Technisches Offizier (Technical Officer), a Kfz-Offizier (Transport Officer) and a 'IVa' (Administrative Officer).

The Geschwader was made up of a number of Gruppen (Groups), normally three in the early part of the war, but later expanded to four. It was not uncommon for the various Gruppen of a Geschwader to be widely dispersed, sometimes even in totally different theatres, depending on operational necessity.

The Gruppe was commanded by a Gruppenkommandeur, usually a senior experienced Hauptmann or a Major, with his own administrative staff (Gruppenstab). At this command level, the commander was very much an active service officer, flying combat missions on a regular basis. A Gruppe would normally have on strength around 40–50 aircraft and approximately 500 personnel. Within the Gruppe would be a number of Staffeln, or Squadrons, with typically between twelve and sixteen aircraft, commanded by a Staffelkapitän, or Squadron Leader, usually an Oberleutnant or Hauptmann. The Staffel would then be subdivided operationally into a number of sections (the Schwarm), normally with four aircraft and flights (the Rotte for fighters and Kette for bombers).

The nomenclature used in period documentation had the unit designation abbreviated. Thus Jagdgeschwader became JG, Kampfgeschwader KG, etc., with a Roman numeral prefix indicating the Gruppe and an Arabic numeral indicating the Staffel.

Hence I./KG3 would indicate I Gruppe of Kampfgeschwader 3, and 2./JG26 would indicate 2 Staffel of Jagdgeschwader 26.

The following types of Geschwader were formed:

JAGDGESCHWADERN (FIGHTER WINGS), ABBREVIATED TO JG

Jagdgeschwader 1 'Oesau'

Operated on the Western Front, seeing action in France, Norway, Holland, on the Eastern Front and in the defence of Germany (Reichsverteidigung) against the Allied bombing campaigns. Initially equipped with the Me 109, it later flew Fw 190s and, in the closing stages of the war, the

A ground crew member carefully paints the Geschwader emblem, a white shield with red letter 'R', on to the fuselage side of a Messerschmitt Me 109 fighter of Jagdgeschwader 2 Richthofen. As with fighter squadrons of all nations, the use of distinguishing emblems was widespread within the Jagdgeschwadern. (*Josef Charita*)

Heinkel He 162 jet. In May 1944 it was officially named after its Kommodore, Walter Oesau, who had been killed in action, but no cuffband was authorised.

Jagdgeschwader 2 'Richthofen'

Saw action in the Polish campaign, the campaign in the west against France and the Low Countries, the Battle of Britain, North Africa, Sicily, Italy and the defence of the Reich. Principal aircraft was the Me 109.

Jagdgeschwader 3 'Udet'

Saw action in the campaign in the west, the Battle of Britain, and the Eastern Front (where missions were flown at major battles such as Cholm, Demjansk, Stalingrad and the Kursk offensive), the Western Front in 1944 (where it participated in the Ardennes offensive) and the final battles in the east. Both the Me 109 and Fw 190 were flown.

Jagdgeschwader 4

Formed in 1943. Saw action predominantly in Italy until late 1944. Subsequently it took part in the Ardennes offensive, and the final battles on the Eastern Front. Equipped with both the Me 109 and Fw 190.

Jagdgeschwader 5

Known unofficially as the 'Eismeer Geschwader' (Arctic Wing). Operated in the far north of Norway and the northern sector of the Eastern Front, though some elements operated in the central and southern sectors. Ended the war in Norway. It was predominantly equipped with the Me 109.

Jagdgeschwader 6 'Horst Wessel'

Formed in late summer 1944 around a cadre from ZG26. It was equipped with the Fw 190 and took part in the defence of the Reich and in the Ardennes offensive before moving to the Eastern Front.

Jagdgeschwader 7

Formed in summer 1944, this unit was equipped with the Me 262 jet fighter. Predominantly involved in the defence of the Reich.

Jagdgeschwader 10

Formed in the spring of 1943, and assigned to the defence of the Reich.

Jagdgeschwader 11

Formed in the spring of 1943 and initially assigned to the defence of the Reich. Elements moved to the Eastern Front in mid-1944. In September 1944 it was once again on the Western Front and took part in the defensive actions at Arnhem, and in the Ardennes offensive, before moving eastwards once again in early 1945. It took part in the defence of Berlin before moving to Schleswig-Holstein in the closing days of the war.

Jagdgeschwader 25

Formed in August 1943 and assigned to the defence of the Reich. Equipped with a high-altitude version of the Me 109 for interception of Allied reconnaissance aircraft. Disbanded in December 1943.

Jagdgeschwader 26 'Schlageter'

Participated in the campaign in the west, the Battle of Britain, North Africa and the defence of the Reich. It ended the war in Schleswig-Holstein. Both the Me 109 and Fw 190 were flown.

Jagdgeschwader 27

Saw action in the Polish campaign, the campaign in the west, the Balkan campaign, the Eastern Front, North Africa, Sicily, Italy, the defence of the Reich and the Ardennes offensive. Having fought on virtually every front, it ended the war in Schleswig-Holstein.

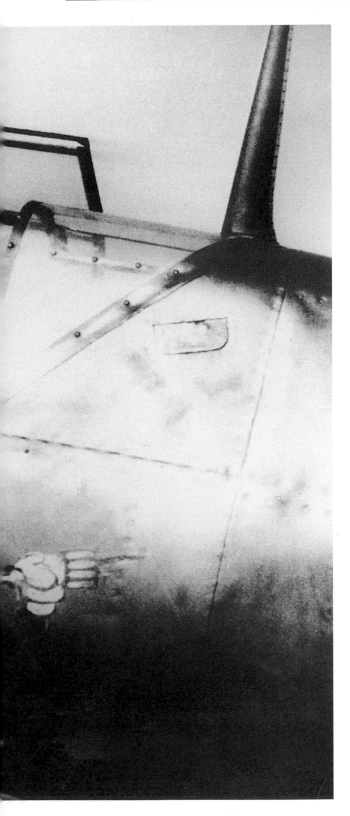

This aircraft from Jagdgeschwader 26 Schlageter carries a wider than usual range of distinguishing insignia. The foremost emblem is a white shield with black Gothic letter 'S' commemorating Albert Leo Schlageter. The snorting bull and Mickey Mouse emblems, particularly the latter, were also widely used in this unit, whose foremost pilot, Adolf Galland, had used the Mickey Mouse emblem since his days in Spain with the Condor Legion. (*Josef Charita*)

Jagdgeschwader 50
Formed in the summer of 1943 and equipped with a special high-altitude interceptor version of the Me 109. Disbanded November 1943.

Jagdgeschwader 51 'Mölders'
Formed before the outbreak of war and saw action in the Battle of Britain before moving to the Eastern Front, where it supported the drive on Moscow. Elements saw action in North Africa, Sicily, Italy and the Balkans, as well as the defence of the Reich. Part of the Geschwader moved to Schleswig-Holstein in the closing days of the war, but much of it went into Soviet captivity. Aircraft flown included the Me 109, Fw 190 and Hs 129 ground-attack fighter.

Jagdgeschwader 52
Saw action in the campaign in the west and actions over the English Channel. From 1941 it served on the Eastern Front, where elements of the Geschwader served on virtually all sectors. At the end of the war, most of its personnel escaped to the west and surrendered to the Americans, but were then handed over to the Soviets and spent many years in captivity. The Me 109 was the principal type flown by this Geschwader.

Jagdgeschwader 53 'Pik As'
Known as the 'Pik-As', or Ace of Spades, wing because of the insignia they carried,

Having joined the Luftwaffe at the age of 18, Leutnant Gerhard Köppen of Jagdgeschwader 52 was decorated with the Knight's Cross in December 1941, while still an NCO pilot, for 40 victories, most of which were achieved on the Eastern Front. He received the Oakleaves while serving with 7./JG52 in February 1942, having reached a score of 72 aerial victories, and was personally promoted to Leutnant by Hermann Göring. He was shot down and killed over the Crimea in May 1942.

this Geschwader saw action in the campaign in the west and the Battle of Britain before moving to the Eastern Front, where it operated in the southern sector. Elements saw action in North Africa, Sicily and Italy and in the defence of the Reich.

Jagdgeschwader 54 'Grünherz'

Taking their title from the green, heart-shaped insignia they carried, this wing was formed in 1940 and took part in the Battle of Britain. It also served on the northern sector of the Eastern Front during the Siege of Leningrad, in centre during the Kursk offensive and in the southern sector in the Ukraine. Elements served in Normandy after the invasion of June 1944, in the defence of the Reich and subsequently in the Ardennes offensive. Both the Me 109 and Fw 190 were flown.

Jagdgeschwader 76

Formed from ZG76 in 1944, when the former unit began to replace its twin-engined aircraft with Me 109s. Took part in the defence of the Reich and in the defence of Hungary in 1945.

Jagdgeschwader 77 'Herz As'

Known as the 'Herz As', or Ace of Hearts, wing because of its formation sign, this unit saw action in the Polish campaign, the campaign in the west, the Battle of Britain, the Balkan campaign, the attack on Crete, the Eastern Front, North Africa, Italy, the defence of the Reich and the Ardennes offensive. At the end of the war, the Geschwader surrendered to the Americans after destroying their aircraft and were promptly handed over to the tender mercies of Soviet captivity.

Oberleutnant Beisswenger. Beisswenger served with Jagdgeschwader 54 and was an accomplished 'expert'. A holder of the Oakleaves to the Knight's Cross of the Iron Cross, awarded on 30 September 1942 after his 100th victory, he is seen here sporting a typical pilot's peaked cap, with the stiffening around the brim removed and the crown crushed to give it a more jaunty appearance. The same fashion was popular in the US Air Force, where it was known as the 'Fifty Mission Crush'. He was killed in action on 6 March 1943.

Hauptmann Wolf Dieter Huy, awarded the Knight's Cross as Staffelkapitän of 7./Jagdgeschwader 77 on 5 July 1941 after his 22nd victory. In March 1942, the Oakleaves were added after his tally reached 40. Huy flew over 400 combat missions before being shot down in North Africa and ending the war as a POW of the British.

Oberleutnant Erwin Clausen of Jagdgeschwader 77. He was awarded the prestigious Oakleaves to the Knight's Cross of the Iron Cross on 23 July 1942 after scoring his 100th victory. Clausen's final score was 132 victories, including 12 four-engined heavy bombers. He was killed in action on 4 October 1943, flying a Focke-Wulf Fw190 in an attack on an Allied bomber formation, minutes after shooting down a B-24 Liberator bomber.

Jagdgeschwader 200

This short-lived Geschwader was formed in June 1944 for duties in the defence of the Reich. It was disbanded six months later.

Jagdgeschwader 300

Formed in mid-1943 for use in the defence of the Reich, this Geschwader was assigned to evening operations in the light summer evenings and so were not true 'night-fighters'. They flew the so-called 'Wilde Sau' (Wild Boar) tactics referred to elsewhere in this book.

Jagdgeschwader 301 'Wilde Sau'

Formed in October 1943 for similar operational use to JG300 on 'Wild Boar' operations against Allied bombers. Some elements also saw service on the Eastern Front in Romania and Bulgaria. The Geschwader ended the war in Schleswig-Holstein.

Jagdgeschwader 302 'Wilde Sau'

The third of the 'Wild Boar' Geschwadern, this unit was formed in November 1943 and flew similar operations to its predecessors. Its second and third Gruppen were disbanded in May 1944; the first Gruppe was ultimately absorbed into the third Gruppe of JG301.

Jagdgeschwader 400

This Geschwader was established in 1942, effectively as a test unit which flew the new, rocket-propelled Me 163 Komet. It saw action against the Allied bomber offensive in the summer of 1944.

Wolfgang Falck was one of a small number of Luftwaffe pilots who achieved 'ace' status flying the Me 110 in daylight operations. His main claim to fame, however, is as the founder of Nachtjagdgeschwader 1, with which the Me 110 eventually played a far more successful role. Falck served as Geschwaderkommodore of NJG1 for over three years before being promoted to the General Staff and is considered by many as the 'father' of the German night-fighting arm. He remained with the General Staff until summer 1944 and spent the rest of the war in various fighter command positions, eventually becoming a prisoner of the Americans in May 1945. After the war, he became a consultant for McDonnell Douglas Aviation. (*Josef Charita*)

NACHTJAGDGESCHWADERN (NIGHT-FIGHTER WINGS)

Nachtjagdgeschwader 1
Formed in 1940. Operated primarily from bases in Holland until 1944, when it was withdrawn into Germany.

Nachtjagdgeschwader 2
Formed in 1941. Initially operated from bases in Holland but some elements served in Sicily and North Africa. Returned to Germany in 1943, when it was used both in the defence of the Reich and, as late as 1945, for long-distance night attacks on Great Britain.

Nachtjagdgeschwader 3
Formed in late 1940. From early 1941 some elements operated from Sicily. Later it was based in Germany, where it was assigned to protect the north German coast.

Nachtjagdgeschwader 4
Formed in 1941. Operated from bases in France until withdrawn into Germany in 1944. Tasked with protective cover for southern Germany.

Nachtjagdgeschwader 5
Formed in late 1942. Operating predominantly from bases in Germany, it took part in the defence of the Reich, attacks on the Normandy invasion front, night operations during the Ardennes offensive and the defence of east Prussia and Silesia.

Nachtjagdgeschwader 6
Formed in 1943. Operated from bases in Germany, with some elements in Romania,

Oberleutnant Prinz Egmont zur Lippe-Weissenfeld from 5./Nachtjagdgeschwader 2. Interestingly, despite its small size, the night-fighter arm contained a number of members of the German aristocracy within its ranks. Lippe-Weissenfeld was decorated with the Knight's Cross on 16 April 1942, and the Oakleaves on 2 August 1943. His final tally was 51 enemy aircraft shot down.

Croatia and Hungary. From late 1944 it was operating on the Western Front in the defence of the Reich.

Nachtjagdgeschwader 7

An understrength unit formed in 1944. Operated from bases in Denmark in the defence of east Prussia.

Nachtjagdgruppe 10

Formed in 1944 as a test unit flying various types, including Me 109, Me 110, Fw 190, Ju 88 and Hs 129 aircraft fitted with experimental radar. Disbanded in 1945 and its remnants absorbed into NJG5.

Nachtjagdgeschwader 11

Formed in summer 1944, it operated from bases in Germany, flying the Me 109 and Fw 190 as high-altitude interceptors. Its 10th Staffel was equipped with the night-fighter version of the Me 262 jet.

Nachtjagdgeschwader 100

Formed in 1942. Operated predominantly on the Eastern Front.

Nachtjagdgeschwader 200

Formed in late 1942. Operated on the Eastern Front. Much of its strength was absorbed into NJG100 in autumn 1943.

ZERSTÖRERGESCHWADERN (DESTROYER WINGS – HEAVY TWIN-ENGINE FIGHTERS), ABBREVIATED TO ZG

Zerstörergeschwader 1

Tracing its origins back to 1935, this Geschwader saw action in the Polish campaign, the campaign in the west, the Eastern Front, North Africa and in anti-shipping missions in the Atlantic. It operated the Me 110, the Me 210 and the Ju 88, as well as at one point using the Me 109 in the fighter-bomber role.

Zerstörergeschwader 2

Originating in 1936, this Geschwader also saw action in the Polish campaign, the campaign in the west, the Battle of Britain, the Eastern Front and in North Africa. As well as the Me 110, it operated both the Me 109 and Fw 190 in the fighter-bomber role.

Zerstörergeschwader 26 'Horst Wessel'

Formed in 1936, this Geschwader took part in the campaign in the west, the Balkan campaign, the Eastern Front, the Mediterranean theatre and in the defence of the Reich. It operated the Me 110, the Me 210, the Me 410 and the Ju 88, as well as the Fw 190 as a fighter-bomber.

Zerstörergeschwader 76

Formed in 1938, this Geschwader took part in the Polish campaign, the attack on Norway, the Battle of Britain, the Eastern Front and the defence of the Reich. Aircraft operated included the Me 110, the Me 410, and the Me 109 and Fw 190 as fighter-bombers.

A Messerschmitt Me 110 bearing the highly distinctive nose art indicating it as an aircraft of the so-called 'Wespengeschwader', the Wasp Wing, Zerstörergeschwader 1. One of the more-extreme colour schemes sported by Luftwaffe aircraft, it consists of a large yellow and black painted wasp motif either side of the aircraft nose. The version shown here has the heavier nose armament consisting of two cannon and four machine guns, and twin, rather than single, machine guns in the rear cockpit. (*François Saez*)

KAMPFGESCHWADERN (BOMBER WINGS), ABBREVIATED TO KG

Kampfgeschwader 1 'Hindenburg'

Formed in 1936, this Geschwader served in the Polish campaign, the campaign in the west, the Blitz on Great Britain, on the Eastern Front, in Sicily and in Italy. Aircraft operated included the He 111, the Ju 88 and the He 177.

Kampfgeschwader 2

This Geschwader took part in the Polish campaign, the campaign in the west, the Blitz on Great Britain and the Balkan campaign, and served on the Eastern Front. Among aircraft operated were the Do 17, Do 217, DO 335, Ju 86, Ju 88, Ju 188 and Me 410.

Kampfgeschwader 3

This Geschwader served during the Polish campaign, the campaign in the west, the Blitz against Great Britain, the Balkan campaign and on the Eastern Front. It was disbanded in August 1944. It appears that its pilots were transferred to fighter operations and others absorbed into the Flakartillerie. Aircraft operated included the Do 17, He 111 and Ju 88.

Kampfgeschwader 4 'General Wever'

This unit took part in the Polish campaign, the attack on Norway, the campaign in the west, the Blitz on Great Britain, the Mediterranean theatre and the Eastern Front. Aircraft operated included the Ju 88 and He 177.

Two Junkers Ju 88A-4 fast bombers warm up their engines before take-off. The Ju 88 was one of Germany's most successful and versatile aircraft. (*Thomas Huss*)

Kampfgeschwader 6

Formed in 1942, this wing took part in the Blitz against Great Britain and also operated in the Mediterranean theatre. From late 1944 it operated on the Eastern Front using Me 109 and Fw 190 fighter-bombers, as well as the Me 262 jet. Medium and heavy bombers operated included the Ju 86, Ju 88 and He 177.

Kampfgeschwader 26

Known as the 'Löwen Geschwader', or Lion Wing, this unit took part in the campaign in the west and the Blitz on Great Britain, and operated in the Balkans, in North Africa, in Italy and on the Eastern Front. Its aircraft included the He 111, Ju 88 and Ju 188. This Geschwader specialised in torpedo strikes against shipping.

Kampfgeschwader 27 'Boelcke'

This Geschwader took part in the Polish campaign, the campaign in the west and the Blitz against Great Britain, and served on the Eastern Front. From late 1944 it flew Me 109 and Fw 190 fighters.

Kampfgeschwader 30

Known as the 'Adler Geschwader', or Eagle Wing, this unit was formed in early 1939. It took part in the Polish campaign and the campaign in the west, and operated on the Eastern Front, in North Africa, in Italy and in the defence of the Reich. Its principal aircraft was the Ju 88, though it also flew the so-called 'Mistel' piggy-back aircraft, combining worn-out Ju 88 airframes with an Me 109 or Fw 190 fighter.

Oberleutnant Gerhard Krems, a Heinkel He 111 pilot from Kampfgeschwader 27. Having taken part in the Battle of Britain, Krems also served with distinction on the Eastern Front and was awarded the Knight's Cross on 25 April 1942. He completed over 250 combat missions on bombers before being attached to the staff of I Fliegerkorps. He survived the war and enjoyed a highly successful postwar career in engineering.

Hauptmann Werner Baumbach of 5./Kampfgeschwader 30. One of the most highly decorated pilots outwith the fighter arm, Baumbach was among the first to use the Ju 88 bomber, with which he sank the French cruiser *Emil Bertin* in April 1940, a feat which was recognised with the Knight's Cross on 8 May 1940. He subsequently enjoyed success in anti-shipping operations, for which the Oakleaves were awarded on 14 July 1941 after he sank 240,000 tons of shipping, and the Swords added to the Oakleaves on 17 August 1942. At this point Baumbach was forbidden to continue combat flying and assigned to staff duties. He was involved in the development of new weapons such as the 'Mistel' combination, and at one point commanded special operations unit Kampfgeschwader 200. He survived the war to die in a plane crash in 1953.

Kampfgeschwader 40

This Geschwader was formed in late 1939 and took part in the campaign in the west and the Blitz against Great Britain, and operated in North Africa. Its principal mission, however, was as a torpedo strike formation to be used against enemy shipping, though some elements took part in the attempts to resupply the stricken 6 Armee at Stalingrad. Among the aircraft operated were the He 111, Ju 88 and Fw 200.

Kampfgeschwader 51

Known as the 'Edelweiss Geschwader' from the edelweiss flower used as its emblem, this unit traces its origins back to 1937. It took part in the campaign in the west, the Blitz on Great Britain and the attack on the Balkans, and served on the Eastern Front, in the Mediterranean theatre and in the defence of the Reich. Its aircraft included

the Do 17, He 111, Ju 88 and Me 410. The Geschwader was one of the first to be equipped with the Me 262 jet fighter, which Hitler had insisted was to be used as a bomber.

Kampfgeschwader 53 'Condor Legion'

This Geschwader took part in the Polish campaign, the campaign in the west and the Blitz on Great Britain. It saw service on the Eastern Front, where it, too, took part in the attempt at resupplying the 6 Armee at Stalingrad. Aircraft operated included the He 111, some of which were configured to carry V1 flying bombs.

Kampfgeschwader 54

The so-called 'Totenkopf Geschwader', or Death's Head Wing, saw service in the Polish campaign, the campaign in the west, the Blitz on Great Britain, in North Africa

Rudolf Roesch, a bomber pilot with Kampfgeschwader 51. Roesch was awarded the Knight's Cross of the Iron Cross on 26 March 1944 as Staffelkapitän of 9./KG51 after completing 100 combat missions. He was posted as missing in action on 28 November 1944.

and on the Eastern Front. Aircraft operated included the He 111, Ju 88 and Me 262 jet.

Kampfgeschwader 55
Known as the 'Greif Geschwader', or Griffin Wing, this unit took part in the Polish campaign, the campaign in the west, the Blitz against Great Britain, and also served on the Eastern Front.

Kampfgeschwader 66
Formed in 1943, this Geschwader operated as a 'pathfinder' unit for bombing attacks on both Western and Eastern Fronts, including target marking for attacks by 'Mistel' combinations.

Kampfgeschwader 76
Formed in 1938, this unit took part in the Polish campaign, the campaign in the west and the Blitz on Great Britain, and also

operated in the Balkans, on the Eastern Front and in Italy. It was used both against ground targets and on anti-shipping strikes. Aircraft operated included the Do 17 and Ju 88.

Kampfgeschwader 77
Formed in 1939, this unit took part in the Polish campaign, the campaign in the west and the Blitz on Great Britain, and served in North Africa, in Italy and on the Eastern Front. Aircraft operated included the Do 17 and Ju 88. The Geschwader was used for anti-shipping strikes as well as attacks on ground targets.

Kampfgeschwader 100
Tracing its origins back to early 1938, this unit took part in the Polish campaign and the attack on Norway and served in North Africa and on the Eastern Front. It carried

out a multitude of tasks, including reconnaissance missions, 'pathfinder' missions, mine-laying and anti-shipping strikes. It also flew bombers equipped with the Hs 293 remote-guided bombs. Principal aircraft of this unit were the He 111, Do 217 and He 177.

Kampfgeschwader 200

Formed in early 1944, this evaluation and test unit flew an amazing assortment of aircraft including the He 59, He 111, He 115, He 177, Ju 87, Ju 88, Ju 188, Ju 252, Ju 290, Ju 352, Ar 96, Ar 196, Ar 232, Fw 44, Fw 189, Si 204, Bü 131, Bü 181 and several others. It also flew a number of captured enemy aircraft, including the Douglas DC-3 Dakota, the Boeing B-17 Flying Fortress and others.

SCHNELLKAMPFGESCHWADERN (FAST BOMBER WINGS), ABBREVIATED TO SKG

Schnellkampfgeschwader 10

Formed in December 1942, this unit saw action in North Africa in the ground attack role, equipped with the Fw 190. It was relatively short-lived, being redesignated Schlachtgeschwader 10 in October 1943.

Schnellkampfgeschwader 210

Formed in 1941, this wing was equipped with the Me 110 and saw action against targets in southern England and against British shipping in coastal waters. It subsequently moved to the Eastern Front, where it served in the ground attack role until early 1942, when it was absorbed into Zerstörergeschwader 1.

STURZKAMPFGESCHWADERN (DIVE-BOMBER WINGS), ABBREVIATED TO STG

Sturzkampfgeschwader 1

Tracing its origins back to 1937, the dive-bomber wing took part in the attack on Poland, the campaign in the west, the Blitz on Great Britain and the attack on Crete,

and saw heavy combat in the Balkans and on the Eastern Front. The Geschwader's III Gruppe was originally designated to be carried on the proposed aircraft carrier *Graf Zeppelin*. In October 1943 it was redesignated

A Junkers Ju 88A-4 of the 'Edelweiss' Geschwader, KG51. Note the unit emblem on the fuselage under the cockpit. The fact that, as far as can be seen on the photo, this example does not seem to have been shot up by enemy fire suggests that this crash-landing was due to some form of technical failure. (*Thomas Huss*)

Kampfgeschwader 200, the Luftwaffe's special operations wing, was responsible for test-flying captured Allied aircraft for evaluation purposes. Shown here is a rare shot of a Vickers Wellington light bomber which was brought down intact and assigned to KG200 for evaluation. Note the German markings applied directly over the original RAF roundel on the fuselage. (*François Saez*)

A very rare shot showing a P-47 Thunderbolt brought down by the Luftwaffe and allocated to KG200 for evaluation. The ungainly P-47, affectionately known as the 'Jug' to its pilots, was a very robust aircraft capable of taking quite heavy punishment. The exact circumstances that resulted in this specimen falling into German hands intact are unknown. The ability to test-fly this aircraft would have given the Luftwaffe invaluable tips on how best to combat it. (*Thomas Huss*)

Schlachtgeschwader 1. The principal aircraft type was the Ju 87.

Sturzkampfgeschwader 2 'Immelmann'

Formed originally as Fliegergruppe Schwerin in 1934, this Geschwader took part in the attack on Poland and the campaigns in the west and in the Balkans. It was heavily engaged on the Eastern Front, where it flew support missions for 6 Armee at Stalingrad. The Geschwader enjoyed considerable success in the anti-tank role. In October 1943 it was redesignated Schlachtgeschwader 2. The principal aircraft type was the Ju 87.

Sturzkampfgeschwader 3

Originating in 1936, like its predecessors this Geschwader saw action in Poland, on the Western Front, in the Mediterranean theatre, the Balkans and on the Eastern Front. It also saw action in North Africa. It enjoyed considerable success in the anti-shipping role. Principal aircraft types were the Hs 123 and Ju 87. In late 1943 it was redesignated Schlachtgeschwader 3.

Sturzkampfgeschwader 5

Formed in mid-1943, this short-lived Geschwader was based in Norway. Originally equipped with the Ju 87, it was redesig-

A Junkers Ju 87B, the first large-scale production variant of this aircraft, in typical early-wartime scheme, green splinter-pattern camouflage with light blue undersurfaces. The rudder and nose are painted bright yellow. The emblem on the fuselage side just ahead of the cockpit shows a red disc with black shield and white rampant lion, the insignia of 1./Sturzkampfgeschwader 3. (*François Saez*)

nated Schlachtgeschwader 5 in February 1944, when it was re-equipped with the Fw 190. Finally it was partially disbanded in May of that year and its remnants absorbed into Kampfgeschwader 200.

Sturzkampfgeschwader 77

Formed in 1936, this unit took part in the attack on Poland, the campaign in the west and the Balkan campaign, and was heavily engaged on the Eastern Front. Its principal aircraft type was the Ju 87. In late 1943 it was redesignated Schlachtgeschwader 77.

SCHLACHTGESCHWADERN (GROUND ATTACK WINGS), ABBREVIATED TO SG

Schlachtgeschwader 1

Formed in 1938, this unit was originally designated Fliegergruppe 10, and shortly afterwards was changed to II./(Schlacht) Lehrgeschwader 2. Using the Hs 123 in the ground attack role, it took part in the attack on Poland and the campaign in the west, after which it also received numbers of the Me 109. It also saw considerable action on the Eastern Front, flying the Hs 123, Hs 129,

Me 109 and Fw 190. In late 1943, Sturzkampfgeschwader 1 was redesignated Schlachtgeschwader 1, and the original elements of this Geschwader thereafter dispersed among other ground attack units.

Schlachtgeschwader 2 'Immelmann'

This Geschwader was formed in 1942 around a number of Me 109s from the former Zerstörergeschwader 1, as well as the fighter-bomber flights from Jagdgeschwader 27 and Jagdgeschwader 53. It saw action in North Africa and on the Eastern Front. When Sturzkampfgeschwader 2 was redesignated Schlachtgeschwader 2 in late 1943, the original elements were dispersed to other ground attack units.

Schlachtgeschwader 4

This unit was formed in late 1943 around a nucleus comprising some of the original elements of Schlachtgeschwader 2. It saw action in Italy and the Mediterranean theatre and on the Eastern Front. It provided support for the abortive Ardennes offensive before returning to the Eastern Front in 1945, where it ended the war.

SCHLACHTGESCHWADER 10

Formed in October 1943 from the former Schnellkampfgeschwader 10, this ground attack unit was equipped with the Fw 190 fighter-bomber. It saw action in North Africa, Italy and Sicily, in attacks on Great Britain and on the Eastern Front.

TRANSPORTGESCHWADERN (TRANSPORT WINGS), ABBREVIATED TO TG

Transportgeschwader 1

This Geschwader began life as Kampfgeschwader z.b.V. 1 and was redesignated in

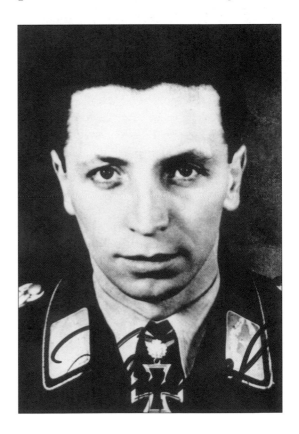

Major Karl Kennel, 5./Schlachtgeschwader 1, was already an accomplished flier, having served with Zerstörergeschwader 2 and 26 in the Me 110 and Me 210. In October 1942 he became Staffelkapitän of 5./SG1 and, flying the Fw 190 predominantly in the ground assault role, was awarded the Knight's Cross after flying 500 combat missions with 28 aerial victories. The Oakleaves followed on 25 November 1944 after his 800th mission. He ended the war with the rank of Major and over 950 combat missions to his credit, with 34 confirmed victories.

Oberstleutnant Alfred Druschel is seen here as Geschwaderkommodore of Schlachtgeschwader 4. Of particular interest in this shot is the shield emblem on his sleeve. This indicates that he served in the fighting in the Crimea between September 1941 and July 1942. Druschel was awarded the Oakleaves with Swords to the Knight's Cross on 19 February 1943, after having flown a total of 700 ground support missions. He took part in Operation Bodenplatte on 1 January 1945, the last great German air attack on the Western Front, during which he was posted as missing in action. (*Josef Charita*)

May 1943. It saw action on virtually every front and in every theatre of operations where the Germans were involved. As well as the early campaigns in Poland, in the west, and the Balkans, it was heavily engaged on the Eastern Front and was involved in the attempts to resupply 6 Armee at Stalingrad and the encircled German forces in the Demjansk cauldron.

Transportgeschwader 2

Originating as Kampfgeschwader z.b.V. 3 and redesignated in May 1943, this unit operated during the invasion of Denmark and Norway, the campaign in the west and the invasion of Crete in May 1941, and also served on the Eastern Front. It saw its final actions around Breslau in 1945.

Transportgeschwader 3

Originally designated Kampfgeschwader z.b.V. 2 and renamed in May 1943, elements of this Geschwader served on virtually every front. It took part in the relief attempt at Stalingrad.

Transportgeschwader 4

Formed in May 1943, and saw action on both Eastern and Western Fronts.

Transportgeschwader 5

Created in May 1943 around elements from Kampfgeschwader z.b.V. 323. Saw action in the attack on Norway, in the west and the Balkan campaign. In late 1942 it was equipped with the enormous Messerschmitt Me 323 Gigant. It was disbanded in August 1944.

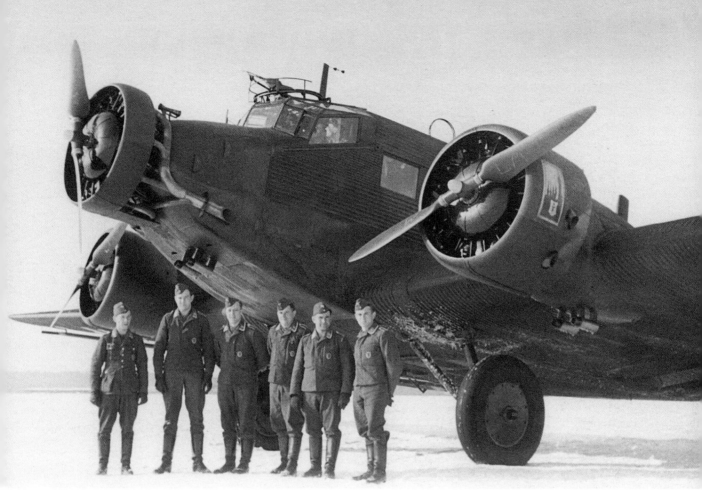

The Ju 52 trimotor was the mainstay of the Luftwaffe's transport arm and gave excellent service from the first day of the war to the last. This early example has had the large wheel spats that were normally fitted removed. Particularly in winter, mud, slush and snow could become packed into the spat and cause problems with the rotation of the wheel. Note also on this example that a machine-gunner position is fitted to the roof of the cockpit canopy. (*Thomas Huss*)

LEHRGESCHWADERN (TRAINING AND DEMONSTRATION WINGS), ABBREVIATED TO LG

Lehrgeschwader 1

Formed in late 1938 as Lehrgeschwader Greifswald, this Geschwader comprised six Gruppen, three of which were equipped with bombers (He 111 and Ju 88), one dive-bomber Gruppe equipped with the Ju 87, one heavy-fighter Gruppe equipped with the Me 110 and one replacement Gruppe equipped with bombers. It saw action in the Polish campaign, the campaign in the west, the Mediterranean theatre, the Blitz on Great Britain and on the Eastern Front.

Lehrgeschwader 2

This unit was formed in 1938. It comprised three Gruppen, one fighter, one ground attack and one reconnaissance. It took part in the attack on Poland and the campaign in the west and was then broken up and its Gruppen assigned to other units for the attack on the Soviet Union.

Although ground combat units were administratively part of the Luftwaffe, when used operationally, they, like those of the

Like most other trainees, Luftwaffe pilots did much of their flying training in biplanes. Here we see one of the most popular trainers, the Heinkel He 72B, about to be given the all-clear signal for take-off. (*Josef Charita*)

Waffen-SS, normally came under the command of an Army Group (Heeresgruppe) and were thus controlled by a senior Army officer, and not directly by the Luftwaffe.

The High Command of the Luftwaffe (Oberkommando der Luftwaffe) was divided into nine departments, known as Abteilungen, as follows:

Department 1   Operations
Department 2   Organisation
Department 3   Training
Department 4   Movements
Department 5   Intelligence
Department 6   Equipment
Department 7   Historical
Department 8   Personnel

Operations, Training and Intelligence were controlled by the Chief of Operations Staff, who was also responsible for strategy as instructed by Chiefs of the Luftwaffe General Staff. Organisation, Movements, Equipment and Personnel were controlled by the Quartermaster General of the Luftwaffe.

CHAPTER THREE

STRATEGY AND TACTICS

The original intention was for the Luftwaffe to play a support role for the Army. It was therefore basically a tactical weapon. The bulk of its front-line combat aircraft were either fighters or medium bombers with limited range, usually enough to operate over the enemy front lines or just beyond, but without the strategic ability to hit deep into enemy heartland. In fact, as early as 1937, both Junkers and Dornier were tasked with developing long-range, strategic heavy bombers (the Ju 89 and Do 19) capable of striking from bases in Germany deep into Soviet Russia, as far as the Urals. Nothing came of the so-called 'Ural Bomber' projects, however, and efforts were concentrated on light to medium tactical bombers. Even when development work on heavy bombers began again, and resulted in the Heinkel He 177 Greif, it was insisted that this heavy aircraft have dive-bombing capability! The He 177 was dogged with technical problems, not the least of which was an alarming propensity for its engines to catch fire, making the aircraft more of a danger to its Luftwaffe crews than to the enemy.

A future development of the Ju 88 design, the Ju 288, was to have been a four-engine type, and even that was delayed as a result of insistence that it should be capable of dive-bombing. The obsession with the need for

dive-bombing ultimately moved even Göring to complain, 'It is complete idiocy to ask of a four-engine bomber that it should dive.' In the event, the plans for the development of this aircraft were shelved.

To the Nazi hierarchy, there was no perceived need for long-range strategic bombers. Hitler had reassured them that Germany would not be at war with Great Britain, so her most likely initial opponents were her direct neighbours. The principal need for combat aircraft, therefore, was in the field of fighters and light to medium bombers most appropriate to Blitzkrieg warfare. The Luftwaffe also pushed the development of new technologies, such as radios, cameras for reconnaissance, and coordination for air support between panzer and Luftwaffe units.

It was not that the potential of strategic bombing was dismissed by the Luftwaffe. There was, in fact, a clear understanding of the value of strategic bombardment, but lack of resources and, more importantly, political interference prevented the creation of a strategic bomber arm. Supporters of the tactical role complained that for every heavy bomber, at least two, or perhaps three, medium bombers could be produced. Göring himself is reported to have said, 'The Führer will never ask me how big our bombers are, but how many we have.' In

1936, the Chief of the Luftwaffe General Staff, General Wever, was killed in an air accident. Wever had been a proponent of the heavy bomber and the loss of such an influential figure to those who supported the strategic role for the Luftwaffe's bombers was devastating.

The creation of a paratroop arm was one of the Luftwaffe's more successful achievements. In the interwar years Germany had observed Soviet paratroop training and had quickly grasped the obvious potential for such operations as an important factor in the strategy of Blitzkrieg. Paratroop units were originally created under Army control but soon passed to the control of the Luftwaffe (apart from those operated by the Waffen-SS and Army Special Forces). Thanks to the efforts of Kurt Student, the Luftwaffe was persuaded to add a glider element to its airborne forces. Initial operations, such as those against the fortress at Eben Emael in Belgium, and operations in Norway, were highly successful. Subsequent operations on Crete, however, though they resulted in victory, were so costly in terms of losses that Hitler forbade future large-scale operations and the elite Fallschirmjäger spent the remainder of the war predominantly in the conventional light infantry role, though they did achieve some impressive results, such as in the defence of Monte Cassino in 1944.

What has become known as the Battle of Britain was effectively a 'softening up' of British defences as a precursor to a planned German invasion. German bombers initially hit defence installations and radar stations as well as coastal shipping. In the second half of August 1940 the focus of attacks switched to RAF air bases and the factories manufacturing the desperately needed aircraft in an effort to gain air superiority. The air battle reached its peak between 8 and 17 August 1940, with the biggest offensive of the war being launched on what was to be known as 'Adlertag', or Eagle Day. Although considerable damage was done, the Luftwaffe suffered severe losses and Hitler subsequently ordered a move away from daylight operations to night bombing, beginning on 7 September 1940. Although the term 'Blitz' (for Blitzkrieg) came into use right at the start of the war with the attack on Poland, it was to be the night offensive on Britain (and, in particular, London) that was to become generally known as 'The Blitz'.

With the cancelling of Operation Sealion (the proposed invasion of Great Britain), the attack on Britain moved from being a softening-up operation prior to invasion, to a long-term strategy intended to wear down the morale and will to fight of the British people. It continued throughout the war, escalating with the introduction of the V1 flying bombs and the V2 rockets, but it is the aerial bombardment of 1940/1 that is forever associated with the Blitz in the minds of most people. Over the course of the Battle of Britain the Luftwaffe lost some 2,300 aircraft, slow-moving bombers and obsolescent aircraft like the Stuka taking the brunt of the losses. The RAF losses mounted to some 900 (mostly fighters). Despite impressive performances by some of the Luftwaffe's top pilots, the air assault on Britain cannot be counted as anything other than a failure – the first major failure of the war and one which severely dented Hermann Göring's pride and status. It was not to be the last time his overconfident boasts concerning the capabilities of his forces were to prove unfounded.

In the summer of 1941, Hitler unleashed his armies against the Soviet Union. Once again, as in Poland, the Luftwaffe met an enemy that was unprepared for the ferocity of its attack. The Red Air Force was poorly organised, with obsolete aircraft and many ill-trained and inexperienced pilots. On the

One of the Richthofen Geschwader's best-known pilots was Major Helmut Wick, an accomplished 'expert' who won the Knight's Cross of the Iron Cross during the Battle of Britain, and the Oakleaves barely two months later, after his 33rd victory. The youngest Major in the Wehrmacht at the time, Wick was shot down over the English Channel in a dogfight and killed on 28 November 1940. In his total of 56 victories, achieved over 168 combat missions, were 26 Spitfires.

first day of the campaign alone, over 1,000 Soviet fighters were destroyed on the ground. German fighter pilots, accustomed to opposing skilled RAF pilots flying quality aircraft such as the Spitfire, had a field day and many aces began running up quite enormous scores, so much so that the 'qualifying point' for the award of the Knight's Cross of the Iron Cross on the Eastern Front rose rapidly. Once awarded for 20–30 victories in the west, it soon required more than double that amount for its award on the Eastern Front. Once again, however, the Luftwaffe was used principally as tactical close support for the Army and did little to prevent the Soviet armaments industry from producing vast amounts of war *matériel* from establishments deep in the Soviet rear areas.

With the turn of the tide against them after the disaster at Stalingrad, and faced with an ever-growing number of Allied bombing raids on their soil, the Germans found that their lack of a strategic bomber force rendered the Luftwaffe unable to strike back with anything approaching the same severity against their enemies. Even Hitler's 'wonder weapons', the V1 and V2, used on Great Britain, never came near to achieving their goals.

The Luftwaffe's fighter arm, designed principally to counter the enemy fighter menace to its own bombers, was now having to cope with the role of intercepting enemy bomber fleets which were themselves not only heavily armed, but provided with powerful escort forces. Despite its best efforts – and those efforts cost the Allies

Prior to the outbreak of the Second World War, Luftwaffe aircrew had gained invaluable combat experience during their participation in the Spanish Civil War in support of Franco's Nationalist forces. Here, two Luftwaffe members wear the uniform of the Condor Legion, and both sport on their right breast pockets the Spanish Cross in Silver with Swords, instituted by Hitler in 1939 to reward participation in the conflict. Both also wear the Spanish Campaign Medal and Spanish War Cross decorations. (*François Saez*)

dearly – the Luftwaffe was incapable of defending German soil, so great had been its losses in experienced aircrew in the first half of the war. Whatever strategic design the Nazi hierarchy had harboured for its Luftwaffe, if indeed there had been any, had failed.

TACTICS

The Luftwaffe, based on experiences gained during the Spanish Civil War, had developed the tactical use of fighters on the basis of the 'Rotte', and the 'Schwarm'. The former consisted simply of two aircraft flying in line astern, with the second fighter protecting the lead fighter's tail. The Schwarm formation simply doubled the Rotte, with two covering aircraft flying behind the two lead aircraft. When an entire Staffel was deployed, the various Rotte and Schwarm would fly at varying altitudes, covering a much greater area of sky and giving greater flexibility than the previous system of flying in 'V' formation.

The Luftwaffe also preferred the inherent accuracy of pinpoint dive-bombing, with aircraft such as the Stuka, on ground support operations, having learned once again in Spain that this gave far better results than the relatively inaccurate area or 'carpet' bombing by medium bombers. Bigger formations of medium bombers were more useful in attacking larger areas of enemy-held territory, major installations, fortresses, etc., but the dive-bomber, aided by a highly developed system of ground-to-air communications with Luftwaffe liaison officers among the ground forces, paid great dividends for the Luftwaffe in the early part of the war. Where the medium bombers were used on the battlefield, they were often flown at low altitude to increase accuracy and also to allow their on-board machine-gunners to lay down suppressing fire on enemy positions. While improving accuracy and effectiveness, such tactics had their own drawbacks, such as susceptibility to enemy return fire, and bomb blast damage from their own payload.

Nevertheless, the relative success of aircraft like the He 111 in Spain helped the Luftwaffe to decide that the medium, rather than heavy, bomber was its preferred weapon. Unfortunately, in Spain, the German fighter aircraft had all but driven the Soviet-supplied Republican fighters from the skies, and the He 111 was more than capable of delivering devastating blows against ground targets when not facing determined fighter opposition. The fast, easy campaigns in Poland and the west would simply confirm the view that the medium bomber was more than adequate. When the Luftwaffe then launched its attack on Britain and the German fighter arm failed to gain the ascendancy, the German medium bombers and dive-bombers would suffer terrible casualties. Fighters had not been developed with the aim of providing long-range cover on strategic bombing missions and were able to provide only limited protection before having to break off action because of lack of fuel.

Experiences in Spain also led the Germans to draw some costly conclusions with regard to the use of aircraft against ships. German bombing raids on shipping actually under way at sea were largely unsuccessful, whereas attacks against ships

Taken in Spain, this photograph shows a Dornier Do 17 of the Condor Legion's Kampfgruppe 88 about to take off on a bombing raid. These aircraft did not carry German markings. As can just be seen on the aircraft in the background, the rudders were painted white with a large black cross. The fuselage and wing markings, in place of the German crosses, featured plain, black discs. (*François Saez*)

moored in port were devastating. The conclusion was drawn that ships at sea were not particularly susceptible to air attack and, initially at least, the anti-aircraft armament fitted to German ships was less than impressive. The Germans at this stage failed to develop any dedicated torpedo bombers and later had to rely on modifying existing designs such as the He 111 and Ju 88. These conclusions also contributed to the decision not to complete the proposed aircraft carrier *Graf Zeppelin* and the ultimate absorption of the intended naval air arm into the Luftwaffe.

Thus, while experiences with the Condor Legion in Spain had led to the development of highly effective fighter tactics, the failure to develop the bomber and maritime arms was to be a costly mistake. The concentration on the Luftwaffe's role as one of close support to ground forces had proven itself valid in Spain and in the early months of the Second World War, but was, in the long run, to prove disastrous.

In the Polish campaign and in the campaign in the west, Germany's opponents faced not only a new, powerful air force, but also a new doctrine of armoured warfare in which tanks were no longer there to support the infantry but were themselves the spearhead force. Working in close cooperation with the rapidly advancing panzers, the Luftwaffe swiftly overcame all effective opposition. On the opening of the campaign, the Luftwaffe launched massed attacks on all Polish airfields in an attempt to destroy the Polish air force on the ground. With the Polish army left without air cover, their chances of resisting German armoured strikes with fighter, dive-bomber and bomber support would be negligible.

In fact, although the Luftwaffe would perform magnificently in close cooperation with the Army (as at Kutno, when a combined air/ground counter-attack following a Polish

assault saw the Poles devastated and over 155,000 surrender, many having broken and run in the face of the sheer ferocity of the German attack), the Germans did not actually succeed in their plan to destroy the Polish air force on the ground. The Poles had become aware of the impending German attack and had removed many of their aircraft to safe areas. These aircraft were then carefully husbanded to provide defensive cover for the coming German assault on Warsaw. In the event it was to be to no avail, as the obsolete Polish aircraft were rapidly subdued by the Germans. The real 'star' in the Luftwaffe's performance in Poland was without doubt the Junkers Ju 87 Stuka, whose pinpoint accuracy in bombing missions in which no effective enemy air opposition was faced was a major factor in several actions.

The Luftwaffe lost just under 200 aircrew and 260 aircraft. Most of the losses were due to anti-aircraft fire rather than action with enemy fighters. In this case, the Luftwaffe's failure to wipe out the enemy air force on the ground was negated by the sheer speed of the campaign. Subsequent such failures, however, were to have disastrous consequences.

During the Norwegian campaign, the Luftwaffe again played a major role, not only in neutralising enemy fortifications by the use of bombers and dive-bombers, but in both transporting troops and dropping paratroops. With much of its small fighter force destroyed on the ground, Norway was able to offer little resistance against the Luftwaffe. Some 700 Luftwaffe aircraft took part in the campaign, though many additional aircraft were used in the resupply role after the main attack. Only fifty or so of the total number were single-engine fighters. Once again, the Luftwaffe had been victorious, but again only against a weak opposition. The most successful aspects of this brief campaign were in the areas of supply and reconnaissance. Fighters and bombers did their job well enough, but were not sorely tested. The Germans also made significant achievements in anti-shipping operations in Norwegian waters, contradicting their earlier beliefs that air attacks against ships under way were not effective.

During the Westfeldzug, the attack on France and the Low Countries, the Luftwaffe fielded approximately 4,000 aircraft against a combined Allied total of less than half that amount. With both sides having around 800 fighters available, it was clear that Allied attempts to interdict German bombing missions were likely to fail. Not only did the numbers of German fighters equal the number of Allied aircraft, but the German aircraft themselves were superior to the majority of Allied types, with the exception perhaps of the Spitfire, which was not yet available in large numbers.

With enemy fighters fully engaged, Luftwaffe bombers were able to wreak havoc on enemy air bases and fortifications and the Luftwaffe's transport aircraft again successfully landed troops and dropped paratroops. The Luftwaffe was even able to land troop-carrying floatplanes on the River Meuse and capture the Willem's bridge at Rotterdam. Initial Luftwaffe operations over France were highly successful, with retreating Allied forces being harried by incessant bombing attacks backed up by intense fighter activity. This was effectively a foretaste of what the Germans themselves would suffer during the Allied invasion of Europe in June 1944, when the invaders enjoyed almost total air superiority. As the rapid

A glider pilot with his DFS 230 glider. This aircraft was capable of carrying up to nine troops. Some 1,600 were built. (*Josef Charita*)

Ground crew load up 250kg bombs on a Junkers Ju 87 Stuka. Note the machine-gun barrel visible just above the top of the undercarriage leg, giving the Ju 87 the means to carry out strafing as well as dive-bombing attacks. (*Josef Charita*)

German advance continued, however, the distances which had to be covered by the Germans increased, while those flown by RAF aircraft shortened, giving them more time over the combat areas.

In the first real major failure of the Luftwaffe, Göring's air force was unable to deliver his promise to Hitler that the Luftwaffe alone could finish off the retreating Allies as they pulled back towards Dunkirk. Over the end of May and beginning of June, Luftwaffe losses actually exceeded those of the Allies. German bombers did, however, succeed in destroying over 240 of the ships being used to evacuate Allied troops from Dunkirk, once again exposing the faulty German theory that air attacks on ships under way were a wasted effort.

Initially successful, the Luftwaffe faltered when it lost air superiority in the skies over Dunkirk. Its bombers were proven to be no match for determined enemy fighter attacks where their own escorting fighters were outnumbered. Nevertheless, in the euphoria of a successful campaign, the Luftwaffe failure was overlooked, Hermann Göring being decorated with the Grand Cross of the Iron Cross and elevated to the unique rank of Reichsmarschall.

In the early part of the war, the Luftwaffe had concentrated on two particular goals. The first of these was the destruction of the enemy's air power, as far as possible 'on the ground' by pre-emptive strikes, and thus attain air superiority. This would support the second goal of providing close support

Ground crew mechanics (known as 'Schwarz Männer', or black men, because of their black coveralls) about to remove the cowling on an early Me 109E for engine maintenance. Note the distinctive snubnose propeller boss and the troughs in the top of the cowling along which the machine guns fired. The Geschwader emblem just visible at extreme left is unfortunately not clear enough to identify the unit. (*Josef Charita*)

to the ground forces; indeed, close support was an area in which the Luftwaffe had excelled in these early campaigns. In all of these, however, the enemy had been swiftly subjugated. In the case where a swift, early victory was not achieved, there was a third stage – that of eliminating an enemy's capability to resist by destroying its industrial capacity and thus its ability to equip and arm its forces. This was something that the Luftwaffe's lack of a strategic heavy-bomber arm rendered it incapable of doing. Although the Luftwaffe rather belatedly acknowledged the usefulness of shipping strikes and used a number of aircraft types in this role, including the He 111, Ju 88 and

Fw 200 Condor to great effect, the failure to strengthen and develop its bomber arm was never fully addressed.

With the onset of the attack on Great Britain, the Luftwaffe was to suffer the consequences of its policy of concentrating on the bomber as a tactical ground support weapon. Even with bases on the Channel coast, the Luftwaffe's fighters would suffer from limited endurance over enemy territory. When aircraft were shot down, its crews were a total loss as, even if they exited the aircraft safely, they would land in enemy territory with virtually no hope of successful escape over the Channel to German-occupied France. Relatively weak defensive armament meant that losses to enemy fighters, given the limited endurance of their own fighter escorts, were high. The original concept of the light bomber being so fast that its speed would enable it to escape enemy fighters was to be proven a total failure. The dive-bomber, though capable of what was considered pinpoint accuracy at the time, was easy prey to enemy fighters unless provided with sufficient escort strength. The so-called 'Destroyers', the twin-engine heavy fighters such as the Me 110, were torn to shreds by RAF Spitfires, giving rise to the ludicrous situation that these twin-engine fighters needed their own single-engine fighter escorts. (The Me 110 would, however, later make a highly effective night-fighter.) Losses reached such proportions that the Luftwaffe was forced to switch to night bombing.

The Germans had also failed to develop an effectively accurate bombsight, so that night operations were faced with the difficulty, first, of finding the target in the blackout, and then hitting it. The Luftwaffe did develop some successful radio direction-finding systems (known as 'Knickebein') to guide their bombers to their targets and became skilled at weather forecasting and the use of 'pathfinders', dropping incendiaries to illuminate the target for the bomber waves following.

At the start of the assault on Great Britain, the Luftwaffe had maintained its normal tactic of hitting the enemy's fighters to reduce opposition to its own bomber forces. To a large degree this was succeeding and RAF Fighter Command losses were crippling. During August/September 1940 it is estimated that around a quarter of the RAF's

A Dornier Do 17 light bomber, known as the 'Flying Pencil' because of its narrow fuselage section. Having delivered reasonable service in Spain and in the early days of the Blitzkrieg against Poland and in the campaign in the west, it was found seriously wanting during the Battle of Britain as a result of its limited payload and vulnerability to enemy fighters. Subsequently, it was used primarily for training purposes and light communication duties. (*Thomas Huss*)

In this wintry scene, a Dornier Do 17 undergoing maintenance has had a propeller removed. This shot clearly shows the forward-firing 7.92mm machine gun operated by the co-pilot. Note also the open cockpit entry hatch visible on the port side of the fuselage. (*Thomas Huss*)

During the attack on the Soviet Union, a number of older aircraft types were still in use, including the Henschel Hs 129. This high-wing 'parasol' monoplane had a crew of two, and was used predominantly as a reconnaissance aircraft. It had two machine guns and could carry 150kg of bombs. (*Josef Charita*)

fighter pilots were lost in action, a totally unsustainable attrition rate. Most of the front-line airfields in the south of England had been hit so badly that they were virtually unusable, reserves were at perilously low levels and Training Command could not keep pace with pilot losses. Then, in early September, the Luftwaffe switched its efforts away from the RAF's fighters to attack its aircraft-production facilities. Its fighters, which had fulfilled the role of tackling their enemy counterparts so well, were now switched to escort duties for the bombers. Having come so close to eliminating enemy fighter resistance to open the way for a successful bombing campaign, the Luftwaffe had now snatched failure from the jaws of success.

German operations in the Balkans in 1941 were once again highly successful, with the now well-tried Blitzkrieg tactics working effectively. Once again, however, the opponents were relatively weak in comparison with the Germans and the campaigns were short-lived. The Luftwaffe was to find that the forthcoming campaign on the Eastern Front was to be a whole different ball game for it.

As the German armies drove through the vastness of the Soviet Union, it became clear that success depended on the ability to maintain supplies. Lines of communication on the ground were stretched perilously thin and were under constant attack from partisans. The Luftwaffe would be capable of supplying much of the Army's needs, but only if its lumbering Ju 52 transport planes were unmolested, which required the Luftwaffe to gain air superiority. Somewhere in excess of 2,800 aircraft were committed to the attack on the Soviet Union and the Luftwaffe succeeded in destroying around 2,000 enemy aircraft on the ground on the first day alone. Nevertheless, so vast was the area the Germans were attempting to control that the Luftwaffe was spread very

The empty bomb cradles on this Heinkel He 111 suggest that it has just returned from a mission. The fuselage emblem just visible shows a white shield with a black bomb being ridden by a bull, indicating that this aircraft is from 4./Kampfgeschwader 1. Although the normal exit was from a door in the port side of the fuselage, as can be seen here a hatch in the cockpit could also allow exit on to the wing. (*Thomas Huss*)

At the start of the Second World War, the Luftwaffe was still using numbers of the older-model Dornier Do 17 as shown here with the rounded, glazed nose and relatively small cockpit. This version of the 'Flying Pencil' was no longer suitable as a front-line bomber by the spring of 1940, when Germany attacked Great Britain, but still gave good service as a training aircraft and in the photoreconnaissance role. (*Thomas Huss*)

thinly. In addition, the German production facilities were now struggling to keep up with wartime production demands. With Germany now fighting a war on two fronts, losses were mounting and soon reached the stage where not only aircraft destroyed but aircrew lost were outstripping Germany's ability to replace them. Ironically, it is estimated that almost as many aircraft were lost as a result of accidents caused by mechanical faults or by inexperienced pilots as by enemy action. It would take almost a full year before reorganisation in the aircraft industry brought about by Generalfeldmarschall Milch would bring aircraft production once again up to levels where they could exceed losses, but by then the war on the Eastern Front, while not yet lost, was no longer winnable.

The quality of the opposition that Germany was facing on the Eastern Front, both in terms of pilots and the aircraft they flew, also improved dramatically. By 1943, although the top aces were still running up huge scores, the average German fighter pilots were finding victories much harder to come by. Here again, the failure of the Luftwaffe to create a strategic capability was to be its undoing. Operating over the front lines, with fighters, light bombers and dive-bombers providing close support to ground forces, the Luftwaffe performed well. Its pilots learned new skills and those who had excelled as dive-bomber pilots now also became adept at 'tank killing'. Unfortunately for the Germans, however, Soviet production facilities were well behind the front line and beyond the capability of its light and medium bombers to reach, so that no matter how efficient the Luftwaffe was at knocking out enemy tanks at the front, the supply of replacements was never halted.

The Luftwaffe's last major offensive operation on the Eastern Front was Operation

The needs of a country at war saw all available aircraft pressed into military service. Among such types was the sole remaining example of the gigantic Junkers G 38. Only two of these aircraft were built. They were so large that passengers were accommodated inside the wings. The aircraft, named 'Hindenburg' (the name can just be seen painted at the nose), has been surrounded by a crowd of sightseers. It was lost in action on the Eastern Front. (*François Saez*)

Ground crew mechanics work on a Messerschmitt Me 109F from Jagdgeschwader 52, showing that unit's famous 'Pik As', or Ace of Spades, insignia on the engine cowling. (*Josef Charita*)

Citadel in July 1943. The operation, which resulted in the biggest clash of armour in history, saw the commitment of around 1,700 Luftwaffe aircraft. Tank-busting aircraft in particular achieved considerable success against enemy armoured units, but it was not long before the initiative was lost and the Luftwaffe forced on to the defensive. Soviet intelligence had, in fact, warned of the impending attack and once the German advance began to be bogged down, carefully husbanded Soviet reserves were committed to battle. Hitler eventually called off the offensive on 10 July 1943.

Once the Red Air Force had wrested control of the skies over Russia back from the Germans, the Luftwaffe's fortunes went into decline. In some areas, German aircraft could operate safely only at night, an almost complete reversal of the situation at the beginning of Operation Barbarossa, where the Luftwaffe ruled the skies and the Soviets were reduced to night-time operations that were of little more than nuisance value.

Things were little better on the Western Front. On 21 January 1943, Unternehmen Steinbock, was launched. This was a fresh bombing offensive against Great Britain, with London as the main target, the Luftwaffe seeking revenge for RAF raids on Berlin. The offensive continued for around fifteen months, eventually petering out in April 1944. Not only was the effectiveness of this mini-Blitz arguable, but the Luftwaffe

Luftwaffe personnel inspect a Soviet Lavochkin fighter which one of their number has shot down. As the war progressed, the quality of both Soviet pilots and aircraft improved dramatically and aircraft such as the Lavochkin were responsible for the demise of many German fighter pilots. (*Josef Charita*)

A Kette of Junkers Ju 87B dive-bombers over the Balkans. The two-tone dark green paint scheme is augmented by a bright-yellow engine cowling and rudder, standard markings for these aircraft during the Balkan campaign of 1941. (*François Saez*)

suffered significant losses to RAF fighters. Thereafter, the Luftwaffe switched the focus of its attacks towards ports in the south of England, where shipping was beginning to gather for the forthcoming invasion of Europe. Here again, results were meagre and achieved only with significant losses.

In June 1944, the Allied landings in Normandy were opposed by a Luftwaffe equipped with just 500 fighters, and by just over a month after the invasion, half of these had been lost.

AFRICA

From a position of neutrality at the outbreak of war, Italy joined the war on Germany's side in June 1940, her main ambition being territorial gains in North Africa. Unfortunately for Mussolini, his troops were soundly defeated by British forces in Libya in December of that year, leaving Hitler with no real option but to come to the aid of his ally. The Luftwaffe's aim was twofold. It would support the ground troops of Rommel's Afrikakorps in North Africa and, from bases in Sicily, along with its Italian allies, attempt to neutralise Malta as a base from which the British could interdict German supply convoys to North Africa.

For the British at this time, defence of the homeland was the first consideration, since the potential for an attempted German invasion still had to be considered, to say nothing of the German air assault. The aircraft allocated to the forces in North Africa, therefore, were second-rate types, including Gloster Gladiator biplanes, US-supplied P-40 fighters and a number of Hawker Hurricanes. All of these aircraft types were more than capable of tackling their Italian counterparts but, on the arrival

of the Luftwaffe, found themselves totally outclassed.

Malta began to suffer heavy aerial bombardment, the Luftwaffe and the Regia Aeronautica pounding both military installations on the island, and convoys attempting to bring reinforcements. Just as it seemed the island would go under, the Luftwaffe transferred resources to the Balkans in June 1941, in preparation for the onslaught against the Soviet Union. This gave the defenders a vital breathing space, but only a very brief one.

With the initial stages of Operation Barbarossa going well, the Luftwaffe soon returned and, as before, the defenders of Malta took a heavy pounding. Once again, however, just as victory was within their

A Messerschmitt Me 109F from Jagdgeschwader 52 in all-over-tan desert camouflage, with pale blue undersurfaces. Dogs were universally popular mascots with fighter pilots and this German Shepherd has been lifted up on to the aircraft's wing to pose for a shot with his owner. Mascots travelled, unofficially of course, to all theatres of conflict with their owners. (*Josef Charita*)

Erhard Jähnert, a ground attack ace from III./Schlachtgeschwader 3. Jähnert served in North Africa and on the Eastern Front, flying his final missions in the Kurland pocket. He was awarded the Oakleaves to his Knight's Cross in April 1945. He survived the war and several hundred combat missions to surrender to British troops in May 1945.

grasp, the Germans were forced to move essential air units away from this sector to reinforce both the Eastern and North African fronts. Shortly afterwards, quantities of Spitfires arrived on Malta, giving the defenders a much-needed boost. With only II Gruppe of JG53 remaining in Sicily to carry on the attack on the island, it was clear that the Germans were no longer in the position of virtually complete aerial superiority that they had previously held, and that any chance of subjugating the island had been lost.

In North Africa, the principal purpose of the Luftwaffe was in ground support, with much of the flying being done at relatively low altitudes, often fighter versus fighter. Here again, the Luftwaffe initially did well, in combat against aircraft that, in general, were inferior to its own. Lack of fuel and spare parts became a problem as Allied naval and air forces took an increasing toll

of German shipping crossing the Mediterranean to bring desperately needed supplies to Rommel. The opposition stiffened significantly in the spring of 1942, when better aircraft such as the Spitfire arrived in North Africa in numbers. This disadvantage was offset somewhat by the introduction of better models of the Me 109, specifically the 'G' or 'Gustav', and the arrival of a number of Fw 190s. This aircraft had been used in North Africa earlier, but as a fighter-bomber. Now it was appearing as a pure fighter.

With the arrival of US forces in North Africa in the Operation Torch landings of 8 November 1942, the pendulum swung irrevocably against the Luftwaffe. Now, instead of combating mediocre-quality aircraft types as it had in the early days of the campaign, it found itself not only outnumbered and short of fuel and ammunition, but up against superb aircraft such as

Mechanics work on a Ju 87 from which the engine cowling has been removed. Note the huge radiator, which necessitated the predominant 'chin' to the nose of the early-model Ju 87s. In later models the movement of the radiators to an underwing position allowed a much more streamlined nose. (*Josef Charita*)

the P-51 Mustang and the P-38 Lightning, as well as the latest Spitfire models. By May 1943, the Axis forces in North Africa had been defeated and the last units of the Luftwaffe were withdrawn to Sicily.

On the home front, Allied bombing raids were becoming ever more intensive. Initially, the US daylight bombing raids concentrated on trying to damage German naval bases in occupied France, with little effect. By January 1943, however, they had moved on to attacking targets in Germany itself, and Germany's failure to develop a strategic fighter force was having dire consequences. Luftwaffe fighter pilots were discovering that these heavy bombers were extremely difficult to shoot down. The machine guns with which most German fighters were armed were just not sufficient for this task.

One expedient which was tried was that of flying an aircraft above the bomber stream and dropping a time-fused bomb. This bomb would then explode in the middle of the bomber pack with devastating results. Other aircraft were fitted with rocket projectiles with similar intent; a direct hit would be devastating but even a near miss would cause significant damage, forcing a stricken bomber out of the pack where it would be easy prey for enemy fighters. The problem with these attempts was that the additional weight and drag factors placed on the German aircraft by carrying these bombs, rockets or the under-wing, gondola-mounted 3cm cannon made their performance sluggish, making them in turn easy prey if they were intercepted by escort fighters.

Although the German fighter defences were taking a heavy toll of Allied bombers, the Allied losses could be quickly made up, while the German losses, particularly of trained pilots rather than the aircraft, could

Mechanics inspect the undercarriage of a Messerschmitt Me 109. The narrow-track, outward-folding undercarriage gave the Me 109 awkward handling characteristics on take-off and landing, making it a difficult aircraft for the novice pilot. The wider-track, inward-folding undercarriage of the Fw 190 made for a much easier aircraft to handle. (*François Saez*)

not. Early US bombing raids, such as that on Schweinfurt in August 1943, where the US aircraft had flown without fighter escorts, depending on the combined fire-power of their own defensive machine guns, had suffered crippling losses of around 25 per cent, although, with each B-17 bomber carrying ten machine guns, the defensive power of the pack was indeed considerable. By the spring of 1943, however, daylight bombing missions were being escorted by P-38 Lightning and P-47 Thunderbolt fighters. This made the task of the German defenders infinitely more difficult, though there were still areas deep inside Germany which, until the advent of the P-51 Mustang

long-range fighter, gave the bombers considerable difficulty. The average daylight bombing raid of this time could see as many as 800 bombers taking part, supported by the same number of escort fighters.

The arrival of escorts such as the excellent P-51 Mustang in 1944 saw losses drastically reduced and from that time on the Germans faced the situation where the numbers of Allied bombers shot down were often matched by their own losses in making the attacks. It has been estimated that as many as 1,000 Luftwaffe fighter pilots were lost between January and April 1944. Once they had achieved control of the skies, the Allied fighters, no longer having to concen-

The pilot of this Me 109F, its fuselage emblem identifying it as from 3 Jagdgeschwader 52, has performed a successful belly-landing. Apart from the deformed propeller blades, the aircraft looks remarkably intact and fit for recovery and repair. From the fact that the cockpit canopy has been jettisoned, it seems that at one point the pilot considered baling out before deciding to try a forced landing. (*Thomas Huss*)

trate on protecting the bombers, could join in on the attack.

The Luftwaffe's night-fighter arm also achieved considerable success. The RAF night bombing raid on Nuremberg in March 1944 suffered 12 per cent losses and resulted in the entire night offensive being temporarily halted. With around 700 operational night-fighters around this time, the Luftwaffe's biggest challenge was obtaining sufficient fuel to keep them operational. It is estimated that by late 1944, the Luftwaffe was only obtaining around 20 per cent of the fuel it actually needed.

German industry, meanwhile, was producing aircraft at a prolific rate. The Allied bombing campaign may have devastated German cities but in fact had little impact on aircraft production. One senior Luftwaffe commander, when promised a manufacturing output of 36,000 aircraft, had commented that he would be hard pushed to be able to use more than 360.

Even at this late stage, however, the Luftwaffe proved itself capable of inflicting serious damage on the Allies. During the Allied airborne operations around Arnhem, German fighters shot down 122 Allied aircraft between 17 and 26 September 1944.

Also around this same time, a number of German fighter aircraft were formed into what were termed 'Sturmgruppen'. These units were equipped with beefed-up Fw 190 fighters carrying two 3cm cannon, two 2cm machine guns and two 12.7mm machine guns. Additional armour was also fitted to give the fighters better protection against defensive fire from the enemy bombers. The heavy armament and armour reduced the top speed and manoeuvrability of these

69

An Me 109 pilot is helped into his flying gear by a member of his ground crew prior to take-off. The cramped confines of an Me 109's cockpit were not the easiest to enter and exit in a hurry. (*Josef Charita*)

It was common for Luftwaffe fighter pilots to christen their aircraft after their wife or girlfriend. This pilot, with the ever-popular German Shepherd mascot, has named his Me 109 'Lisl'. (*Josef Charita*)

The young fighter pilots of the Luftwaffe were little different from those of other nations in enjoying the use of open-top, 'sporty' vehicles. The pilot, still wearing his flying boots and jerkin, is from Jagdgeschwader 53 'Pik As', and is fortunate enough to have the use of a Mercedes tourer from his unit motor pool. (*François Saez*)

aircraft, however, making them vulnerable to escorting fighters. To counteract this, each group of Fw 190s would be escorted by two groups of Me 109G fighters to fend off the escorts while the Fw 190s attacked the bombers.

On occasion, they scored phenomenal successes. On 27 September 1944, a force of some twelve B-17 bombers from 445 Bombardment Group were hit by a Sturmgruppe of Fw 190 fighters. Within just two minutes, ten of the B-17s had been shot down. Such successes, however, were not attained without losses and attrition in these Sturmgruppen reached levels of over 300 per cent during their short lifespan. In desperation, some of these units were even instructed to ram the enemy bombers if firepower alone was insufficient to bring them

down. Despite the desperate efforts of the German defensive units, some sense of the hopelessness of the situation may be gauged by the fact that between June and September 1944, the Luftwaffe had flown over 32,000 combat sorties and had lost approximately 3,500 pilots. The Allies, on the other hand, had flown over 200,000 sorties for the loss of just 500 pilots.

As the Allied advance through occupied Europe began to be bogged down because of overextended supply lines, the Luftwaffe was given something of a breathing space and began to remuster its resources. Remarkably, despite the efforts of the Allies to destroy German industry, the aircraft factories had no problem in meeting the need for replacement aircraft. The major problems were in finding sufficient fuel,

71

The crew of a Heinkel He 111 of Kampfgeschwader 27 celebrate the completion of their 100th successful combat mission, somewhere on the Eastern Front. Such celebrations were routinely carried out as morale-boosting events, often combined with the presentation of commemorative silver schnapps tumblers, and also often formed the 'milestones' by which the crews qualified for various awards, Front Front Flight Clasps, etc.

and more importantly, trained pilots of a good standard.

Attempts to build up a strong enough force to tackle the Allied bombing offensive were thwarted when Hitler launched his offensive in the Ardennes. In order to support this offensive the Luftwaffe was ordered to carry out a massed attack on Allied airfields so as to prevent any Allied counter-attack from receiving air support. On 1 January 1945, over 900 Luftwaffe aircraft set out on Operation 'Bodenplatte'. The results were disastrous. Although 200 Allied aircraft were destroyed (a loss which could quickly

and easily be made good), the Luftwaffe lost 300 aircraft of its own. In addition, as the Allied aircraft had been destroyed on the ground, no pilots were lost, but the 300 Luftwaffe aircraft which had been shot down took irreplaceable aircrew with them.

On the Eastern Front, after the great Kursk offensive, Germany had gone on to the defensive, and by the summer of 1944 the Luftwaffe was spread dangerously thin. Defending a front line of some 1,500 miles, it could offer only 400 fighters. The speed of the Soviet advance often saw airfields having to be abandoned at a moment's

Luftwaffe crews on the Eastern Front often fought alongside the air forces of allied nations. Romania also operated the Me 110, and here a number of Luftwaffe aircrew from a Zerstörergeschwader pose for a photograph along with their Romanian comrades. Luftwaffe aircrew were often to be seen wearing Romanian or Bulgarian aircrew badges. (*Josef Charita*)

This Junkers Ju 88 has come to grief in a collision with a Henschel Hs 126. It is difficult to ascertain exactly who collided with whom in this case but from the angle of the Henschel it would appear that the Ju 88 may have collided with it while taxiing. One would have expected damage to the Henschel's propeller had it struck the Junkers while on the move. The fragile nature of the glazed nose section on the early Ju 88 models is amply illustrated by this accident. (*Thomas Huss*)

The military funeral, with full military honours, of fighter ace Walter Nowotny. His honour guard was made up of fellow highly decorated fighter aces. Nearest the camera is Gordon Gollob carrying the orders pillow, a traditional method of displaying a deceased soldier's decorations. (*Josef Charita*)

notice, precious aircraft being obliged to take off and fly westwards while the ground crew, fuel, munitions, etc. were left to their fate. In January 1945, an additional 600 fighters were moved from the Western Front, but it was far too little to have an effect at this stage of the war. Fuel shortages were such that at times only 5 per cent of a Geschwader's aircraft strength could be flown.

In the last stages of the war, history was made when operational jet and rocket-propelled fighters went into combat for the first time. Germany developed several jet aircraft, but two in particular were effective against enemy aircraft. The Me 163 Komet, an astonishingly fast rocket-propelled aircraft, could reach combat height within just two minutes of being launched. Here,

after firing off its ammunition, and with its fuel exhausted, it glided back to earth (at speeds of over 500kph) and had to land on a crude skid under the fuselage. It is reckoned that accidents with the Me 163 claimed more of its pilots' lives than did enemy action. However, in the hands of skilled pilots, the Komet did succeed in downing enemy aircraft and thus earned its place in the history books.

The Me 262, though still suffering from developmental teething problems, could also inflict serious damage in the hands of skilled pilots, and a number of Luftwaffe 'Experten' joined the history books as the world's first jet fighter aces. In one raid over Germany in March 1945, twenty-nine jet fighter sorties were flown against US bomber formations.

CHAPTER FOUR

THE NIGHT-FIGHTING WAR

The Luftwaffe first began to develop its night-fighter arm in the spring of 1940. Prior to this, night combat was seen by the Luftwaffe to be the domain of the bomber on the offensive, not a defensive role for fighters. For the defence of the Reich, the Luftwaffe had to depend on the abilities of the Flakartillerie.

A training unit, or Lehrgeschwader, had been established at Griefswald in 1938 to trial the use of the Me 109 fighter for night attacks in cooperation with ground-based searchlight units. The style of night-fighting would require two basic factors – the illumination of the enemy in order that the fighters might find and attack them, and a good, clear sky.

Thanks to Ernst Udet, a fighter wing, (N) JG53, was given the task of developing night-fighting techniques, albeit with obsolete Arado Ar 68 open-cockpit aircraft with no electronic direction-finding/target location equipment. Based on the experience gained with (N) JG53, it was decided to

Hauptmann Rudolf Sigmund, night-fighter ace with II./Nachtjagdgeschwader 1. Sigmund was decorated with the Knight's Cross on 2 August 1943 when, refusing to bale out of a stricken aircraft and leave his badly wounded radio operator behind, he nursed his Me 110 back to its base, saving the life of his comrade. Sigmund was shot down and killed by his own flak after attacking enemy bombers over Munich on 31 October 1943, having achieved a score of 28 enemy bombers shot down.

form dedicated night-fighting groups, which were initially based in Norway and Denmark. These early units were equipped with aircraft such as the Me 109D, an obsolescent model unsuitable for blind night flying, something which perhaps indicates the low priority given to such operations by the Luftwaffe High Command. After all, Göring himself had said in 1939, 'Night fighting? It won't come to that!'

In the early stages of the war, the RAF's attentions were concentrated on leafleting raids and were of little effect. The Me 109D aircraft used against them had their canopies removed to avoid searchlight glare reflecting from the Plexiglas. The Luftwaffe's attempts to intercept the enemy aircraft were as ineffectual as the leafleting raids themselves. Only when the RAF began its night bombing campaign against Germany, and the combination of Flak-artillerie and searchlights, however skilful, was shown to be an inadequate answer, did attention focus once again on the development of the night-fighter.

In April 1940, Wolfgang Falck, later to become considered as the 'father' of the night-fighters, was tasked by Göring with forming a night-fighter force, and this included the conversion of his own 1./Zerstörergeschwader 1 to night-fighting. On 20 July 1940, the first aircraft to be destroyed by a dedicated Luftwaffe night-fighter unit was shot down. In the same month, Generalmajor Josef Kammhuber was appointed to establish the so-called Nacht-verteidigung, or night protection, of Germany. A defensive barrier which became known as the Kammhuber Line was established, consisting of a double line of both searchlights and flak artillery. Meantime, combat tactics were being developed by the Luftwaffe's night-fighter pilots.

Early night-fighting tactics were far from effective. The Me 109D had been replaced by an aircraft with far better prospects as a night-fighter, the Me 110. A larger, twin-engine aircraft with a much greater endurance, it could carry fairly powerful armament, had sufficient speed to outpace its intended target and, importantly, a second crew member to handle radio and, ultimately, radar, while the pilot concentrated on flying the aircraft and firing at the enemy. Although a failure in its original intended role as a heavy day-fighter the Me 110 would, in the hands of some of the Luftwaffe's finest Nachtjagdflieger, go on to become a highly successful night-fighter.

Even with a better aircraft at their disposal, however, the night-fighter pilots had a difficult task to perform. In order to avoid being blinded by glare from searchlights, the fighters had to attack their prey from below, with the disadvantages that climbing would reduce their speed and that moving into the searchlight beams themselves left them open to distracting glare and the perils of friendly fire.

Night-fighter forces were strengthened by the addition of some Ju 88s and Do 17s, their original glazed noses now solid and fitted with heavier armament, but still, the limited range of tactics available to them meant that successes were meagre. Nevertheless, the night-fighting war moved from being a purely defensive one to one in which the Germans took the offensive, with Luftwaffe night-fighters attacking enemy bombers over Great Britain as they returned from raids over Germany. Only relatively small successes were achieved, however.

Initially, three basic types of ground-based radar were used by the Germans, one to give early warning of the enemy approach, one to locate the bombers and a third to guide the night-fighter. In 1941, tests began with the use of aircraft-mounted interception radar, and the first kill credited to a Luftwaffe night-fighter equipped in this way was on 9 August 1941. It was not, however, until February 1942 that this form of radar was placed into volume production. The night-fighter pilots were not all impressed with the new equipment, which was prone, like many new developments, to faults and teething troubles.

Up until this point, enemy bombers made their approach to their targets individually, making them difficult for the night-fighters to find, since the ground-based guidance radar would only take them to the approximate position of their prey. Thereafter, until the advent of effective interception radar on the aircraft itself, much depended on the good eyesight of the night-fighter pilot. Cloudy conditions would often make the prey almost impossible to find.

Then, in May 1942, enemy tactics changed with the first of the so-called thousand-bomber raids. Far from the enemy being difficult to detect, the German radar was swamped with images and the night-fighters overwhelmed by sheer weight of numbers. A large quantity of enemy bombers flying in tight formation could bring a fairly effective combined weight of defensive fire to bear, making attacks on large formations much more dangerous than those on single aircraft.

Earlier in 1942, the FuG 212 Lichtenstein radar had been trialled, but was not universally popular. Some experienced night-fighter pilots felt that any advantage gained from the new radar equipment was offset by the loss of speed suffered due to the weight it added to the aircraft and preferred hunting their prey visually rather than by electronic means. Rapid develop-ment of new systems and tactics followed the beginning of the RAF's thousand-bomber raids.

In October 1942, the FuMG 65 system, known by the code-name of Würzburg-Gerät, came into service. A powerful radar system

US troops examine the support posts for the radar antennae on a captured Messerschmitt Me 110 night-fighter. Note the openings for the nose-mounted cannon between the two lower antennae posts. Also of note here are the shrouded exhausts on the engine cowlings, and the underwing drop tanks giving the aircraft extended endurance. (*National Archives*)

The ground element of the radar aircraft detection system often consisted of the Wurzburg FuMG (Flak) 39d, as shown here. Relatively small, with a 3m parabolic dish, it was easily portable.

for its day, it had a range of around 35km, later that same year extended to 70km.

A major part of the defence system was the Himmelbett radio apparatus. This involved the use of radio beacons for orientation, backed up by Freya apparatus with a range of 60 to 150km, used as an early warning system. Himmelbett and Freya assisted the Würzburg radar to track the signals of approaching aircraft and establish data regarding range, altitude, speed, etc., which was then transmitted to ground control. Here, a red beam was projected on to a glass table overlaid with a map of the area covered, giving a visual tracking of the enemy as they approached. In turn, ground control was connected to further Würzburg radar equipment which sent this data to the night-fighters, giving them the enemy position and at the same time transmitting their own position relative to the enemy back to ground control, where it was displayed as a blue beam projected on to the glass table. Generally, one night-fighter would be in the air, in a designated holding area awaiting vectoring to the enemy target, another would be ready for take-off on the ground, and a third waiting in reserve.

Although the whole of Germany was covered by a network of Himmelbett, Freya and Würzburg , a shortage of night-fighters meant that not every approaching bomber force was intercepted. Then, the RAF development of electronic countermeasures against the German systems made matters even worse for the Luftwaffe.

In June 1943, one of the Luftwaffe's accomplished bomber aces, Major Hajo Hermann, suggested an idea which was instantly seized upon by Göring. Instead of enforcing a blackout on potential target areas, Hermann suggested that they be fully lit, increasing the chances that the enemy aircraft would be spotted visually by dedicated, fast, single-engine fighters which would see their targets silhouetted against the brightly lit cities below. Searchlights would also be used, but no flak, meaning that the fighters would have no fear of being hit by friendly fire; they would, theoretically at least, have a much better chance of achieving hits than the flak in any case. The new tactics were known as 'Wilde Sau', or Wild Boar, and were carried out by Me 109 and Fw 190 fighters, fitted with drop tanks to give them an extended flight time.

The first operation took place in July 1943. Hermann and his comrades assembled in the skies over the predicted target in the Ruhr, safe in a flak-free zone, and awaited the enemy. Unfortunately the RAF had other ideas and attacked Cologne. Hermann and his colleagues sped to the actual target area, which of course was not a designated flak-free zone, and had to cope with heavy fire from German guns as well as defensive fire from enemy aircraft. Nevertheless the operation was a complete success: twelve enemy bombers were shot down and only one German fighter lost.

In July 1943, Luftwaffe night-fighters, scrambled to intercept an RAF bomber formation heading for Hamburg, were baffled to find their radar equipment showing thousands of contacts. The RAF was dropping aluminium foil, code-named 'Window' and designed to give the same radar signature as a bomber aircraft. As the night-fighters struggled in vain to find a real target, Hamburg was hit by a thousand-bomber raid. Eventually, the smarter Luftwaffe crews were able to differentiate between a 'Window' signal (which appeared to move unnaturally fast) and a true signal from a slow-moving bomber, but the initial confusion was immense.

An additional threat to the Nachtjagd-flieger was the increasing number of RAF night-fighters now escorting their bomber streams. The British had developed equipment that would detect the German search radar. As the Luftwaffe night-fighters approached the area in which the enemy had been reported and switched on their own search radar, they would be 'lit-up' to the escorting RAF night-fighters, who were waiting to pounce.

Göring was delighted with the results of Hermann's tactics and immediately authorised the formation of a new wing of Wilde Sau fighters, Jagdgeschwader 300, with Hermann as Geschwaderkommodore. These tactics were responsible for some significant successes. On 17 August 1943, 40 enemy bombers were shot down and a further 30

damaged. Six days later, during an RAF raid on Berlin, 56 enemy aircraft were shot down, and between 1 and 4 September 1943, also over Berlin, 73 bombers were downed. The Wilde Sau tactics finally came to an end in 1944 when a new radar system, Lichtenstein SN-2, was introduced and saw the night-fighters return to a more traditional tactic of being vectored towards their intended targets from the ground.

A number of combat tactics were developed by the pilots for the actual attacks. One had the pilot approaching the enemy bomber from below, some 500m lower than the intended victim. Once below the bomber, the fighter would pull up sharply. This would have the effect of reducing the fighter's speed so that, as the bomber passed over them, its unprotected belly exposed, the fighter would have a second or two more 'on target'. The tactic also had its disadvantages, needing expert flying skills to time the manoeuvre to perfection, to say nothing of the risk of colliding with the victim.

The most effective tactic to be introduced was the use of the so-called 'Schräge Musik' (jazz music or, in German, quite literally 'slanting' music). The name came from the fact that aircraft thus equipped had a number of upward-firing cannon mounted at a slanted angle in the main fuselage. Fighters so equipped could approach the enemy bomber, once again from below, usually undetected, and once in position simply fire the cannon in the fuselage up into the enemy bomber.

The concept had been first tried in 1942 with a radar-equipped Do 17 but the tests were not considered successful and the project was shelved. However, the main proponent of the tactic, Oberleutnant Schönert, fitted his Me 110 night-fighter with two 2cm MG 151/20 cannon, which he had attached to the rear of his cockpit. With

This close-up of the nose of a Junkers Ju 88R night-fighter shows an incredible array of radar antennae. The larger outer antennae are for the Lichtenstein SN-2, while the inner mounts, each with four dipoles, are for the FuG Lichtenstein 202.

this arrangement, he succeeded in shooting down a bomber in May 1943. Shortly afterwards, given command of II./NJG5, he was given authority to have three Do 217 aircraft fitted with upwards-firing armament in the fuselage.

The Schräge Musik system was first used on operations on 17 August 1943, when German night-fighters intercepted RAF bombers on their way to attack the research establishment at Peenemünde in the Baltic. The last of three waves of bombers were hit by night-fighters using Schräge Musik and

lost 29 bombers out of a total of 166 aircraft, a 17 per cent rate of loss. The rate at which losses were considered by the RAF to be unsustainable was 10 per cent, so it can be clearly seen that the successful use of Schräge Musik tactics could have the potential to cause havoc to the Allied night bombing offensive. Bombers rarely had any advance warning of the attack and only British advances in anti-radar detection equipment prevented even more serious damage to Bomber Command's efforts. With the concept now proven to be effective, more and more aircraft began to be fitted with upward-firing fuselage armament and by 1944 it is estimated that fully one-third of night-fighters carried Schräge Musik, using ever more powerful cannon.

In March 1944 an RAF night bombing raid on Nuremberg by almost 800 bombers was hit by night-fighters. A total of 94 bombers were shot down, 79 of them by night-fighters. No matter how badly wounded the Luftwaffe was, it was still capable of turning and inflicting devastating blows on occasion.

In the spring of 1944, the Siemens firm introduced the FuG 227 radar system, code-named Flensburg. Using wing-mounted antennae, it allowed the German night-fighters to home in on the tail warning radar which was carried on RAF bombers. Unfortunately for the Germans, on 13 July 1944 a Ju 88 night-fighter fitted with this equipment lost its way and landed by mistake at RAF Woodbridge. With the German aircraft available for examination, the British were soon able to remove the threat to the bombers by simply ordering that the tail warning radar be removed.

On 4 March 1945, around 200 Ju 88 aircraft from the Luftwaffe's Nachtjagdflieger took off from their airfields at the beginning of what was designated as Unternehmen Gisela. This time, instead of attempting to intercept Allied bombers as they approached their targets, the Germans would follow the aircraft home and hit them when they were at their most vulnerable, when landing.

A combination of factors allowed a significant German success. First, the night-fighters succeeded in crossing the North Sea and entering British airspace undetected. Then, in a display of complacency, convinced that the war was all but won, the Allied bombers switched on their navigation lights as they approached their airfields, not believing they were in any danger of attack from what was believed to be a defeated Luftwaffe. Thirdly, the night in question was clear, with no cloud formations to conceal the bombers from the night-fighters' attentions. A total of nineteen bombers were shot down, in addition to a further nine which had been lost during the raid on Germany. Eventually, British night-fighters that had been scrambled managed to drive off the intruders.

It has been estimated that somewhere around 100,000 Allied aircrew were lost during the RAF bombing offensive against Germany. It has also been estimated that approximately 1 million casualties were suffered by Germany during these raids. Certainly the raids against Germany and German-occupied areas inflicted far greater casualties than were ever suffered in German raids against Great Britain. The intent of the raids was twofold: to destroy the German economy and to break the morale of the German people. The first was only barely achieved towards the very end of the war. German production was still high and only lack of fuel and trained pilots kept so many German aircraft on the ground. The morale of the German people, like that of the British during the Blitz, was never broken.

The original night-fighter wing, Nachtjagdgeschwader 1, achieved over 2,300 aerial victories during the war (145 of them in daylight), an indication of just how effective and skilled the pilots of the Nachtjagdflieger had become. As with the day-fighter arena, Germany also took night-fighting into a whole new dimension by using a radar-equipped version of the Me 262 jet fighter. Equipped with this aircraft, 10 Staffel of NJG11 downed forty-three enemy aircraft in just seventy sorties, an extremely high kill rate for this late stage of the war.

CHAPTER FIVE

THE AIRCRAFT

At the opening of the Second World War the Luftwaffe was equipped with less than fifty major operational aircraft types, many of which were already obsolescent, and including a number of biplanes. By 1945, the Luftwaffe had produced over 190 aircraft types, including helicopters, two operational jets and one rocket-propelled fighter. Although a number of obsolescent types such as the Heinkel He 111 and Junkers Ju 52 remained in service throughout the war, through sheer necessity as no volume production of suitable replacements had occurred, by the end of the war the Germans also fielded some of the world's most advanced aircraft. War, inevitably, gives considerable impetus to technical advancement and nowhere was this as apparent as with the Luftwaffe. Although the speed with which some types were rushed into production meant that they were dogged by technical problems, Luftwaffe aircraft wielded considerable influence on post-war Allied aircraft design.

By the closing stages of the war, some of the finest early types such as the Messerschmitt Me 109 had reached the limits of the development potential of their airframes, while others like the Focke Wulf Fw 190 had gone way beyond what had been originally envisaged, to evolve into the superlative Ta 152. It was perhaps a failing on Germany's part that, when under the greatest pressure, she expended far too much time and effort on research and development work for advanced new types, when applying the same resources to creating more of the basic, well-proven designs might well have served the nation's military needs better. The speed with which the Allies rushed to grab the top German scientists and designers at the end of the war is testament to the respect in which their abilities were held.

Space restrictions mean that only a representative selection of some of the most important aircraft types from among the huge number manufactured can be covered here.

Note: Standard German nomenclature for aircraft types allocated a name for each lettered variant. Thus, for example, the A variant would be known as the 'Anton', the B as the 'Bertha' and so on, as follows:

Letter	Name
A	Anton
B	Bertha
C	Clara
D	Dora
E	Emil
F	Friedrich
G	Gustav

Letter	Name
H	Heinrich
I	Ida
J	Julius
K	Konrad
L	Ludwig
M	Martha
N	Nordpol
O	Otto
P	Paula
Q	Quelle
R	Richard
S	Siegfried
T	Theodor
U	Ulrich
V	Viktor
W	Wilhelm
X	Xanthippe
Y	Ypsilon
Z	Zeppelin

ARADO AR 196

By the outbreak of the Second World War, the Arado Ar 196 was the standard shipboard floatplane carried on most large German warships, replacing the older Heinkel He 60 biplanes that had previously been used. Development had begun in 1936 and the first prototype had flown the following year. Full volume production began in 1939.

A low-wing, two-seater monoplane, the Ar 196 was powered by a single BMW Bramo radial engine giving it a top speed of just

An Arado 196 floatplane, with wings folded, is hoisted aboard a heavy cruiser. Note the small rudders at the rear of each float, allowing the aircraft to be steered when on the water.

over 300kph, a reasonable performance given the huge drag factor of the fixed floats. It had a more than adequate range of around 1,000km and was armed with two 2cm cannon in the wings, a 7.92mm machine gun in the engine cowling and two 7.92mm defensive machine guns in the rear cockpit. It could also carry two 50kg bombs.

The Ar 196 was an extremely popular plane with its crews. It flew well, but had the advantage of good handling not only in the air, but on the water too. In addition to being carried on the major warships, the Ar 196, with its folding-wing facility, was widely used as the shipboard aircraft on Germany's auxiliary cruisers. Not having the luxury of a catapult to launch their aircraft as on the larger warships, the auxiliary cruisers had to hoist the seaplane out of its hangar by crane and deposit it on the water for take-off. Its use by these ships saw it take to the skies in areas as far afield as the Pacific Ocean.

Initially its use was principally by major units of the German fleet, but over time, as these ships were lost in action or decom-missioned, much of the combat use of the Ar 196 was from shore-based locations, from where it was used for coastal patrols and anti-submarine work. It was in fact an Ar 196 which forced the surrender of the British submarine HMS *Shark* in 1940.

In general, the Ar 196 is considered to have been superior to its Allied equivalents, although it would not, of course, have stood much chance against fighter aircraft carried on Allied escort carriers. Well over 500 Ar 196s were built. Production took place not only at Arado, but at SNCA in France and at Fokker in the Netherlands. Production ceased in 1944.

DORNIER DO 17

The Dornier Do 17 was the result of the firm's attempts to gain a contract from Lufthansa for the production of a fast mail plane with capacity for up to six passengers. However, attempts to reduce the cross-sectional dimensions of the fuselage as far as possible, to reduce drag and improve aerodynamics, made the interior too cramped

Most numerous of the Luftwaffe's pre-war bombers was the Dornier Do 17. Early examples of the type saw service in the Spanish Civil War, where it performed well despite weak defensive armament, its relatively high speed keeping it out of trouble. This example has come to grief and, with wings and undercarriage removed, is being recovered for repair. Note the crumpled nose.
(*François Saez*)

This revised model of the Dornier Do 17 was widely used during the Battle of Britain. This version had a much larger cockpit and an angular, glazed nose. The codes on this aircraft suggest that it belonged to either IV./KG76 or IV./KG40. This aircraft, too, suffered at the hands of enemy fighters and was later relegated to the heavy night-fighter role, where it enjoyed more success.

and uncomfortable for passengers, so the design was rejected by Lufthansa. Nevertheless, the Luftwaffe saw the potential of the aircraft as a light bomber and reconnaissance aircraft.

The earliest versions to enter production, the Do 17E bomber and Do 17F reconnaissance aircraft, instantly gained the nickname 'the Flying Pencil' because of the very thin fuselage section. Bomb-carrying capability was a meagre 500kg.

The German concept of having a light, fast bomber that did not require heavy defensive armament, since it was fast enough to outrun any enemy fighters, seemed to have been proven when a Do 17 came in first at the Zurich air competition in 1937, beating all of the fighters entered in the competition. Various engine types were tried on the aircraft in the months that

followed in an attempt to provide a better balance between speed, fuel economy and payload capacity. The Do 17P was tried in Spain with the Condor Legion but with its weak defensive armament suffered at the hands of Republican fighters. A new version, designated Do 17S, was produced, with a much larger cockpit extending below the lower fuselage level, producing the gondola structure later found on a number of other German types. The Do 17S also had a much more effective defensive armament.

The definitive model, the Do 17Z, appeared in time for the opening of the Second World War. It featured more powerful engines, an increased payload of 1,000kg and heavier armament. It performed well enough in the campaign against Poland, its relatively good speed and beefed-up armament just enough to keep it out of trouble.

A Dornier Do 217 about to take off on a night mission. The much-enlarged and heavily glazed nose and cockpit area are markedly different from earlier models of the Do 17 'Flying Pencil' which preceded it.

With the opening of the campaign in the west of 1940, however, it faced the faster, heavily armed Spitfires and Hurricanes of the RAF and was slaughtered in large numbers. Production ceased during that year and surviving examples were used either as test beds for new equipment, or converted to night-fighters. Those so converted were given solid noses into which were fitted up to four 7.92mm machine guns and two 20mm cannon. Do 17 night-fighters served on until around 1942, often as test beds for new radar equipment, before finally being phased out with the arrival of the Do 215 and Do 217.

The Dornier Do 215 had actually been intended as an export version of the Do 17Z and a number were constructed before the outbreak of war for sale to Sweden. The major difference between the Do 17 and Do 215 was in the provision of more power-ful engines which boosted not only its top speed but also its service ceiling. When war broke out, those destined for Sweden were taken over by the Luftwaffe. Around 100 or so Do 215s were completed, most of which went on to serve with the night-fighter arm.

Visually, they were almost identical to the Do 17.

Well before the outbreak of war, Dornier were aware that the Do 17 would not be able to compete with the performance of aircraft like the Junkers Ju 88 and development work had begun on a new, improved version, the Do 217. Once again, this aircraft was visually very similar to the Do 17Z model, but with a far superior performance. The first examples flew in 1938 and the aircraft entered Luftwaffe service in 1940. It was not until the closing stages of the Battle of Britain in 1941, however, that it first saw combat action. As a bomber, it was capable of carrying the 'Fritz' glider bomb with which Do 217s sank the Italian battleship *Roma*. It also served as a night-fighter in its J and M versions, with powerful nose-armament featuring four 7.92mm machine guns and four 20mm cannon, and could also carry the 'Schräge Musik' slanted, fixed-firing guns in the rear fuselage. Production ceased in 1943, by which time it was clear that what Germany desperately needed was a series of purpose-built, true night-fighters, rather than converted bombers.

DORNIER DO 24

This flying boat first flew in 1937, having been developed as an export project on behalf of the Netherlands, for use as patrol aircraft in the Far East. It first entered volume production in Holland under licence, but when the factory was captured, shortly after Germany's attack on France and the Low Countries, subsequent production went to the Luftwaffe.

The Do 24 had a wingspan of 27m, and length of 22m. It was powered by three engines, either Pratt & Whitney or BMW Bramo, giving it a top speed of between 340kph and 400kph, dependent on the engine type fitted, a ceiling of between 5,900m and 5,600m, and a range of between 2,900km and 3,200km. The military version carried a crew of four, with armament consisting of one 2cm cannon and two 7.92mm machine guns. The Do 24 was well liked by its crews and had superb handling characteristics on the water. Construction continued briefly after the war, with a further twenty built for German civilian use, and a number were also sold to Spain, where they remained in service until 1967.

FIESELER FI 156 STORCH

This superb light communications and observation aircraft was introduced in 1936. Aptly named Storch (Stork) because of its long, spindly undercarriage legs, it had short take-off and landing (STOL) capabilities which made it a first-class type for operating out of battlefield locations – front-line airstrips, roads, or just about any small field or unobstructed piece of ground. With only the lightest of headwinds, the Storch could take off in just 60m and land in just 20m. Indeed, the Storch was one German aircraft that was never bettered by

A Dornier Do 24 flying boat in a steep climb. These aircraft were built for use by the Dutch forces in the Far East and built under licence in Holland. They were only taken into wider use by the Luftwaffe after the Dutch manufacturing facility was overrun by the Germans in 1940.

Not as glamorous as the fighters, but certainly one of the finest aircraft of its type ever to be made, was the superb Fieseler Fi 156 Storch. With short take-off and landing capabilities, the Storch could operate not only from airstrips but from roads, fields or just about any small piece of reasonably level ground. It was the favoured personal aircraft of many senior commanders. (*Josef Charita*)

any Allied equivalent type throughout the entire war.

A high-wing monoplane with a spacious, large, glazed cabin, it was powered by an Argus As10C-3 engine, giving it a top speed of just 175kph, slow flying speeds being no disadvantage for observation duties, a ceiling of 4,600m and range of 385km. It was armed with a single 7.92mm machine gun in the rear cockpit for self-defence.

The Storch was extremely popular with senior commanders, who often had one as their personal aircraft and used them to command their troop movements from the air. Among those who considered the Storch

an invaluable tool and used the aircraft with considerable frequency were some of Germany's best leaders – Rommel, von Manteuffel, Model, Kesselring, von Richthofen and others. Even Field Marshal Montgomery is said to have been most impressed on testing out a captured Storch in North Africa.

Capable of flying in almost all weathers, as well as general communication/ observation duties, the Storch found itself employed as a photoreconnaissance aircraft and an air ambulance. It also had towing capabilities for light gliders. Of course, such light, slow-moving aircraft did make excellent targets for the enemy, and many were shot down – often by ground fire. The commander of 3 SS-Panzer Division 'Totenkopf', SS-Obergruppenführer Theodor Eicke, was killed when his Storch was shot down by Russian ground fire while he was on a forward reconnaissance. Generalfeldmarschall Walter Model and General Ludwig Crüwell were also shot down when flying in a Storch. The former escaped unscathed, while the latter was taken prisoner.

The Storch gained fame during the audacious rescue of Italian dictator Benito Mussolini from his prison at Gran Sasso by SS-Sturmbannführer Otto Skorzeny. The Storch was safely landed on a tiny, flat plateau on the mountain and took off again successfully, carrying the giant Skorzeny and the less-than-slim Italian dictator, surely testing the aircraft to the limits of its carrying capacity when taking off in such dangerous circumstances.

Interestingly, a Storch was the last German aircraft to be shot down in a 'dogfight' in the Second World War. In this unique event, a Storch was spotted by its US counterpart, a Piper Cub artillery observation plane. The Cub went into the attack, with its occupants shooting at the Storch with their .45-calibre Colt automatics, damaging the Storch sufficiently to bring it down. Not only was the Storch the last plane to be brought down, but the only one to be downed by pistol fire.

A total of just under 3,000 examples were built during the Second World War, and so successful was the aircraft that the Storch was constructed postwar in France by Morane-Saulnier as the 'Cricket', albeit with the in-

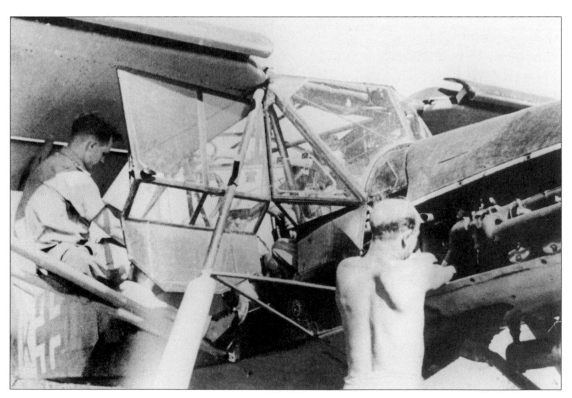

As mechanics work on the engine of this Storch, a good view is afforded of the large, glazed cockpit offering the type of superb visibility essential in a good spotter aircraft. (*Josef Charita*)

line engine replaced by a radial type. Production also continued in Czechoslovakia after the war and the design was further copied by the Russians and the Japanese.

FOCKE WULF FW 189

Designed by Kurt Tank as a replacement for the ageing Henschel Hs 126, this reconnaissance aircraft entered service in 1941. It featured a distinctive twin-boomed tail, a central fuselage and a substantial level of glazing to the roomy cockpit, giving the excellent degree of visibility essential to a reconnaissance aircraft. The Fw 189 was twin-engined, and carried a crew of three or four members.

The aircraft had excellent handling and its good manoeuvrability and armament made its destruction a difficult proposition for enemy aircraft. It was also capable of absorbing a huge amount of damage while still remaining airborne. Around 845 examples were manufactured.

FOCKE WULF FW 190

Even if many of Germany's aces preferred the Me 109, the aircraft designed to be its successor, the Focke Wulf Fw 190, is believed by many to have been the finest aircraft produced by Germany during the Second World War. Designed by Kurt Tank as a successor to the Me 109, the first prototype flew in 1939 and production of the Fw 190A began in the following year. Known as the Würger (Butcher Bird, or Shrike), it was a low-wing monoplane typified by the large cowling of a radial engine, in this case the BMW 801. The aircraft also had its undercarriage legs mounted in the wings, folding inboard, giving a much greater width of track and thus increased stability on take-off and landing. The Fw 190 did have some disadvantages, however. Forward visibility when on the ground during take-off and landing, taxiing, etc., was poor because of the angle at which the aircraft sat and the large cowling. Pilots often claimed that the aircraft became uncomfortably hot and that, in emergencies, the canopy could be difficult to open against the slipstream. Explosive cartridges had to be fitted to aid in opening the canopy when flying at speed.

Nevertheless, the Fw 190A was a fine aircraft. It had a top speed of 653kph and a powerful armament of two 13mm heavy machine guns and four 20mm cannon. When it appeared in action against the RAF in 1940, the Fw 190A outclassed anything

The Fw 189 reconnaissance aircraft was a highly successful design that gave sterling service, particularly on the Eastern Front, in its intended role. Well liked by its crews, it was robust and capable of taking considerable punishment.

A Focke Wulf Fw 190A. Particularly noticeable is the wide track of the undercarriage, which folds up inwards, rather than outwards as on the Me 109, making the aircraft far more stable on take-off and landing. Note the gun barrels visible at the wing root and also just by the top of the undercarriage leg. (*Josef Charita*)

Britain could offer, making even the current, improved model of the Spitfire, the Mk V, look sluggish in comparison.

A large number of sub-variants of the Fw 190 were produced as this highly versatile design was adapted, and saw the Fw 190A carry bombs, rockets, heavy cannon in wing-mounted pods, and even a torpedo. A twin-seat trainer version was also produced, as was a night-fighter version. With drop tanks fitted, the Fw 190 had an extremely useful range of around 950 miles.

A number of the new aircraft saw service in North Africa and on the Western Front in an attempt to combat the newly introduced Spitfire Mk V. The latest Spitfire was completely outclassed by the Fw 190, and so impressed were the British that they actually planned a commando raid on a German airfield in occupied France in an attempt to steal one for evaluation. In the event the plans proved unnecessary as on 23 June 1942 a Luftwaffe pilot who had lost his way landed his Fw 190 on an English airfield by mistake. For a time, it seemed that whenever the RAF received a new, improved version of the Spitfire, the Luftwaffe outdid it with a better version of the Fw 190. The most successful types, the Fw 190A-5 and Fw 190A-8, between them had over twenty sub-variants, including fighter-bombers, reconnaissance aircraft and rocket-armed fighters.

For an aircraft which, it was felt, would not be able to surpass the Me 109, the Fw 190A earned a solid reputation as a first-class aircraft. Fw 190s were even used on hit-and-run bombing raids on England. It also

The side view of an Fw 190A shows the teardrop canopy to good advantage. Lacking the heavy angular framing of the Me 109, it gave the pilot far greater visibility. One disadvantage of the Fw 190 was the lack of forward vision for the pilot when taxiing, his view being obscured by the cowling of the large BMW radial engine. (*Josef Charita*)

earned the respect of Allied aircrew. An interesting anecdote relates that when a US manufacturer produced a spoof poster of the Fw 190 with the tag line 'Who's afraid of the big bad Wulf?', they received back a copy of the poster signed by a large number of aircrew with the message, 'We are!'

In 1943, the so-called 'long-nosed' Fw 190D began to appear, the 'Dora'. Fw 190B and Fw 190C models had been proposed but never reached production. This aircraft had a lengthened forward fuselage into which was mounted an in-line rather than radial engine, though the basic appearance remained similar because of the large, annular radiator fitted in front of the engine. In fact the Fw 190D-9 (in the numbering system, the D-9 followed the A-8) was effectively a stop-gap measure in the programme that would ultimately lead to the Ta 152. Capable of speeds of up to 685kph, this much-improved version brought the FW 190

back its superiority over most other existing fighters in its class. With many of its top aces by now having been lost in action, however, the Luftwaffe was in the position of having one of the finest aircraft in existence but no longer having quite so many of the top-quality pilots to fly them. Nevertheless, on their very first combat mission, Fw 190D-9s downed four Lancaster bombers and a Mosquito fighter. Around 700 Fw 190Ds were produced.

The ultimate development of the Fw 190 was the high-altitude interceptor, which was given a Ta, rather than Fw, prefix in honour of its designer, Kurt Tank. With a speed of 755kph and a ceiling of 15,000m, the Ta 152 was armed with a 30mm cannon, firing through the propeller spinner, and a 20mm cannon in each wing. Thankfully for the Allies, only 150 or so Ta 152s were completed before the war ended and only very few of these saw combat; this aircraft would

Without doubt one of the finest aircraft of the war, the Focke Wulf Fw 190 was far more stable on take-off and landing than the Me 109. As can be seen from this view, however, the nose-high attitude and the large cowling for the radial engine badly obstructed the pilot's forward view on taxiing. (*National Archives*)

have had a devastating effect on the Allied bomber formations attacking German targets had it seen service in significant numbers.

In all, some 20,000 Fw 190s of various types were produced, of which around 7,000 were the fighter-bomber variants. A small number were provided to German allies, including 75 to Turkey, where they served until 1948, 72 to Hungary, a small number to Romania and evaluation examples to Japan. It is also believed that the Red Air Force captured sufficient Fw 190s intact at the end of hostilities to maintain a few operational squadrons of them after the war. A number of airframes were also completed by the French after the war, but did not remain in service for any length of time because of reliability problems with the engines.

Approximately a dozen Fw 190s still exist in collections today, of which four are long-nose 'Dora' variants, though none are thought to be in flying condition. Though it never came to replace the Me 109, and indeed many Me 109 pilots much preferred their aircraft to the Focke Wulf, the Fw 190 is considered by many to have been the best German fighter aircraft of the Second World War.

FOCKE WULF FW 200 CONDOR

This highly successful aircraft started life as a civilian transport plane. Design work started in 1936 and the first prototype flew in 1937. The Condor flew with Lufthansa, with Danish airline DDL and with a Brazilian airline. It carried nine first-class and seventeen second-class passenger seats. In 1938, Lufthansa flew one of its Fw 200s non-stop from Berlin to New York, a flight lasting around 25 hours. It later also flew on the Tokyo route, a flight (with stops) lasting over 40 hours. Its potential as a long-range reconnaissance aircraft was immediately obvious to the Luftwaffe.

A large aircraft, some 23m in length and with a wingspan of nearly 33m, it was powered by four BMW Bramo engines. Volume production began with the Fw 200A and continued with the more powerful, but heavier, Fw 200B, and the Fw 200D, with increased fuel capacity.

The basic Fw 200B transport version was also taken into military use and several served as VIP transports for senior officials, including Hitler himself. Hitler's personal aircraft was one of the original Fw 200A types, named Immelmann III, commanded by his personal pilot, Hans Bauer, a veteran First World War fighter ace. Bauer had flown civil aircraft for Lufthansa after the war but came to Hitler's notice and was transferred to the SS. Hitler's personal Condor featured armour plating and a downward-firing ejector seat which would launch its passenger out through the floor of the aircraft. The head of the SS,

The Fw 200 Condor. These aircraft bear the distinctive insignia of Kampfgeschwader 40. The massive size of the Condor and its origins as a civilian airliner are very apparent.

Bernhard Jope was one of the Luftwaffe's top Focke Wulf Condor pilots. Serving with Kampfgeschwader 40, Jope was decorated with the Knight's Cross of the Iron Cross on 30 December 1941 in recognition of his bombing of the 42,000-ton troop transporter *Empress of Britain* on 24 October of that year. He later received the Oakleaves on 24 March 1944 and became Kommodore of Kampfgeschwader 100. After the war, Jope returned to civil aviation and was a pilot with Lufthansa.

Reichsführer-SS Heinrich Himmler, also had his own personal Fw 200, a C-4 variant.

In 1939, a military version with more powerful engines, the Fw 200C Condor, appeared. This version had actually begun life as an export project on order for the Imperial Japanese Air Force. However, the outbreak of war saw the project taken over for German use. It was intended for long-range maritime reconnaissance. With a crew of up to eight, the FW 200C-3 version was typically armed with one 20mm cannon in a turret just abaft the cockpit, three machine guns in a dorsal gondola and two in the mid-fuselage. It could also carry a bomb load of up to 2,000kg under the wings and some examples were even adapted to carry Hs 293 guided missiles. Its range was up to 3,560km and it had a top speed of some 360kph.

Unfortunately the alterations made to the aircraft's structure to produce the military version resulted in a weak fuselage and several of these huge aircraft broke up as a result of the stress induced by the impact on landing, the fuselage fracturing just aft of the wing. The long endurance of the civilian version was also drastically reduced by the excessive weight produced by the military requirements, and stood at around 14 hours. Addition of Hohentweil radar equipment increased the weight even further. The inherent weaknesses in the structure of the military version also meant that if the aircraft took violent evasive measures to avoid attack by enemy aircraft it was liable to break up.

The Fw 200C entered service with Kampfgeschwader 40, operating from near Bordeaux in occupied France. In the first two months of anti-shipping operations alone, Fw 200 Condors sank an estimated 90,000 tons of enemy shipping. Initially, their extreme long range allowed them to attack convoys well out of the range of land-based air cover. The advent of a more disciplined convoy system with aircraft carrier escorts allowed the Allies to counter this threat successfully, however, as the large, slow Condors, despite their heavy defensive armament, were no match for Allied fighters. Nevertheless, well over 360,000 tons of Allied shipping is reckoned to have been lost to attacks by the Condor. Churchill himself referred to the aircraft as the 'scourge of the Atlantic'.

Losses eventually led, in 1941, to its role changing from maritime bomber to maritime reconnaissance. Condors were thereafter specifically ordered to avoid action with the enemy. Instead of attacking enemy shipping, they were to locate enemy convoys and stand off, shadowing the enemy while U-boats were homed in on them. A few examples did return to maritime strike duties armed with the Hs 293A anti-shipping missile but were not particularly successful.

Their achievement in combined operations with the U-boats was illustrative of what might have been achieved if the Navy had been allowed to have its own air element, akin to Britain's Coastal Command. Unfortunately, Göring's insistence that 'Everything that flies belongs to me!' ensured that cooperation between the Luftwaffe and Kriegsmarine was kept to a minimum. Far from being helpful to the Navy, he was positively obstructive to combined operations between the two.

The Fw 200 Condor had been a first-rate civilian aircraft and had provided sterling service to the military. It had not been designed with military use in mind, however, and the aircraft's structure was put under tremendous strain by the type of use it saw as a combat aircraft. Increasingly robust defences available to Allied shipping saw surviving Condors relegated to transport duties once again in the second half of the war, and some were involved in attempting to keep 6 Armee in Stalingrad supplied. Nevertheless, it remained one of the more successful aircraft in terms of the damage it inflicted on enemy shipping compared with other aircraft adapted for maritime use.

Production ended in 1944, by which time around 270 Fw 200s of all types had been produced. This is not a large number by any standards, but despite its faults the Condor certainly achieved successes out of proportion to the small numbers in service. Remaining examples soldiered on in transport duties through to the end of the war. A further development intended to result in an even larger version, the Fw 300, did not progress beyond the design stage. There are no surviving Condors in flying condition known to exist today. In 1999, however, a Condor was raised from a fjord in Norway but disintegrated during the lifting operation. The recovered fragments are currently undergoing restoration in Germany, where it is hoped to produce a complete aircraft, but one which will be a static display piece only.

HEINKEL HE 111

The mainstay of the Luftwaffe's bomber arm in the Second World War, the Heinkel He 111 began its life in the early 1930s when its designer, Ernst Heinkel, sought to design what was intended as a fast passenger plane. The result was a successful single-engine aircraft, the Heinkel He 70, which broke several records. Introduced in 1932, it carried four passengers at around 320kph, extremely fast for its day.

The Luftwaffe then instigated development of a larger passenger aircraft with the specification that it be easily converted for military use. Work commenced on a larger, twin-engine version of the He 70, which would develop into the He 111. Although

The Eastern Front in winter, and ground crew prepare to load bombs into a Heinkel He 111. Considerable time and effort was required to keep aircraft in flying condition in winter on the Eastern Front, when engine blocks would often freeze solid, and trays of burning oil were placed on the ground under the engines to thaw them out. (*Josef Charita*)

bigger, the He 111 clearly shows its lineage, with many design similarities to the smaller aircraft. The He 111 entered service with Lufthansa in 1936 as a civil airliner in its V2 and V3 versions (a bomber variant of the V3 was also produced). At the same time, however, the airframe was being developed as a bomber. The area used as a smoking compartment in the civil version, immediately aft of the cockpit, had become the bomb bay of the military variant. Although the civilian version was successful, the added weight requirements of the military version resulted in an aircraft that was underpowered, having a top speed of only 275kph. Only a small number of He 111A were made, these eventually being sold to China.

The first major military variant was the He 111B, which had a greatly improved

97

performance, the original BMW engines being replaced by more powerful Daimler-Benz units, giving the aircraft a top speed of 365kph. At this speed they could outrun many of the fighter aircraft of the day. Around 300 were produced, some of which saw service with the Condor Legion during the Spanish Civil War. This version carried a payload of around 1,500kg. A number of early examples of the He 111 were also sold to Turkey.

The next major variant saw a redesigned, fully glazed nose replacing the cockpit atop the fuselage of the earlier models. Improved engines increased its top speed to around 400kph, and large numbers were ordered. Entering service in 1938, this new version was built in substantial quantities, so that over

700 He 111s were available for action in the attack on Poland. With losses low and production rapid, even greater numbers were available for the 1940 campaign in the west.

Further improvements to the powerplant resulted in the most prolific version, the He 111H. Carrying a crew of five, it had a single machine gun in the nose, one in a dorsal position that would eventually be replaced by a powered turret and one in a ventral gondola. Guns could also be mounted to fire from the fuselage side-windows. The bomber version could carry a payload of over 3,000kg. Although the vast majority built were intended as conventional medium bombers, a function the aircraft carried out successfully, it was also capable of carrying torpedoes as a maritime strike

Aircrew gather under the nose of a Heinkel He 111 to celebrate the end of a successful sortie. The Luftwaffe's bombers carried much less defensive firepower than Allied bombers and the attrition rate was high when they encountered determined enemy fighter opposition. (*Thomas Huss*)

aircraft. In the event, however, most anti-shipping strikes by He 111s involved the use of bombs rather than torpedoes.

One bizarre version, the He 111Z (the 'Z' standing for 'Zwilling' or 'Twin') consisted of two He 111s, joined together by a common central wingspan between the two fuselages, and was used as a tug for towing the enormous Messerschmitt Me 321 Gigant glider. The subsequent decision to add engines to the Gigant made the equally gigantic He 111 Zwilling redundant and plans to create a bomber version of this huge aircraft came to nothing.

A further He 111 variant, the H-22, of which around 100 were made, was adapted for launching the V1 flying bomb in flight rather than from the conventional fixed launch ramps which would be introduced later. Well over 400 attacks with V1s were made from He 111 aircraft.

What had been a highly successful bomber during the campaigns against Poland and in the west began to show its inadequacies during the attack on Great Britain. Its defensive armament was ineffective against the Spitfires and Hurricanes of the RAF and the limited range of the Messerschmitt Me 109s that provided escort for the bombers meant that they were often left unprotected. Operating over friendly territory, the RAF fighters could land, quickly refuel and rearm and take off again to continue the attack, while the German fighters were forced to break off and return to their bases in France when fuel and munitions ran low. Following the heavy losses suffered in the Battle of Britain, the He 111 gradually began to be replaced for daylight operations by the Ju 88. The Heinkel then took over as the predominant night bomber, as well as seeing heavy use as a transport aircraft.

Production eventually ceased in 1944, by which time well over 7,000 had been produced. By that time it was well outdated, but the lack of a suitable replacement (the larger Heinkel He 177 Greif being a major disappointment and suffering from multiple problems) meant that it remained in service until the end of hostilities.

One of the He 111's greatest moments was on 21 June 1944, when bombers of the type attacked the Soviet airfield at Poltava. The airfield was packed with American B-17 bombers and their P-51 Mustang escorts, which had landed there after a bombing raid on the Ploesti oilfields in Romania. Some sixty-five enemy aircraft, including forty-five B-17 bombers, were destroyed in the surprise attack.

Production of the design also continued under licence in Spain as the Casa 2.111. Over 200 of this Spanish variant were manufactured and the aircraft remained in service until 1965. It was surviving examples of the Spanish-built variant which were used in the movie *The Battle of Britain*. Ironically, the Spanish version of the He 111 was powered by engines from the firm that also provided engines for the Spitfire aircraft that destroyed so many He 111s during the Battle of Britain – Rolls-Royce.

The last airworthy He 111 (actually a Spanish-built CASA) crashed in 2003. It is believed that a further example is under restoration to flying condition at the time of writing, but currently there are no examples of the He 111 still flying.

HEINKEL HE 162 SALAMANDER

Although not spectacularly successful, the He 162 earned its place in history as one of the handful of jet-powered aircraft to see combat service and actually achieve aerial victories against the enemy.

On 10 September 1944, the Air Ministry issued a requirement for a single-seat jet aircraft which was to be easy to build and cheap to manufacture in large quantities, the intent being simply to scrap any damaged or faulty aircraft rather than waste time and resources on costly repairs. Proposals were to be lodged within ten days and the fighter to be in production by 1 January 1945. The new fighter was to be known as the 'Volksjäger', or 'People's Fighter'. The concept was wholeheartedly supported by Hermann Göring, who went so far as to suggest that the new aircraft could be piloted by Hitler Youth boys, who had at best had only rudimentary training on powered aircraft, having spent most of their flying time on gliders. More sensible voices objected, unhappy at resources being diverted from proven designs like the Me 262, but were overruled.

Most major German aircraft manufacturers submitted tenders but it was the Heinkel firm which was, in the event, successful. The firm was given an order for 1,000 of the new fighters, to be produced by April 1945. The aircraft was to be powered by a single BMW-003 turbojet, attaining a speed of 760kph, and armed with two 2cm or 3cm cannon.

The resultant aircraft carried the engine in a large pod on top of the fuselage, the intake being just behind the cockpit. It featured a tricycle undercarriage and twin tail fins (to avoid the jet engine exhaust), and was of composite construction, with a metal fuselage but wings and tail fins made from wood.

The first prototype was flown in December 1944 and, although it performed well, highlighted some of the problems faced by Germany at this stage of the war when one of its laminated wooden undercarriage doors fell off in flight. It had been the victim of poor-quality bonding agents. The Luftwaffe faced similar problems with

The Heinkel He 162 Salamander, an aircraft which might have had considerable potential had it not been rushed into volume production far too soon. The huge engine mounted behind the cockpit seriously hindered the pilot's view of any aircraft approaching from the rear, although because of the He 162's speed, the chances of any enemy coming from that quarter were minimal. (*Thomas Huss*)

its Moskito night-fighter, an almost direct equivalent to the Mosquito used by the RAF, and also made predominantly of wood. Germany just could not source the correct constituents for good-quality glues at this point in the war.

Nine days after the first flight, the prototype was being put through its paces when the glue on one of the wings failed and the aircraft lost an aileron. Out of control, it crashed to the ground, killing the pilot. Another danger facing pilots of the He 162 was trying to bale out of a cockpit which was immediately in front of the jet engine intake. To avoid the pilot being sucked into the engine, the He 162 was fitted with an ejector seat.

A number of improvements were made over the next few prototypes, in particular the strengthening of the wings, to which downturned tips were added to improve stability, and strengthening the nose to cope with the recoil from the 3cm cannon. By the end of January 1945, the first production aircraft were ready.

The He 162A was capable of a top speed of 900kph, much faster than the original specification had called for, despite being heavier as a result of the various improvements made to the design. In February 1945, just under fifty of the new fighters were delivered to a test and evaluation unit, Erprobungskommando 162, commanded by top ace Heinz 'Pritzl' Baer. Later that month, the first examples were also delivered to a front-line combat unit, I./Jagdgeschwader 1, replacing its Focke Wulf Fw 190 fighters.

It was March 1945 before all the pilots operating these aircraft were fully familiarised with their new jet fighters. At the beginning of April, I./Jagdgeschwader 1's airfield was heavily bombed by US B-17s, forcing it to move to a new location near the Danish border. Around this time

II./Jagdgeschwader 1 also began to receive the He 162. The new jets finally went into combat service in mid-April and scored their first success on 19 April when an He 162 shot down an RAF Tempest. Unfortunately the He 162 itself was also shot down during the return flight to its base.

Over the remaining few weeks of the war, He 162s succeeded in shooting down a few more Allied aircraft, but only at the cost of at least thirteen of their own number. It should be noted, however, that most of these losses were due to the failure of the aircraft engines or structure, rather than to enemy action. Many of the pilots who flew the He 162 considered it to be a first-class aircraft. Although the design itself was sound, the type had been rushed into service in an incredible three months from the issuing of the original requirement, meaning that little or no time had been allowed to iron out the type of flaws which dog almost all new products. One RAF pilot was killed after the war while flying an He 162 at an air display, when one of the wooden tail fins broke off.

The He 162 had a very limited endurance, because of its thirsty jet engines and its inability to carry a large fuel load. The substantial engine mounted on top of the fuselage behind the pilot also blocked his view in that direction, though at the time there were no Allied aircraft capable of enough speed to pursue and attack an He 162 from this position. It seems reasonable to assume, however, that had more time been available properly to develop the aircraft and address some of its more significant flaws, the result might have been an impressive aircraft. As it was, the He 162 was yet another example of 'too little, too late' for the Luftwaffe.

Jagdgeschwader 1 surrendered most of its He 162s intact at the end of the war, so several still exist in museum collections, in Europe and the USA. None are in flying condition and, given the inherent dangers in operating this aircraft, it is unlikely that any attempts would ever be made to bring one to a state of airworthiness.

HEINKEL HE 177 GREIF

Design work on this most unfortunate aircraft, ultimately the only heavy bomber that Germany would produce, began in 1938. As a result of political interference and the lack of support for a strategic heavy-bomber programme, ridiculous demands were placed on the design, including the requirement that it be able to perform as a dive-bomber! Such outrageous suggestions resulted in considerable delays and the aircraft would not enter service until 1942.

The He 177 was a large aircraft with a 31m wingspan and 22m in length. It carried a crew of six, had a maximum speed of 472kph, a ceiling of just over 7,000m and a range of up to 5,000km. Armament consisted of a single 7.92mm machine gun in the glazed nose, two further machine guns in forward and rear dorsal turrets, a machine gun in the tail and two more at the rear of the ventral gondola. The He 177 could carry up to 6,000kg of bombs internally. It could also carry two Hs 293 guided missiles under the wings, as well as mines or torpedoes in the anti-shipping role.

One of the most interesting, and problematic, features of the He 177 was its engines. In order to give it the performance demanded of it, two 2,950hp Daimler-Benz DB 610 units were fitted, each made up of two twelve-cylinder liquid-cooled engines coupled to a single propeller. This arrangement was horrendously prone to catching fire. Six of the eight prototypes were lost to crashes, as were the majority of the pre-production examples.

Although some He 177s took part in the bombing campaign against Great Britain in the dive-bombing role (albeit a very shallow dive), the majority ended up on the Eastern Front. Here they were even used as tank-busters with 5cm or 7.5cm anti-tank guns fitted.

Around 850 He 177s were built, of which 130 were manufactured under licence by Arado. Heinkel did attempt, without official sanction, to redevelop the design, with four individual engines replacing the trouble-some twin units. This aircraft, designated

Crew members gather around the nose of a Heinkel He 177 Greif prior to take-off on another mission. An aircraft which might have had great potential had it been given adequate development time, it was dogged by technical problems which made it more dangerous to its crews than to the enemy.

A nose view of the Heinkel He 219 Uhu. Note how the cockpit is to the extreme forward end of the fuselage, and the high nose wheel of the tricycle undercarriage. The weapons pack is just visible in a gondola under the fuselage. The openings in the nose are for radar antennae.

the He 277, did actually reach prototype stage and a further version, the He 274 high-altitude bomber, was in an advanced enough stage that an example was actually completed and flown after the war ended.

Interestingly, it was the He 177 that was earmarked as the aircraft to carry Germany's atomic bomb, had it succeeded in building one.

HEINKEL HE 219

The Heinkel He 219 Uhu, or Owl, was produced in response to a request from General Kammhuber during 1941 for a new dedicated night-fighter aircraft. Despite having his designs rejected by the Air Ministry, Heinkel went ahead and con-

structed a prototype from his own funds and in November 1942 the He 219 flew for the first time.

The aircraft was a two-seater, 15.6m long, with an 18.5m wingspan. The cockpit was placed right at the very nose of the aircraft. It was twin-engined, featuring a tricycle undercarriage and twin tail planes. Maximum speed was 620kph, with a ceiling of 9,300m and a range of 1,500km. Armament of the production version consisted of four 20mm cannon, two 30mm cannon and two further 30mm cannon in 'Schräge Musik' form in the rear fuselage. The aircraft was fitted with Lichtenstein radar.

The first prototype was demonstrated to Kammhuber, who, highly impressed, ordered its immediate production. Despite a number of teething problems, by June 1943 early production aircraft were being handed over to front-line units for operational testing. The He 219 proved itself in combat almost immediately. On its first combat mission, it shot down five enemy bombers, with twenty more following in the next ten days, including several de Havilland Mosquitos, considered to be almost untouchable.

Despite these successes, political machinations by Erhard Milch, who had been enraged by Kammhuber ordering the He 219 into production against his wishes, saw all sorts of obstacles placed in the way of increased production, including the removal of Kammhuber himself from his position. Fortunately for the night-fighter arm, Milch, too, was removed soon afterwards and Armaments Minister Albert Speer

gave the production of the He 219 his full backing.

Just over 300 He 219s were produced. It was not without its faults but was certainly one of the better German aircraft of the Second World War and far superior to the range of former bombers/fighters which had been pressed into service as night-fighters prior to its arrival. Had it entered service earlier and not been dogged by political interference, it might have had a far more significant impact on the Allied bomber offensive.

HENSCHEL HS 129

Intended as a ground attack aircraft to support the already obsolescent Ju 87 Stuka, this aircraft entered service in 1942. It had a top speed of just over 400kph and a range

A Henschel He 129 captured intact by the Americans at the end of the war and shipped to the USA for evaluation. This aircraft achieved some success as a tank-buster on the Eastern Front, with a 7.5cm anti-tank gun slung below the fuselage. (*National Archives*)

The Junkers Ju 52 had provision for a defensive machine-gunner's position in the rear fuselage. The exposed single 7.92mm machine gun was not much of a defence against determined enemy fighter attack and was rarely used. (*François Saez*)

of 560km. It carried two 7.92mm machine guns and two 20mm cannon in the nose and was capable of carrying a 350kg bomb-load. Various armament combinations were later introduced, including a ventral tray with four machine guns and, subsequently, a single 7.5cm anti-tank gun, replacing the 3cm version.

The aircraft was extremely well protected, with the pilot sitting in an armoured tub behind a 3in-thick armoured-glass cockpit screen, but this welcome feature (from the pilot's viewpoint, at least) resulted in sluggish performance from its Daimler Benz engines. Refitting with Gnome-Rhône engines, which became available after the fall of France, solved this problem, however, and allowed the aircraft a reasonable, if not outstanding, performance. Around 865 examples were constructed.

JUNKERS JU 52

Probably one of the best known of the Luftwaffe's aircraft in the Second World War, the distinctive trimotor Ju 52, known affectionately to the troops as 'Tante Ju', or Aunty Ju, began its life in 1928 when the first prototype was flown. This was a basic commercial transport aircraft with a single engine in the nose. A second prototype was completed as a seaplane. Orders for the new aircraft were not forthcoming, however, and construction ceased after only seven examples had been completed. Only one was sold, to Canada, and the remainder were later delivered to the Luftwaffe and used as target aircraft.

With little demand for their transport aircraft, Junkers decided to develop the design as a passenger-carrying aircraft and two additional engines were fitted in the wings. Almost immediately, an order was received from Bolivian airline LAB. The first trimotor Ju 52 flew in March 1932. The aircraft, with its distinctive corrugated skin, was an instant success and was purchased not only by Lufthansa, where it became the principal aircraft type of the company, but by Argentina, Belgium, Brazil, Denmark, Ecuador, Estonia, Greece, Hungary, Italy, Mexico, Norway, Peru, Romania, South Africa, Spain, Uruguay and even the UK. Around 400 examples were sold. In 1937, a Ju 52 became the first passenger aircraft to fly over the Pamir mountains en route from Germany to China.

With the creation of the Luftwaffe in 1935, it was decided that, as well as being suitable as a transport aircraft, the Ju 52 would serve as a makeshift bomber until suitable bomber aircraft could be produced. This version was fitted with a defensive machine-gun position in the rear upper fuselage, and one in the lower fuselage in a retractable 'dustbin' position. The passenger cabin was converted to provide a bomb bay. Only light, 50kg bombs were carried, with a capacity for thirty-two of these in the bomb bay. Around 1,200 of the bomber variant were ordered. A number of these aircraft served with the Condor Legion during the Spanish Civil War, where their versatility as

As well as normal entry doors, the Ju 52 had large fuselage panels which could fold up, as shown here, to give greater access to the interior for easier loading and unloading. It was the principal aircraft type of the Luftwaffe's transport fleet and was in service from the first day of the war until the last. The distinctive corrugated surface of the type is clearly seen in this shot. (*François Saez*)

As well as regular transport duties, the Ju 52 was widely used as an air ambulance, bearing large, clearly visible Red Cross markings. Ju 52s such as these were responsible for evacuating large numbers of wounded German troops before the final collapse at Stalingrad in 1943. (*François Saez*)

transport aircraft was confirmed but their suitability as bombers shown to be over-optimistic, being far too slow and lightly armed to deal with enemy fighters. Based on experiences in Spain, the production of the bomber variant of the Ju 52 was halted.

The Ju 52 was a large aircraft, spanning some 29m and being 19m in length. It had a fixed undercarriage, which occasionally had streamlining spats fitted. Its corrugated Duralumin skin was extremely robust but its uneven surface increased drag. The top speed of the aircraft was just 277kph. Range was 1,000km and ceiling 5,900m. It carried a crew of two. The final version, the Ju 52/3m g14e, carried the heaviest defensive armament, but even that was relatively light. It comprised a single machine gun fired from an open rear dorsal position, one machine gun fired from each side of the fuselage and one forward-firing

machine gun in a small, fixed cupola above the cockpit.

The Ju 52 would become the standard transport aircraft of the Luftwaffe and this military transport version was also sold abroad, being taken into service in Spain, Hungary, Switzerland and Portugal, many serving well after the Second World War. A Ju 52 production plant in occupied France continued production after the war where the aircraft, produced by Amiot, was designated the AAC1 Toucan. Sweden and Czechoslovakia also used the Ju 52 after the Second World War. In Spain, the Ju 52 was built under licence as the CASA 352 and used into the 1970s. The Swiss air force only finally retired its last military transport Ju 52s in 1984.

Germany produced just under 5,500 Ju 52s, predominantly for use as military transports. As well as a standard freight-carrying transporter, the Ju 52 was the normal mode of transport for delivering paratroopers. Among the more unusual variants produced was the minesweeper version, the Ju 52/3m (MS), which had a huge metal ring affixed under the fuselage. A small motor in the fuselage was used to generate a magnetic field in this ring which would detonate magnetic mines as the aircraft flew low over the water.

A seaplane transport was also produced, the Ju 52/3m (See), which had the undercarriage replaced by two large floats. Skis could also be fitted in place of wheels on the undercarriage struts for operating over frozen terrain. Ju 52s would serve with the Luftwaffe from the first day of the war to the last, and on every front. They would drop paratroops over Eben Emael and on Crete and would deliver desperately needed supplies to the beleaguered 6 Armee at Stalingrad. Hitler also had his own personal Ju 52.

JUNKERS JU 87

The Ju 87 Stuka began life in September 1935 as the Ju 87V. It was, to say the least, an unusual aircraft and a particularly ugly one at that. It featured cranked wings and a fixed undercarriage shrouded in stream-lined 'spats'. The original prototype was fitted with a Rolls-Royce Kestrel engine, which required a large radiator intake at the nose of the aircraft, and had a V-shaped twin tail fin.

The first volume production model, the Ju 87A, entered service in 1937, and by then was powered by a Junkers Jumo engine. The aircraft carried a single machine gun in each wing, and a rearwards-firing machine gun in the cockpit. It carried a crew of two, pilot and rear gunner/radio operator. It could carry a bomb load of 250kg (or 500kg if only the pilot was aboard). The Ju 87 was capable of diving at 90 degrees, dropping its bomb and then pulling out against forces of

up to 6G. It was certainly an impressive aircraft for its day. Apart from a few which were sent to Spain with the Condor Legion, this variant did not see combat action. Just over 260 were built.

By the outbreak of war, the Ju 87B had been developed. This version had improved and strengthened undercarriage, a more powerful engine and a redesigned nose, though still featuring the distinctive large radiator housing on the 'chin'.

On 1 September 1939, three Ju 87s from Stuka Geschwader 1 carried out the first offensive act of the Second World War when they successfully precision dive-bombed a blockhouse controlling the demolition charges which the Poles had set up to deny the Germans use of a strategic bridge. The Ju 87B performed well during the attack on Poland, the fear their appearance created being enhanced by the addition of a siren attached to the port undercarriage leg, producing a mournful wailing sound when the aircraft went into its dive.

It is also interesting to note that it was the Ju 87 which scored the first aerial victory of the Second World War when an aircraft from Stuka Geschwader 1 shot down a Polish PZL P11 as it took off to intercept the German formation.

The Ju 87, commonly referred to as the Stuka (an abbreviation of **Sturzka**mpfflugzeug), did have several less impressive qualities, however. Its rate of climb was very slow, its manoeuvrability poor and its defensive armament weak. Although it served its purpose well during the campaign in the west, during the Battle of Britain it suffered heavy casualties in action against Spitfires and Hurricanes of the RAF.

Two sub-variants of the Ju 87B were also produced. The Ju 87R was a long-range version. It was visually similar to the Ju 87B but had increased fuel tank provision within the wings. The Ju 87C was designed to be operated from an aircraft carrier and was fitted with a tail hook, folding wings and undercarriage legs that could be jettisoned if the need to ditch in the sea arose. In the event, the carrier never entered service and any Ju 87Cs which had been completed were used in the conventional role.

The next major variant of the Ju 87 was the Ju 87D. A new powerplant saw the radiators moved to the wings and the original large radiator housing in the nose replaced by a much smaller oil cooler housing. All this gave the aircraft a much more streamlined appearance. Defensive armament was increased from one to two machine guns, offensive armament changed from machine guns to cannon and bomb carrying capacity was also improved.

After the mauling that Stuka units had taken during the Battle of Britain, they performed well again in the opening phases of the war on the Eastern Front, at least until the quality of both Soviet aircraft and pilots improved.

The method of operation of the Ju 87 in the dive-bombing role was rather interesting, as much of the operation was effectively automated. The release gear for the bomb-load, the dive brakes and the elevator control were all linked to the bomb-sight. Before going into his dive, the pilot would set the height at which the bomb was to be dropped. The operation of the dive brakes by the pilot automatically adjusted the elevators, putting the aircraft into a dive. The pilot would judge the angle

An interesting shot of one of the early models of Ju 87. Note the massive undercarriage spats distinctive of this early A type and the twin, rather than single, antennae masts to the rear of the cockpit. These early types were used in Spain (though the example shown bears regular Luftwaffe, rather than Condor Legion, markings) but were already being phased out of combat duties before the outbreak of the Second World War. (*François Saez*)

This Ju 87 seems to have come to grief by overshooting the runway and ending up nose-down in a ditch, rather than having crashed through enemy action. Note the barrel of the machine gun just above the undercarriage leg. The dive brakes used during the dive-bombing manoeuvre can also be seen under the leading edge of the wing. Clear also from this image is just how large an aircraft the Ju 87 was. (*Thomas Huss*)

of his dive by lining the horizon up against aiming marks in the glass of the canopy and, having reached around 90 degrees, would direct the aircraft straight at the target through the sight. Once the predetermined height was reached, the bomb, on its cradle, would be swung out and dropped, and at this point the elevators would automatically adjust to take the aircraft out of its dive. Typically, bomb-release height would be around 900m. It would then normally take around 500m of airspace for the Ju 87 to pull out of its dive at around 400m and begin climbing again.

The last major version of the Stuka was the Ju 87G. By the time this aircraft was introduced, in 1943, it had been removed from the dive-bombing role and reallocated to ground attack use. For this task, the dive brakes were also removed. The Ju 87G model was capable of carrying a 37mm cannon, with a muzzle velocity of some 850m/s, mounted in a pod under each wing.

Although the fitting of these weapons and a degree of armour protection increased the aircrafts' weight and drag, reducing speed and manoeuvrability, they became extremely successful as 'tank hunters'. The 37mm cannon fitted were obsolete in the ground role, but when fired from the air, into the weakly armoured top surfaces of enemy tanks, they were devastating. Ju 87Gs were used to good effect in support of the German armoured offensive at Kursk in 1943. The most successful German pilot of the war, Oberst Hans-Ulrich Rudel, holder of the Knight's Cross with Golden Oakleaves, Swords and Diamonds, flew the Ju 87G, his personal score including some 519 enemy tanks destroyed.

As well as those produced for the Luftwaffe, a small number of Ju 87s were also exported to the air forces of Germany's allies, and examples flew with the Italian, Bulgarian and Hungarian air forces. A number were also exported to Japan for evaluation. These export models were designated Ju 87K. An unarmed trainer, the Ju 87H, was also produced.

Production of the Ju 87 finally ceased in October 1944 after some 5,700 of the type had been built. Surviving examples of the Ju 87 are extremely rare and all are thought to be non-flying static display pieces.

JUNKERS JU 88

Design of the Junkers Ju 88 began in 1936, the aircraft being intended as a 'fast bomber'. Work progressed with impressive

The crew of a Junkers Ju 88A of Kampfgeschwader 51, the so-called 'Edelweissgeschwader', pose in front of their aircraft. (*François Saez*)

speed and, in fact, the first prototypes flew in that same year. Interestingly, two American designers on contract to Junkers were involved in its development. Despite the relatively large size of the aircraft, it was initially fitted with dive brakes so that it could also act as a dive-bomber. Still under test through the late 1930s, the Ju 88 did not see action in the Spanish Civil War or during the Polish campaign.

So great was the enthusiasm of the Luftwaffe for this new aircraft that in 1938 it was decided that it would become the standard bomber aircraft and orders were placed for a large number, with estimated construction rates of around 300 per month. This was far too much for Junkers to cope with and production was also farmed out to a number of other manufacturers, including Arado, Heinkel, Dornier, Henschel and even the Volkswagen motor works.

The Ju 88A series, with a crew of four, had an impressive performance, its twin Junkers Jumo engines giving it a top speed of 517kph, with a payload of up to 2,000kg at altitudes of up to 8,200m, and a range of up to 2,730km. There was no large internal bomb bay, most of its payload being slung underneath the wings.

Defensive armament consisted of two 7.92mm machine guns firing from the rear of the cockpit, one firing towards the rear from a ventral gondola, one in the glazed nose and even one in the front of the cockpit that could be fired by the pilot.

This shot gives an excellent view of the underside of the Ju 88 and the ventral gondola. Entrance to the aircraft was by a ladder attached to a glazed hatch at the rear of the gondola. (*François Saez*)

Nevertheless, despite performing well during the campaign in the west, it suffered a fairly high attrition rate during the Battle of Britain. Losses of Ju 88s, however, were far lower than those of its counterpart Heinkel and Dornier bombers, as the Ju 88's speed, especially in a steep dive which its airframe was designed to withstand, often allowed it to escape from trouble. The aircraft did suffer considerable teething problems in the first half of its career, having been rushed into service far too quickly. At one point it was claimed that it was 'not the enemy the crews are frightened of, it's the Ju 88'. Nevertheless, the Ju 88 was able to match the speed of the much lighter and smaller Me 110 heavy fighter, while carrying a much more substantial payload and with a much greater range. A Ju 88B, featuring a redesigned cockpit area, was developed but only a handful made. They did, however, form part of the development work which would ultimately lead to the Ju 188.

A new model, the Ju 88C, began to appear in 1941. This version had a solid nose in which were fitted three machine guns and a 20mm cannon, giving the new version a fairly hefty punch, certainly as good as many fighters. Among the roles carried out by this version were coastal patrols and anti-shipping strikes. The Ju 88C was the first version to be used on night-fighting operations.

Further variants included the Ju 88D long-range reconnaissance aircraft and the Ju 88G night-fighter. As well as beefed-up armament in the nose, and more powerful 1,700hp BMW engines, some Ju 88Gs were fitted with the so-called 'Schräge-Musik', a set of up to six fixed 20mm cannon fitted into the rear fuselage, firing upwards at an angle of 60 degrees and operated when the aircraft flew under an enemy bomber. Revised forward-firing armament was also fitted, with two cannon on the right-hand side of the nose and four more in a weapons tray that replaced the ventral gondola. The night-fighter variants also carried short-range Lichtenstein radar fittings in the nose which would allow them to home in on enemy aircraft after being directed to their location by ground-based, long-range Wurzburg radar. Although the fitting of the radar antennae to the nose increased drag and reduced top speed slightly, it led to a much higher success rate in interceptions of enemy aircraft.

It was in the night-fighter role that the Ju 88 would truly excel. Although the Me 110 remained in service as a night-fighter to the end of the war, along with a few other advanced units built in smaller numbers, such as the Heinkel He 219 Uhu, from 1944 the Ju 88 was in numerical terms by far the predominant and most successful of the night-fighters, destroying more enemy aircraft than all other types combined. Improvements in the Ju 88G night-fighter continued throughout the war, with engines, armament and radar systems under continual development.

A Ju 88H version, with extended fuselage and range of over 5,000km, was produced in limited numbers for maritime reconnaissance duties. A tank-busting version, the Ju 88P, was also produced, which carried variously a 7.5cm, 5cm or two 3.7cm forward-firing cannon in the ventral gondola. It was used operationally in small numbers on the Eastern Front, usually in the 'train-busting' role. The drag caused by the additional housing for the anti-tank gun adversely affected the aircraft's performance, making it more vulnerable to enemy fighters, so the housing was made jettisonable through the use of explosive bolts. It was also known for the blast from the heavy anti-tank weapon to crumple the nose area of the aircraft, or even bend the propeller blades.

One of the more interesting variants was the so-called 'Mistel' combination. This consisted of a worn-out Ju 88 airframe, on to the back of which was constructed a large cradle. Into this cradle was loaded a single-engine fighter such as the Me 109 or Fw 190. The Ju 88 was not crewed in this instance, being controlled by the pilot of the 'piggy-back' fighter. The Ju 88 was packed with explosive, to the extent that the aircraft itself became the 'bomb' carried by the fighter. When the destination was reached, the fighter simply released the Ju 88 to drop on to its target, and flew off on its own. It was generally used against fixed-structure targets such as bridges, rather than enemy vehicles or troops. Approximately 250 such 'Mistel' combinations were produced, some of which were used against the British landing areas during the invasion of Normandy in June 1944.

Over 15,000 Ju 88s were eventually built, in over sixty different versions, and the aircraft also led to the development of the advanced Ju 188. In addition to the Luftwaffe, Ju 88s served in the air forces of Bulgaria, Romania, Finland, Hungary and Italy.

JUNKERS JU 188

The high-performance Junkers Ju 188 evolved from what had been an alternative design developed alongside the Ju 88 as the Ju 88B, with a larger, more streamlined cockpit. By the outbreak of war, the Air Ministry had already planned for a new

A 'Mistel' combination. Various aircraft types were used in such units. Here, a Focke Wulf Fw 109a sits 'piggy-back' atop a worn-out Junkers Ju 88.

Despite the redesigned nose and cockpit area, the origins of the Junkers Ju 188 are clear from this shot, the aircraft retaining many distinct similarities to the Ju 88 that preceded it. (*National Archives*)

bomber that would ultimately replace the current aircraft types and Junkers had plans for its own proposals to this end, the Junkers Ju 288. Delays in the project resulted in the firm being asked to revise its Ju 88B design as an interim measure, and this became the Junkers Ju 188.

In the summer of 1940, a number of standard Ju 88 airframes, but with extended wingspan, elongated cockpit and more powerful engines, were produced but failed to impress the Air Ministry, though the aircraft were placed into service in the long-range reconnaissance role. By 1942, with the new generation of bombers still no nearer realisation, Junkers were asked to consider further developments of their Ju 88 design once again.

The resultant aircraft was formally designated the Ju 188 and in October 1942 was authorised for production. By February 1943, the first production aircraft were rolling off the line and by the end of the year almost 300 had been delivered. Unfortunately, however, the Ju 188 was not the aircraft it should have been. Despite the improved performance and load-carrying capacity, it had the same bomb bay as the Ju 88. Any additional payload had to be slung from shackles under the wings, the resultant increase in drag somewhat negating the advantages of the new aircraft.

By the start of 1944 it had been decided to focus on the reconnaissance versions of the aircraft, where the problems with payload were not so important. Subsequent

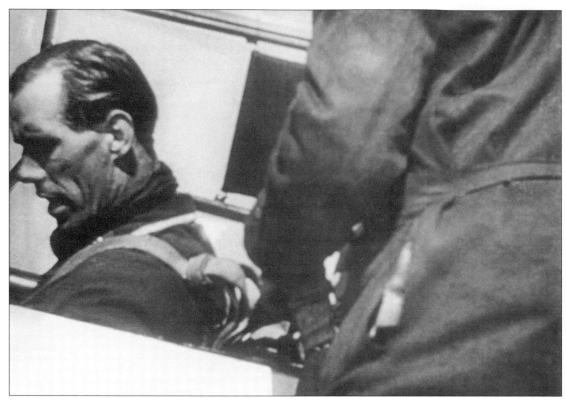

Messerschmitt test pilot Fritz Wendel sits in the cockpit of what appears to be an Me 109. The life of a test pilot was difficult and dangerous. Wendel test-flew most Messerschmitt aircraft, including the Me 262 jet fighter, and at one time held the world speed record, setting a standard that was not beaten for thirty years. (*Josef Charita*)

development work was carried on under a new designation, the Ju 388.

MESSERSCHMITT BF (ME) 109

Ranking as one of the most famous aircraft of all time, the Messerschmitt Me 109 began life as the brainchild of Prof. Willi Messerschmitt. Designed in 1934, the earliest version, somewhat ironically, was powered by a Rolls-Royce Kestrel engine. The first production version was the Me 109B (there was no Me 109A).

German involvement in the Spanish Civil War gave the Luftwaffe an ideal opportunity to test new aircraft under real combat conditions. Accordingly, examples of the early B and C variants saw active service with the Condor Legion in Spain, gaining much invaluable combat experience. The B variant initially had a wooden, two-blade propeller and was lightly armed, with only two machine guns, while the C variant had the machine-gun armament increased to four, and a larger radiator for better engine cooling.

By the outbreak of war, the interim D version, of which just 200 were built, was in service, all of these early types having a twin-bladed propeller. The B and C types had fuselage-mounted guns, firing through the propeller arc, and provision for a third gun firing through the propeller boss (though after problems with overheating, this was removed, to be replaced in later models). The C and D models also had wing-mounted guns.

The Me 109 was a very advanced aircraft, featuring all-metal structure, compared to the high incidence of wood and canvas still being used by other nations. The design, as was proven in the year to come, was capable of constant upgrading and modification as new powerplant and armament were developed. The only real drawback to the Me 109 design was the very narrow track of the undercarriage. The undercarriage legs were mounted at the wing roots and lifted outwards, whereas many of its contemporaries had the legs mounted in the wings, lifting inwards. This narrow track and the fact that the wheels sat at an angle to the ground rather than perpendicular, gave it some interesting handling characteristics on take-off and landing, which some pilots found difficult to master. Nevertheless, it became the favoured 'mount' of many aces even after the advent of newer, more advanced aircraft.

With the arrival of the much-improved E model in early 1939, the 109 had achieved world-beating status. Featuring a three-bladed, variable-pitch, metal propeller and a top speed of 560kph, this model could also carry drop tanks to increase its range and was capable of carrying a small bomb-load. It was the E (or 'Emil') model that formed the backbone of the Luftwaffe fighter arm

A Messerschmitt Me 109E, the type most commonly flown during the campaign in the west and during the Battle of Britain. The aircraft is being prepared for flying (the engine crank handle can be seen projecting from the cowling). Note the blunt-nosed spinner with the opening through which a 2cm cannon is fired. (*François Saez*)

Aircrew pose beside an Me 109E. Instantly recognisable features include the snub-nosed spinner, with the cannon firing through its centre, and the square air intake on the port side of the cowling. The 'Emil' was the predominant Luftwaffe fighter type until the introduction of the F in 1941. (*Josef Charita*)

during the campaign in the west and during the Battle of Britain. As a fighter it was superior to the Hurricane of the RAF and an equal to the Spitfire. Nevertheless, although the Me 109 was claimed to have a theoretical cruising range of 640km, in combat flying it had a true effective radius of only around 160km, giving it just 95 minutes' flying time.

Improvements continued with the F model, introduced in late 1940. This variant, with an aerodynamically stream-lined shape, now had a top speed of 630kph (nearly 160kph faster than the first production B models.). Armament consisted of two machine guns in the cowling and a 20mm cannon firing through the propeller spinner. Just over 2,000 F variants were built.

In 1942 the G (or 'Gustav') model arrived. This was to be the most successful of all variants. It once again featured beefed-up armament, with heavier-calibre 13mm machine guns in the cowling, as well as the ability to carry rockets or additional cannon in underwing gondolas, and some even featured pressurised cockpits. Over 24,000 of the G variant were built.

The final production version was the K, which featured a supercharged engine, giving a top speed of 725kph and had a very heavy armament in the shape of three 30mm cannon. It was designed to be used primarily as a 'bomber-killer'. Some late-war Me 109s were fitted with a modified canopy which gave a far greater degree of visibility to the pilot than the original, with its heavy, angular framing. This so-called 'Galland' hood also substituted clear armoured glass for the armoured metal plate that was evident on earlier canopies.

An Me 109F pilot taxies his aircraft past watching comrades on a rain-drenched airfield. The unit emblem on the fuselage side just ahead of the air intake cowl identifies the aircraft as belonging to III Gruppe of Jagdgeschwader 3. The aircraft bears a two-tone dark/mid-green splinter-pattern camouflage, and black spinners with white centres. (*Thomas Huss*)

A Messerschmitt Me 109F with a dramatic winter camouflage scheme. The Me 109F was very similar in appearance to the G model, the latter differing in featuring two large bulges to the engine cowling just in front of the canopy, to accommodate the breeches of the cannon, which fired through the propeller arc, thanks to interrupter gear. This example has also been fitted with a 2cm cannon in a gondola under each wing. These gave the fighter a very powerful punch, something badly needed to take down a robust, four-engine bomber like the B-17, which could take very heavy punishment. (*Josef Charita*)

The pilot of an Me 109G relaxes in a deck chair next to his aircraft. Note the bulges over the cowling just in front of the canopy which, in conjunction with the earlier-style canopy, identifies this type. The mottled, rather than splinter-style, camouflage to the fuselage was typical of the second half of the war. (*Josef Charita*)

A special version of the Me 109, the Me 109T, was also created for use on the proposed German aircraft carrier *Graf Zeppelin*, with short take-off and landing capability, and was fitted with an arrester hook at the tail. More unconventionally, Me 109s were used as the control aircraft in the 'Mistel' combinations (see Ju 88) and a twin-bodied 'Zwilling' version was also contemplated.

The Me 109 flew in every theatre in which the Germans were engaged from the first day of the war until the last. Over 33,000 were built, the type remaining in production throughout the war. A few Me 109s still survive in museum or private collections and although most are now static display pieces, a handful are still in flying condition and occasionally take to the air.

The Me 109 was a fine aircraft, and a design that was proven to have massive potential for development and improvement. Even so, by the end of the war it had outlived its usefulness, and should have been replaced by the superior Fw 190 or the new-generation jet fighters. Inability to keep up with the demand for the Focke Wulf and development problems with newer types, however, would mean that Me 109 production would be maintained well past the point where it should have been superseded. After the war, production

A Messerschmitt Me 109F is prepared for take-off by ground crew. Note the engine crank handle inserted through the starboard side of the cowling. The broad, rounded spinner clearly differentiated the F model from the preceding E type. (*Josef Charita*)

continued in Spain, where it was built by the Hispano firm as the HA 1109. The latest versions were powered by Rolls-Royce Merlin engines and their production finally ceased in 1956. The aircraft served until the mid-1960s.

The following other nations are known to have operated the Me 109:

Bulgaria. Me 109E and later Me 109G models.

Croatia. Me 109G.

Czechoslovakia. Produced after the war by Avia as the S-199. These were in fact left-over wartime Luftwaffe aircraft, refurbished by the Czechs with whatever engines were available. Some of these aircraft were later sold to Israel, resulting in battles between Israeli-flown former Luftwaffe Messerschmitts and Spitfires of the Egyptian air force during the Six-Day War. Czech aircraft served until 1952.

Finland. Me 109G, in service until 1952.

Hungary. Me 109G. Both German-supplied and Hungarian licence-built machines were used.

Japan. A handful of Me 109E and G for evaluation.

Romania. Me 109G. A small number of these were supplied by the Germans and an equally small number (less than twenty) built under licence.

Switzerland. Me 109G.

Note: The terminology used to describe this aircraft may seem confusing, the terms Me 109 and Bf 109 both being widely used. The prefix 'Me' of course indicates 'Messerschmitt', while 'Bf' signifies 'Bayerisches Flugzeugwerke'. The 'Bf' prefix was the original and is commonly used in many text books when referring to the 109 (and indeed the 110 and other Messerschmitt types). With the increase in fame of the Messerschmitt designs it was suggested that in future the firm's name be changed to Messerschmitt AG, and the 'Me' prefix used for all future aircraft designs. Strictly speaking then, the 'Bf' 109 designation should have continued but, in reality, many original German wartime documents used the 'Me' prefix rather than 'Bf' in official correspondence on this aircraft.

MESSERSCHMITT BF (ME) 110

Design work on the Me 110, intended as a heavy, twin-engine fighter classed as a Zerstörer, or Destroyer, began in 1934 and the first Me 110A prototype flew in May 1936. The twin-engine, two-seat fighter had a maximum speed of 560kph and a range of 1,120km, which could be extended by carrying additional fuel in underwing drop tanks. It was armed with four 7.92mm machine guns, two 20mm cannon in the nose, and a single 7.92mm machine gun in the rear cockpit.

The Me 110 was intended for deep-penetration missions behind enemy lines and therefore needed not only a long range, but sufficient speed, firepower and manoeuvrability to face any single-engine, light enemy

An early Me 110C parked up on a grassy airstrip. Note, under the nose, the two ports for the 2cm cannon. On the top part of the nose are four 7.92mm machine guns, two with their exposed barrel ends visible. A further 7.92mm defensive machine gun was fitted to the rear of the long cockpit canopy of such early versions of the Me 110. (*Thomas Huss*)

fighters it encountered. Göring saw the Zerstörer as the elite branch of the fighter arm and had many of his best and most experienced pilots transferred to the Zerstörergeschwadern.

Well armed, the first volume production variant, the Me 110C, was successful in the attack against Poland and in interception duties in late 1939, when Me 110s shot down nine RAF Wellington bombers over the Heligoland Bight. During operations in the west in the spring of 1940, the Me 110 was beginning to meet much stiffer opposition in the form of Spitfires and Hurricanes of the RAF, which were much faster and more manoeuvrable. With the onset of the German air offensive against Great Britain in 1940, Me 110s suffered heavy losses against RAF fighters.

Although packing a powerful punch with its nose-mounted armament, the slower Me 110 was vulnerable to attack from the rear, having only a single machine gun in its rear cockpit. The ridiculous situation arose that these twin-engine heavy fighters then required their own protective escort of Me 109 single-engine fighters. Over 120

Me 110s were shot down in August 1940 alone. This state of affairs could not be allowed to continue and the Me 110s were withdrawn from daylight combat flying. Most were transferred to the Mediterranean theatre, where at that time the Spitfire was still a rarity, and later to Russia. This was, however, far from being the end of the combat career of this aircraft. As the need for night-fighter defences against RAF bombing attacks became more urgent, and with the Me 109s which had been allocated to this role proving unsuitable, the Me 110 was to find a new lease of life.

One of the most famous Me 110 pilots was the Deputy Führer, Rudolf Hess, who used an Me 110 to make his unauthorised flight from Germany to Scotland on 10 May 1941, in an attempt to bring about a negotiated peace without Hitler's prior approval.

Heavy fighter, fighter-bomber and reconnaissance versions of the Me 110C were built. The Me 110D was a special long-range version and the E and F variants were fighter-bombers with strengthened airframes. The first purpose-built night-fighting version was of the Me 110F-4 sub-variant,

Another Messerschmitt Me 110 with the full 'antler'-type Lichtenstein SN-2 radar antennae fitted. These antennae added considerably to the drag factor, reducing the aircraft's performance.

This Me 110 belongs not to a Zerstörer Geschwader, as one might have expected for an aircraft of this type, but, as shown by the nose emblem, to Jagdgeschwader 53, the 'Pik As', or Ace of Spades, wing. (*Thomas Huss*)

now carrying a third crew member to operate the aircraft's radar equipment.

The most advanced version to see service was the Me 110G-4, carrying two 20mm and two 30mm cannon in the nose, two 20mm 'Schräge Musik' oblique upward-firing cannon in the fuselage, and twin 7.92mm defensive machine guns in the rear cockpit. It was even possible to fit a further two 20mm cannon in a special armaments pack fitted to the belly of the aircraft. This heavy firepower was capable of delivering a devastating amount of punishment to Allied bombers. This version was also occasionally used on daylight missions, most famously when providing air cover for the escape of the battleships *Scharnhorst* and *Gneisenau*, and the cruiser *Prinz Eugen* in the so-called 'Channel Dash' of 12 February 1942.

Attempts to improve the basic Me 110 concept resulted first in the Me 210. With a conventional single rudder and redesigned fuselage with the cockpit in the nose, the aircraft was not particularly successful, suffering from several major problems. It was extremely unstable in flight and many pilots considered it impossible to fly. A bomb bay in the nose was capable of carrying a 1,000kg payload and up to four 20mm cannon could be fitted in the nose. Defensive armament, unusually, consisted of one machine gun in a remote-controlled barbette either side of the fuselage. Although 1,000 aircraft were ordered, it was so bad that production was ceased after only ninety had been built. Me 210s were also built under licence in Hungary and, strangely enough, the Hungarians were able, by making a few design alterations, to produce a first-class aircraft. The Germans took advantage of this and incorporated the Hungarian improvements into a new design, designated the Me 410, but visually very similar to its ill-fated predecessor.

The Me 410 entered service in mid-1943. Although well liked by its crews, it still could not compete with Allied equivalents, such as the de Havilland Mosquito. Four variants of this fine aircraft were built. The Me 410A was a standard fighter/fighter-bomber with a number of sub-variants, including a camera-equipped reconnaissance fighter and a variant equipped with a 50mm cannon for destroying enemy bombers at extreme range. The Me 410B was basically similar but with improved armament and engines. An anti-shipping torpedo bomber sub-variant of the Me 410B was also produced in small numbers. The Me 410C was a high-altitude interceptor with increased wingspan, and the Me 410D had a number of metal panels replaced by wood to conserve essential strategic metals. A total of 1,160 Me 410s were built.

Despite its inherent failings, the Me 110 had performed excellent service for Germany as a night-fighter, being the preferred machine of many of the top night-fighter aces, and production continued until March 1945. As well as in the Luftwaffe, the Me 110 served in the air forces of Italy, Hungary and Romania.

Of the 6,100 built, only around nine Me 110s still survive in various collections, all in Europe, and only as static display pieces. It is not thought that any still survive in flying condition. Two Me 410s are known still to exist, one in Europe and one in the USA.

This view of a Messerschmitt Me 210 clearly shows the rotating barbettes that held the rearwards-firing 2cm cannon. The actual weapons have been removed on this captured aircraft. (*National Archives*)

The rarely seen Me 310, of which only a very small number were constructed, is identifiable from its four-bladed propellers.

MESSERSCHMITT ME 262

Work on what was to become the world's first fully operational jet fighter began in 1938. The resultant aircraft was a streamlined, low-wing monoplane with swept-back wings, powered by a BMW turbine engine in a nacelle slung under each wing. The earliest prototypes, in fact, had a single, nose-mounted propeller and were used to test the airframe design before the new jet engines became available. These were test flown in 1940. The first purely jet-propelled prototypes first took to the air in July 1942, having been preceded by a version with both a nose-mounted piston enginc and jet turbines.

The BMW engines were later replaced by Junkers Jumo turbojets. These early jet engines were unreliable and even those that were operated correctly had a very limited life, somewhere around twelve hours of flying. This was partly because of the lack of availability of the required heat-resistant materials in wartime Germany. Although the earliest versions had standard undercarriage with a tailwheel (necessary for ground clearance with the nose-mounted propeller),

production models featured tricycle undercarriage. One who had the opportunity to fly this phenomenal aircraft was General-leutnant Adolf Galland. Galland was extremely enthusiastic, clearly seeing the tremendous potential for this aircraft. His comment after test flying the Me 262 was that it 'felt as if the angels were pushing'.

Mass production of the Me 262 was finally authorised in 1943, but only after Hitler insisted that the aircraft be developed as a bomber! His irrational orders were ignored and full-scale production of the Me 262 A-1a fighter version, known as the 'Schwalbe', or Swallow, went ahead. On discovering that his orders had been disobeyed, Hitler flew into a rage and ordered all fighters already built to be converted into Me 262 A-2 fighter-bombers, known as 'Sturmvogel', or Storm Birds.

Though without doubt a superb and highly advanced aircraft for its day, the Me 262 was not without its problems. The jet engines were prone to failure and when this happened the resultant loss of power left the aircraft vulnerable to attack from standard piston-engine aircraft. Misuse of the revolutionary fighter was also the cause of much

The sleek, shark-like lines of the Messerschmitt Me 262 are evident from this shot of one of several examples which were captured intact at the end of the war and returned to the USA and UK for evaluation. (*National Archives*)

Hauptmann Georg-Peter 'Schorsch' Eder. Eder was a skilled pilot with many victories with both the Me 109 and Fw 190 to his credit, including several enemy tanks as well as aircraft. Towards the end of the war, Eder flew with Jagdgeschwader 7, piloting the Me 262 jet fighter, with which he achieved 24 aerial victories and 40 enemy aircraft destroyed on the ground in the course of 150 jet missions. He became Germany's leading ace in terms of four-engined bombers shot down, accumulating a tally of 36. He was shot down on 22 January 1945 as he came in to land, but survived to spend the rest of the war in hospital.

frustration. Hitler's insistence that this plane be used as a bomber, negating most of its advantages in speed and manoeuvrability, since it struggled to carry a 500kg bomb-load, saw its eventual use as a devastating fighter, as intended, much delayed. The Me 262 carried four nose-mounted 30mm cannon, giving it a savage punch. Its top speed was 870kph, reduced to 755kph in the bomber version.

A two-seat, night-fighter version, the radar-equipped Me 262 B-1, was also produced and saw operational use before the end of the war, downing several enemy heavy bombers. This version could also carry 'Schräge Musik' oblique upwards-firing cannon in the rear fuselage, as well as, in the day-fighter role, forty-eight rocket projectiles, a 50mm

cannon, or a battery of Jagdfaust mortar rounds, all of which could be devastating in use against enemy bombers.

Over 1,400 Me 262s were produced, but many of these were destroyed on the ground during bombing raids or rendered inoperative as a result of shortages of fuel. Only around 300 are believed to have become operational. Units using the Me 262 operationally were Jagdgeschwader 2, Jagdgeschwader 7, Nachtjagdgeschwader 11 and Jagdverband 44.

Probably the best-known unit to operate these aircraft was Jagdverband 44, the so-called 'Squadron of Experts' under Adolf Galland, where most of the pilots were highly decorated aces. A total of forty Me 262 pilots became jet fighter 'Experten'

This photograph shows a captured example of the rare Messerschmitt Me 262 twin-seat, jet-powered night-fighter. It is equipped with FuG 218 Neptun radar. Only a small number were built but they did see combat action and succeeded in shooting down a number of enemy aircraft. (*National Archives*)

after qualifying as aces all over again in jet-powered aircraft.

A substantial number of Me 262s survived the war and were seized by the Allies for evaluation, so that several still exist today, though none are thought to be in flying condition. At the time of writing, however, a US-based business is manufacturing five exact replicas of the Me 262 as fully functional flying aircraft. At least one has already been test-flown and granted a certificate of airworthiness. One has apparently been sold to a German buyer, so the sleek lines of the Me 262 will be seen again in the skies over Germany at some point in the not-too-distant future.

The Japanese were also developing a jet fighter, the Nakajima Kikka, inspired by the Me 262 (Japanese officials had witnessed some Me 262 test flights), which bore a strong resemblance to the German jet. Only one prototype of the Japanese version ever flew, however, in August 1945, and crashed after an aborted take-off. In excess of twenty others were at various stages of completion but the war ended before any were flown.

MESSERSCHMITT ME 163 KOMET

One of the war's most amazing aircraft, the Komet was the first, and only, rocket-powered aircraft to serve operationally in the Second World War. It was designed by Alexander Lippisch as a single-seat interceptor. Work began on the concept as early as 1938 with the Dfs 194 test plane, which

The Messerschmitt Me 163 Komet on its take-off dolly. Although a retractable tail wheel was fitted, the aircraft had no main under-carriage. Once the Komet was airborne, the wheeled dolly was jettisoned, and subsequent landing was by a simple skid fitted under the fuselage. (*National Archives*)

eventually developed into the Komet. When Lippisch moved to the Messerschmitt firm in 1939, work began on developing the concept aircraft as a fighter. The first prototype, the Me 163A, was ready in late 1940 and was in test throughout late 1940 and 1941. One of the test pilots, Haupt-mann Heini Dittmar, broke the world speed record with a top speed of 1,004kph in a Komet in October 1941. It was not until 1942, however, that the Me 163B appeared and two further years of testing improve-ments were required before the type entered service with JG400 in May 1944. The speed at which this tiny aircraft could zoom up into the air led to it being com-pared to a rocket-powered flea, some Luft-waffe personnel referring to their Me 163 as 'the Mighty Flea'. The unit emblem, in fact, of JG400 was just such an insect, with the legend 'Wie ein Floh, aber Oho!' (Like a flea, but Oh Ho!).

Despite its futuristic concept, the Komet was a simple aircraft, made from wood with a canvas covering. It was a small, tail-less aircraft with swept-back wings and no under-carriage, but rather a simple skid under the fuselage for landing. The aircraft was posi-tioned on a jettisonable, wheeled trolley for take-off, which would be from the hard-top runway of an airfield, while the landing, using the skid, would be on the grassy verges. The Komet's wingspan was just 9.3m and length 5.7m. A 3m-long flame would emerge from the tail on take-off, with the exhaust reaching temperatures of around 1,800 degrees centigrade.

The Me 163's powerplant was a Walter HWK 509A-2 rocket motor, powered by mixing two different chemicals – 'T-Stoff' (hydrogen peroxide) and 'C Stoff' (hydrazine/methanol) – producing 1,700kg of thrust. The bulk of the fuel was carried in a tank in the fuselage, with two smaller tanks either side of the pilot. This gave the aircraft a top speed of 960kph (596 mph) and an astonishing climb rate of 5,000m/minute. However, heavy fuel consumption meant that its operational endurance was only around 100km.

The phenomenal rate of climb meant that the Komet could reach high-flying enemy bombers very quickly. It was armed with two 30mm cannon, one in each wing root, but could carry only 60 rounds of ammunition for each. Unfortunately the rapid rate of consumption of fuel meant that once it had reached its target area, it only had two to three minutes of endurance before the fuel expired. The Komet then had to be glided back to base. Being so small and moving incredibly fast, the Komet was a difficult target for Allied escorting fighters. But its speed was also a dis-advan-tage, as it approached its target extremely fast, giving the pilot little time to line up and take aim before overshooting and passing his victim. If he missed, he would not have much time for a second pass.

Allied pilots became aware that there was little point in trying to intercept a fast-moving Komet on its way towards its target. Instead, they waited until, its fuel spent, the rocket fighter glided in to land at its base. The Germans were, in fact, forced to allo-cate regular piston-engine fighters to rocket- and jet-fighter bases to protect such aircraft from being 'bounced' by enemy fighters during the landing phase, when the advantages provided by their great speed were negated.

The extremely volatile rocket fuel mix was also a dangerous factor for the Komet pilot to consider. A bumpy landing on the aircraft's simple landing skid could and often did cause an explosion. In fact it has been estimated that more Komets were lost to explosions on take-off or landing than to direct enemy action. Komet pilots were also painfully aware that the fuel mix would ignite after only a few seconds if it came into contact with organic material. Komet crews were issued with nylon overalls which being synthetic, would not ignite. The material was still porous, however, so any major fuel leaks as a result of enemy fire or a crash landing could mean that fuel soaked through the nylon to meet organic materials – such as the pilot's skin!

Although over 300 Me 163Bs were constructed, less than 100 were operational and it is estimated that only around 16 enemy aircraft were shot down by Komets. A further development, the Me 263, was planned and would have featured retractable undercarriage, a pressurised cabin and greater fuel capacity, but the war ended before it could be brought into being.

The first operational use of the Me 163 came in July 1944, when aircraft from JG400 attacked a formation of B-17 bombers near Merseburg. Units using the Me 163 included Erprobungskommando 16, a test unit based at Peenemünde but which did use its bright-red painted Komets in action against an Allied bomber formation during May 1944, and Jagdgeschwader 400.

An Me 163 was sent to Japan for evaluation but the U-boat carrying it was sunk en route. The Japanese did, however, develop their own copy of the Me 163, designated the Mitsubishi J8M. This never entered service. A good number of Me 163s survived the war and at least eleven are known to be on display in various museums at this time.

One of the largest aircraft operated by the Luftwaffe was the incredible Messerschmitt Me 323 Gigant. Bizarrely, this aircraft was first designed as a glider, but was so large and heavy that it required a twin Heinkel He 111 to tow it. A six-engined, powered version, as shown here, was introduced and was a successful freight carrier, but extremely vulnerable to Allied fighters, and most were shot down. The fixed undercarriage consisting of a row of wheels along the bottom of the fuselage can be clearly seen. (*Josef Charita*)

MESSERSCHMITT ME 323 GIGANT

The aptly named Messerschmitt Me 323 Gigant truly was an aerial behemoth, initially designed as the Me 321, a glider intended to facilitate large-scale troop movements in the intended invasion of Great Britain. It had a simple, canvas-covered, tubular-steel frame, with a massive 55m wingspan. It was 28m long and 10m in height. It had a fixed undercarriage consisting of ten wheels grouped in rows of five either side of the fuselage. It was manned by a crew of five, and carried an armament of five machine guns in the nose, with a further six mounted in the fuselage.

Powered by six 14-cylinder Gnome-Rhône engines, the Gigant could carry up to 120 fully equipped troops. Alternatively it could comfortably accommodate a large 8-ton semi-track with its towed 10.5cm artillery piece, two 4-ton trucks or even a light tank, such as the Mk II panzer. The aircraft was loaded via massive 3.4m-high doors in the nose. Provision was also made for jet-assisted take-off when carrying particularly heavy loads. The Gigant entered operational service in May 1942, with around 200 being produced.

AIRCRAFT WEAPONRY

The standard aircraft armament, defensive in bombers and larger aircraft, and offensive in fighters, was, at the beginning of the war, the machine gun. Typically, German machine guns were of 7.92mm calibre, the same as that of the standard infantry rifle or carbine, in the same way as the standard

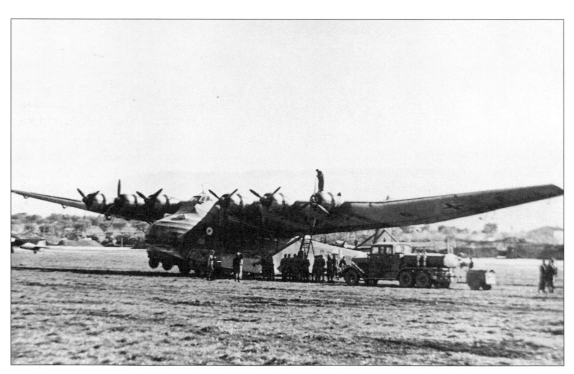

The diminutive figures surrounding this Me 323 Gigant give some indication of the sheer size of this behemoth. Even more incredible is the fact that it began its life as a glider!

A Messerschmitt Me 109 is mounted on trestle stands with its undercarriage raised while its armament is zeroed. Accurate alignment of the aircraft's weapons was essential. Many of the top aces, Marseille being a perfect example, were incredible marksmen capable of shooting down an enemy plane with only a handful of shells. (*Josef Charita*)

machine gun calibre on early RAF aircraft was the .303in.

Early aircraft carried the 7.92mm MG (Maschinengewehr) 17, introduced in 1936, as standard armament. Fitted as fixed armament in the wings or cowling of a fighter, it was belt-fed, the ammunition contained in a tray or trough adjacent to the weapon and spent cartridge cases removed through an ejection port, out of the aircraft. As a defensive weapon on a flexible mount, it was normally fed by a single- or twin-drum magazine, and spent cartridge cases collected in a canvas pouch attached to the ejector port on the weapon to avoid their cluttering the inside of the aircraft.

These machine guns, with a rate of fire of around 1,200 rounds per minute, could put out a substantial volume of fire and, in the early part of the war, this was certainly sufficient to eliminate most of the enemy aircraft encountered. As armour protection and robustness of build on enemy aircraft increased, however, the basic machine gun was often found wanting, although improved versions such as the MG 171, introduced in 1942, went some way to rectifying this. This fired a much heavier 13mm round, but retained a high rate of fire, not far short of that of the MG 17. It was not too heavy a weapon and could easily fit into the same location on the aircraft as the earlier, lighter calibre machine guns (i.e. in the wing or under the engine cowling). This weapon remained in service from its introduction until the end of the war.

Towards the latter part of the war, a number of fighter aircraft types were equipped with 2cm (as here) or even 3cm cannon. This gave them a very powerful punch but the extra weight of these weapons and the gondolas into which they were fitted adversely affected the handling of the aircraft, so that many pilots preferred not to have them. (*Josef Charita*)

The MG FF was already in service at the outbreak of war. Based on the Swiss Oerlikon cannon, it fired a powerful 20mm shell. It was a heavy piece of ordnance, however, with a slower rate of fire of just 520 rounds per minute.

In an attempt to upgrade from the MG 17, a new 15mm-calibre weapon, the MG 151/15, was introduced. Although this new weapon featured a much greater muzzle velocity than the MG FF, it suffered from a lower rate of fire than the standard MG 17, at 900 rounds per minute, and was soon replaced by the MG 151/20. This was a 20mm version that was a significant improvement over the previous weapons,

and was especially effective when fitted to first-rate new aircraft like the Fw 190, which could carry several, enabling it to deliver a savage punch. Although the rate of fire was lower than the MG 17, at 750 rounds per minute, it was much faster than the previous 20mm weapon, the MG FF.

To counter the Allied bombers which were notoriously tough to shoot down, the MK (Maschinenkanone) 108 was introduced. A relatively lightweight weapon, two, or sometimes even four, could be carried by a single fighter. It proved extremely effective, with a rate of fire of 660 rounds per minute.

In the latter part of the war, a number of Reichsverteidigung aircraft were equipped with the devastating MK 101, which fired a 30mm projectile at long range, enabling the German fighters to tackle the heavy bombers from outside the range of their defensive machine guns. A later version of this, the MK 103, had an improved electrical firing system allowing a greater rate of fire of 420 rounds per minute, compared to 250 for the MK 101.

The problem with most of these heavier-calibre weapons was their low rate of fire. Machine guns were light, had a high rate of fire and substantial amounts of ammunition could be carried, allowing a fighter to pour a significant amount of shot on to the target. However, its small calibre meant that a robust enough enemy aircraft could often withstand this punishment and escape, even if damaged. The heavier-calibre weapons fired a much more devastating shot, which could often down an enemy aircraft with only one or two hits. Its slow rate of fire, though, and the limited supply of ammunition that a fighter could carry meant that considerable accuracy, and luck, were required. Typically, German fighter aircraft would carry a mix of both machine guns and heavier cannon.

BOMBS

The Luftwaffe was no different from any other air force in using a variety of bombs, depending on the intended target and purpose. Bombs were designated by their size, so that SC1200 would be a 1,200kg general-purpose bomb. The heaviest produced for the Luftwaffe were 2,500kg. The following categories of bombs were used:

Luftwaffe ground crew prepare to load bombs into the bomb bay of a Dornier light bomber. Lack of a heavy bomber capable of carrying an effective payload was to be a major factor in the strategic failure of the Luftwaffe in the Second World War. Small bombs such as these were useful enough in close tactical support operations with the Army, but in a strategic bombing campaign were of much less impact. (*François Saez*)

135

Bomb Type	Description
B (Brandbombe)	Incendiary.
BC (Sprengbrand bombe)	Explosive incendiary.
LM (Luftmine)	Aerial mine with delayed activation mechanism and magnetic fuse.
PC (Panzerbombe Cylindrisch)	An armour-piercing bomb used mostly against enemy ships or fortified positions.
SC (Sprengbombe Cylindrisch)	A general-purpose bomb within a relatively lightweight cylindrical casing, used for general demolition. A fitting on the nose of the bomb ensured that no extreme penetration of the ground occurred and that the greatest blast effect occurred above ground.
SD (Sprengbombe Dickwandig)	A semi-armour-piercing fragmentation bomb with a much thicker casing, used as anti-personnel bombs or armour-piercing bombs.

Ground crew prepare to load a 500kg bomb on a Junkers Ju 87B. The bomb was held in a cradle under the fuselage which swung clear when the bomb was about to be released. Provision was also made for carrying smaller, 50kg bombs under the wings. (*Josef Charita*)

The Luftwaffe, possessing no heavy bomber force, never developed any bombs to match the huge 'blockbuster'-type bombs used by the Allies. They did, however, develop some extremely sophisticated winged bombs and guided missiles, of which the two most important were the Hs 239 and the PC 1400 Fritz.

The PC 1400 Fritz was a glider bomb intended for use against large targets such as battleships or aircraft carriers. It consisted of a standard PC 1400 armour-piercing bomb, to which four stabilising fins were fitted. A control unit and tail unit with operating control surfaces allowed the bomb to be 'steered' to its target by radio control.

The Hs 293 was an anti-shipping missile which, like the Fritz, was guided to its target by radio control, although a wire-guided version was also developed. The Hs 293 was the first successful guided missile, sinking the sloop HMS *Egret* on 27 August 1943.

ROCKETS

In the latter part of the war, some aircraft assigned to Reichsverteidigung duties were equipped with rocket projectiles. Although technically air-to-ground as well as air-to-air, they seem to have been most successfully used against enemy bomber streams. Designated the R4/M, the projectile was 81cm in length and carried a 0.520kg explosive charge. It achieved speeds of over 500m/s and had a range of 1,500m. The effect of several salvoes of these rockets fired by attacking aircraft into a bomber stream could be devastating.

CHAPTER SIX

AIRCRAFT MARKINGS

The colour schemes used on Luftwaffe aircraft were often extremely complex and would take a huge amount of space to cover in depth; indeed entire multi-volume works have been written on this subject alone. The purpose here is to give the reader a very basic overview of the general schemes used. Examples will always be found of aircraft which do not fit the general rules, new schemes often being applied at local level over the top of the original factory-applied scheme. This was often unavoidable as aircraft moved from, for instance, the European theatre, for which the basic schemes were intended, to the desert terrain of North Africa or the snow-covered landscape of a Russian winter.

On the outbreak of war, the Luftwaffe used a basic three-colour scheme. Undersurfaces were painted a light blue colour, while upper surfaces were in a two-tone dark green/black-green splinter pattern. Only the top part of the fuselage was camouflage-painted, the sides remaining in the light-blue colour of the undersurfaces.

In 1940, the scheme altered slightly for most aircraft. Undersurfaces were still in light blue but the camouflage pattern was executed in grey-green/grey-violet. In addition the previously pale blue sides of the fuselage were painted with a mottled pattern of blotches on the camouflage colours. The intensity of the mottle varied from aircraft to aircraft.

Colours changed again in 1944, with camouflage patterns being executed in a mix of dark green/light green/brown-violet. The bands of camouflage colour on the upper surfaces were not now the sharp angles and straight lines of the splinter pattern but employed more curves. The main camouflage patterns now extended down over much of the fuselage sides, replacing the older mottled patterns over the base pale blue, though some mottling was still often evident. This last scheme lasted until the end of the war.

Bomber aircraft started the war with the same basic two-tone green splinter over pale-blue undersurfaces as used by fighters and other light aircraft. On the beginning of the night bombing campaign against Great Britain, the pale-blue undersurfaces and sides of bombers on night operations were overpainted in black. In 1943 a new scheme appeared, with black undersurfaces complemented by pale grey upper surfaces over which a mottled camouflage scheme in dark green or dark grey was applied.

Night-fighters began the war using the same scheme as day-fighters. In 1940 some aircraft began to appear with all-black upper surfaces and light blue undersurfaces. A number of night-fighters were also painted all black. In late 1942 a new scheme appeared, with the whole aircraft in pale grey, and upper surfaces painted with a dark grey mottled pattern; and finally, in the latter part of the war, black undersurfaces were combined with mottled grey upper surfaces. Aircraft operating in North Africa were originally painted in plain sand colour over pale blue undersurfaces. Mottled camouflage patterns were later added, in olive green, over the upper surfaces and fuselage sides.

The national markings on German aircraft consisted, of course, of the so-called 'Balkenkreuz' black cross on the upper and lower wings and fuselage sides, and the swastika on the tail. A significant number of variants existed for these insignia, however. Initially, both the fuselage and wing crosses were in black, with white edges and a very narrow black outer border. This style of marking was used until 1943, when the

narrow black outer edges were deleted. In 1944, the black crosses themselves were deleted from the fuselage and upper wings, leaving just the white outer edges of the arms of the cross. The undersurfaces of the wings retained the black cross with outer white edges. Towards the end of the war, the fuselage and wing-undersurface crosses, which had already lost their black centres, had the white outer edges changed to black, but still devoid of a centre. The swastika on the tail at this point lost its white outer edge and became solid black.

In addition to the basic colour scheme and national markings, all Luftwaffe aircraft carried unit codes or tactical markings flanking the fuselage cross, and also, on larger aircraft, on the wing undersurfaces. Tactical markings were carried by fighter aircraft and consisted of a series of chevrons and bars flanking the fuselage cross as follows:

Basic Luftwaffe national emblems, from top left to bottom right: the early form of Balkenkreuz featured a central black cross with white edges and black outer borders; post-1943 Balkenkreuz with outer black edges removed; basic Balkenkreuz with no borders; 1944-style cross in black; 1944-style cross in white.

Geschwader Kommodore	Double chevron and horizontal bar ahead of fuselage cross, single horizontal bar to rear of cross.
Geschwader Adjutant	Single chevron and vertical bar ahead of fuselage cross.
Geschwader Operations Officer	Single chevron and horizontal bar ahead of fuselage cross.
Geschwader Technical Officer	Single chevron, vertical bar and circle ahead of fuselage cross.
Geschwader Staff	Single chevron and two vertical bars ahead of fuselage cross.
Gruppe Kommandeur, I Gruppe	Double chevron ahead of fuselage cross.
Gruppe Adjutant, I Gruppe	Single chevron ahead of fuselage cross.
Gruppe Technical Officer, I Gruppe	Single chevron and ring ahead of fuselage cross.
Gruppe Staff, I Gruppe	Single chevron and numeral '1' ahead of fuselage cross. ahead of fuselage cross, horizontal bar to rear of cross.
Gruppe Kommandeur, II Gruppe	Double chevron
Gruppe Adjutant, II Gruppe	Single chevron ahead of fuselage cross, horizontal bar to rear of cross.
Gruppe Technical Officer, II Gruppe	Single chevron and ring ahead of fuselage cross, horizontal bar to rear of cross.
Gruppe Staff, II Gruppe	Single chevron and numeral '2' ahead of fuselage cross.
Gruppe Kommandeur, III Gruppe	Double chevron ahead of fuselage cross, vertical bar to rear of cross
Gruppe Adjutant, III Gruppe	Single chevron ahead of fuselage cross, vertical bar to rear of cross.
Gruppe Technical Officer, III Gruppe	Single chevron and ring ahead of fuselage cross, vertical bar to rear of cross.
Gruppe Staff, III Gruppe	Single chevron and numeral '3' ahead of fuselage cross.

Note: III Gruppe could be indicated by either a vertical bar to rear of cross or a wavy line.

Gruppe Kommandeur, IV Gruppe	Double chevron ahead of fuselage cross, solid black circle to rear of cross.
Gruppe Adjutant, IV Gruppe	Single chevron ahead of fuselage cross, solid black circle to rear of cross.
Gruppe Technical Officer, IV Gruppe	Single chevron and ring ahead of fuselage cross, solid black circle to rear of cross.
Gruppe Staff, IV Gruppe	Single chevron and numeral '4' ahead of fuselage cross.

Note: IV Gruppe could be indicated either by a solid black circle to rear of cross or a small black cross.

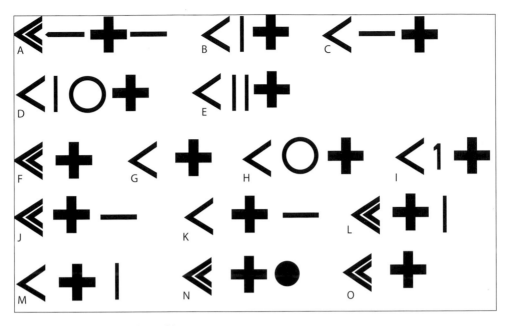

Typical fighter aircraft tactical markings:

a. Geschwaderkommodore, b. Geschwader Adjutant, c. Geschwader Operations Officer, d. Geschwader Technical Officer, e. Geschwader Staff, f. Gruppe Kommandeur – I Gruppe, g. Gruppe Adjutant – I Gruppe, h. Gruppe Technical Officer – I Gruppe, i. Gruppe Staff – I Gruppe, j. Gruppe Kommandeur – II Gruppe, k. Gruppe Adjutant – II Gruppe, l. Gruppe Kommandeur – III Gruppe, m. Gruppe Adjutant – III Gruppe, n. Gruppe Kommandeur – IV Gruppe, o. Gruppe Kommandeur – IV Gruppe, alternative.

Non-fighter units used an alphanumeric system to identify the unit. This generally consisted of two black-painted characters before the fuselage cross (white on black-painted aircraft, such as night-fighters), followed by one character to the rear of the cross. Larger units had the letter before the numeral, smaller units or sub-units of larger formations, vice versa.

Identified units include:

A1	Kampfgeschwader 53	
A2	Zerstörergeschwader 52, II Gruppe of Zerstörergeschwader 2	
A3	Kampfgeschwader 200	
A5	Sturzkampfgeschwader 1, Schlachtgeschwader 1	
A6	Aufklärungsgruppe 120	
B3	Kampfgeschwader 54	
B4	Nachtjagdstaffel Finland	
B7	Wettererkundungsstaffel 1	
C1	Erprobungskommando 16	
C2	Aufklärungsgruppe 41,	

	Nahaufklärungsgruppe 3	
C6	Kampfgruppe zbV 600	
C8	Transportgeschwader 5	
C9	Nachtjagdgeschwader 5	
D1	Seeaufklärungsgruppe 126	
D3	Nachtschlachtgruppe 2	
D5	Nachtjagdgeschwader 3	
D7	Wettererkundungsstaffel 1	
D9	Nachtjagdgeschwader 7	
E2 to E7	Erprobungsanstalt Rechlin	
E8	Nachtschlachtgeschwader 9	
F1	Kampfgeschwader 76, III Gruppe	

141

	of Sturzkampfgeschwader 77	T3	Bordfliegerstaffel 196, Bordfliegergruppe 196
F6	Aufklärungsgruppe 122	T5	Wettererkundungsstaffel-Oberbefehlshaber der Luftwaffe
F8	Kampfgeschwader 40		
G1	Kampfgeschwader 55		
G2	Aufklärungsgruppe 124	T6	Sturzkampfgeschwader 2, Schlachtgeschwader 2
G6	Kampfgruppe z.b.V. 2, Transportgeschwader 4	T9	Versuchsverband-Oberbefehlshaber der Luftwaffe
G9	Nachtjagdgeschwader 1		
H1	Aufklärungsgruppe 12	U2	Nahaufklärungsgruppe 5
H4	Luftlandgeschwader 1	U5	Kampfgeschwader 5
H7	Sturzkampfgeschwader 3	U8	Zerstörergeschwader 26
H8	Aufklärungsgruppe 33	U9	Nachtschlachtgruppe 3
J2	Nahaufklärungsgruppe 3	V4	Kampfgeschwader 1
J4	Transportstaffel	V7	Aufklärungsgruppe 32
J6	Kampfgruppe z.b.V. 500	W2	Grossraumlastensegler-gruppe 321
J9	Sturzkampfgeschwader 5		
K6	Küstenfliegergruppe 406	W7	Nachtjagdgeschwader 100
K7	Aufklärungsgruppe Nacht	X4	Lufttransportstaffel See 222
L1	Lehrgeschwader 1	Z6	Kampfgeschwader 60
L2	Lehrgeschwader 2		
L5	Kampfgruppe z.b.V. 5	1A	Wettererkundungsstaffel 5
M2	Küstenfliegergruppe 106	1B	Wetterurkundungskette – Luftflotte 5
M7	Kampfgruppe 806		
M8	Zerstörergeschwader 76	1G	Kampfgeschwader 27
N3	Stab Kampfgruppe 3, Kampfgruppe z.b.V. 172	1H	III Gruppe/Kampfgeschwader 26
		1K	Nachtschlachtgruppe 4, III Gruppe/Kampfgeschwader 27
P1	Kampfgeschwader 60		
P2	Aufklärungsgruppe 21	1L	Nachtschlachtgruppe 10
P4	X Fliegerkorps	1T	1 Staffel/Kampfgruppe 126, Kampfgeschwader 28
P5	Küstenfliegergruppe 406		
P7	Seenotstaffel 5, Seenotstaffel 51	1Z	Kampfgeschwader z.b.V.1, Transportgeschwader 1
Q9	Schlachtgeschwader 5		
R4	Nachtjagdgeschwader 2	2Λ	II Gruppe/Nachtjagdgeschwader 2
S1	Sturzkampfgeschwader 3		
S2	Sturzkampfgeschwader 77, Schlachtgeschwader 2	2C	I Gruppe/Zerstörergeschwader 1
		2F	II Gruppe/Zerstörergeschwader 26, Kampfgeschwader 54
S3	Transportgruppe 30		
S4	Küstenfliegergruppe 506, Kampfgruppe 506	2H	Versuchsstaffel 210, III Gruppe Zerstörergeschwader 1, II Gruppe/Zerstörergeschwader 26
S7	Sturzkampfgeschwader 3, Schlachtgeschwader 3		
		2J	Zerstörergeschwader 1
S9	Erprobungsgruppe 210, Schnellkampfgeschwader 210, Zerstörergeschwader 1	2N	I, II and III Gruppen/Zerstörergeschwader 26
		2S	III Gruppe/ Zerstörergeschwader 2
T1	Aufklärungsgruppe 10		

2U	Zerstörergeschwader 1		7A	Aufklärungsgruppe 121
2Z	Zerstörergeschwader 2,		7J	Nachtjagdgeschwader 102
	Nachtjagdgeschwader 6		7R	Seeaufklärungsgruppe 125
3C	Nachtjagdgeschwader 4		7T	Kampfgruppe 606
3E	Kampfgeschwader 6		7U	Kampfgruppe z.b.V. 108
3K	Minensuchgruppe		7V	Kampfgruppe z.b.V. 700
3M	I Gruppe/Zerstörergeschwader 2		8H	Aufklärungsgruppe 33
3U	Zerstörergeschwader 26		8L	Küstenfliegergruppe 906
3W	Nachtschlachtgruppe 11,		8Q	Transportgruppe 10
	IGruppe/Zerstörergeschwader 2		8T	Kampfgruppe z.b.V. 800,
3Z	Kampfgeschwader 77			Transportgeschwader 2
4D	Kampfgeschwader 25,		8V	Nachtjagdgeschwader 200
	Kampfgeschwader 30		9K	Kampfgeschwader 51
4E	Aufklärungsgruppe 13,		9P	Kampfgruppe z.b.V. 9
	Nahaufklärungsgruppe 15		9V	Aufklärungsgruppe 5
4F	Kampfgruppe z.b.V. 400		9W	Nachtjagdgeschwader 101
4N	Aufklärungsgruppe 22			
4R	Nachtjagdgeschwader 2			
4T	Wettererkundungsstaffel 51			
4U	Aufklärungsgruppe 31			
4V	Kampfgruppe z.b.V. 9,			
	Transportgeschwader 3			

Following the fuselage cross, a further character, combined with the use of colours, identified the Gruppe and Staffel within the Geschwader, as follows:

5D	Aufklärungsgruppe 31	
5F	(F) Staffel/Aufklärungsgruppe 14	
5H	(H) Staffel/Aufklärungsgruppe 14	
5J	Kampfgeschwader 4	
5K	Kampfgeschwader 3	
5M	Sturzkampfgeschwader 76	
5T	Kampfschlachtgeschwader 1	
5W	Seenotstaffel 10,	
	Wettererkundungsstaffel 76	
5Z	Wettererkundungsstaffel 26	
6G	Sturzkampfgeschwader 51	
6I	Küstenfliegergruppe 76,	
	Seeaufklärungsgruppe 130	
6J	Nachtschlachtgruppe 8	
6K	Aufklärungsgruppe 41	
6M	Aufklärungsgruppe 11	
6N	Kampfgruppe 100,	
	Kampfgeschwader 100	
6R	Seeaufklärungsgruppe 127	
6T	Küstenfliegergruppe 706	
6U	Zerstörergeschwader 1	
6W	Seeaufklärungsgruppe 128,	
	Küstenfliegergruppe 196	

A	Blue	Geschwader Stab
B	Green	I Gruppe Stab
C	Green	II Gruppe Stab
D	Green	III Gruppe Stab
F	Green	IV Gruppe Stab
G	Green	V Gruppe Stab
H	White	1 Staffel/I Gruppe
K	Red	2 Staffel/I Gruppe
L	Yellow	3 Staffel/I Gruppe
M	White	4 Staffel/II Gruppe
N	Red	5 Staffel/II Gruppe
P	Yellow	6 Staffel/II Gruppe
R	White	7 Staffel/III Gruppe
S	Red	8 Staffel/III Gruppe
T	Yellow	9 Staffel/III Gruppe
U	White	10 Staffel/IV Gruppe
V	Red	11 Staffel/IV Gruppe
W	Yellow	12 Staffel/IV Gruppe
X	White	13 Staffel/V Gruppe
Y	Red	14 Staffel/V Gruppe
Z	Yellow	15 Staffel/V Gruppe
Q	White	16 Staffel
J	Red	17 Staffel

O	Yellow	18 Staffel		M	Blue	4 Staffel/I Gruppe
E	White	19 Staffel		N	White	5 Staffel/II Gruppe
I	Red	20 Staffel		P	Red	6 Staffel/II Gruppe
				R	Yellow	7 Staffel/II Gruppe

Some amendments were made to this coding in the late stages of the war, resulting in the following final coding version:

				S	Blue	8 Staffel/II Gruppe
				T	White	9 Staffel/III Gruppe
				U	Red	10 Staffel/III Gruppe
				V	Yellow	11 Staffel/III Gruppe
A	Blue	Geschwader Stab		W	Blue	12 Staffel/III Gruppe
B	Green	I Gruppe Stab		X	White	13 Staffel/IV Gruppe
C	Green	II Gruppe Stab		Y	Red	14 Staffel/IV Gruppe
D	Green	III Gruppe Stab		Z	Yellow	15 Staffel/IV Gruppe
F	Green	IV Gruppe Stab		Q	Blue	16 Staffel/IV Gruppe
G	Green	V Gruppe Stab		J	White	17 Staffel/V Gruppe
H	White	1 Staffel/I Gruppe		O	Red	18 Staffel/V Gruppe
K	Red	2 Staffel/I Gruppe		E	Yellow	19 Staffel/V Gruppe
L	Yellow	3 Staffel/I Gruppe		I	Blue	20 Staffel/V Gruppe

CHAPTER SEVEN

TECHNICAL DEVELOPMENTS

As early as 1936, the Luftwaffe was sponsoring research into rocket-powered aircraft. Dr Eugen Sänger was commissioned to build an aerospace research institute in Trauen, where he was to design and develop a manned aircraft capable of reaching orbital height above the earth, powered by liquid-fuel rocket engines the design of which he had already perfected. These engines were capable of producing a thrust in excess of that achieved by the later V2 ballistic missiles.

The resultant design was for an aircraft capable of supersonic flight reaching up into the stratosphere. With short, wedge-shaped wings and a horizontal tailplane at the end of the fuselage, the aircraft was to have been launched from a 2-mile-long ramp by means of a rocket-powered sled. After take-off, having reached an altitude of around 5,000m, it was to have attained a speed of around 1,750kph. The main engine would then ignite and accelerate the aircraft to a speed of some 22,100kph at an altitude of over 145km.

The aircraft, having reached its peak velocity, would then start to decelerate and lose altitude, eventually hitting denser atmosphere and bobbing over like a stone skipping along the surface of water. Eventually, it would simply glide back to its designated landing spot, where it would come down on normal aircraft landing gear. The whole concept bore many similarities to the space shuttle of today. Estimated range from take-off to landing was around 23,500km. Intended to be capable of carrying a bomb-load of up to 3,600kg, the aircraft carried no defensive armament. It was hardly likely to need any, as no aircraft in existence would have been capable of catching it.

Development work continued until the time of the invasion of the Soviet Union, at which point it was halted, all resources being needed for the development and construction of conventional aircraft for the war effort. The aircraft, had it been successfully built, would have given Germany the capability to strike directly at the USA.

The introduction of such advanced aircraft as the Me 163, Me 262, He 163 and others amply demonstrate the high level of technical advancement achieved by the Luftwaffe during its short life. Less well known perhaps are some of the other, sometimes very futuristic, aircraft that were under development but did not enter service before the war ended. In many cases, these aircraft never progressed beyond the drawing-board stage, though the capture of developmental research material by the Allies at the end of the war meant that much of the theoretical work done by the

Luftwaffe was incorporated into postwar aircraft development by the Allies.

Some of these projected aircraft have an almost science fiction aspect to them, flying wings, vertical take-off types and others. The number of projects was quite astonishing, but limitations of space make it possible to describe only a few of the more important types, which either actually reached prototype stage and flew, or for which the development continued by the Allies after the war resulted in an actual completed and serving aircraft type.

FOCKE WULF TA 183 HUCKEBEIN

Another jet fighter, this aircraft was allocated a 'Ta'- rather than 'Fw'-type number in recognition of its designer, Kurt Tank. Development work began in 1942. The final design resulted in a relatively short fuselage with a large air intake in the nose, passing under the cockpit to feed the turbojet engine in the rear. The wings, containing fuel cells and mounted mid-fuselage, were swept back at 40 degrees, and the tailplane mounted atop the large tail fin. A pressurised cockpit was provided for the pilot, with a bubble canopy providing good all-round visibility. The aircraft was to have been provided with four 30mm cannon and the capacity to carry a useful bomb-load in a compartment partially recessed into the fuselage, thus reducing drag.

The design was accepted in February 1945 and production ordered of a number of prototypes. It was intended that the first of these would fly in May/June 1945 and full-scale production begin in October of that year. The war, of course, ended before any were completed, the production facilities being overrun by British troops in early April.

It was not to be the end of the Huckebein story, however. On capturing Berlin in May 1945, the Soviets discovered a full set of design drawings at the Air Ministry. Impressed by the potential of the design, they ordered production of a number of prototypes, the first of which flew in July 1947, powered, ironically, by a Rolls-Royce Nene turbojet engine. The Soviets were impressed, but not entirely satisfied with the performance of the aircraft. They made some minor modifications of their own, including moving from having a single, large tailplane at the tip of the fin, to single tailplanes each side, a little way down from the top. The resultant aircraft entered service with the Red Air Force (and with the air forces of many Soviet satellite states) as the Mig 15.

Meanwhile, after the war, Kurt Tank had been invited to Argentina, where he was asked to design a new jet fighter for the

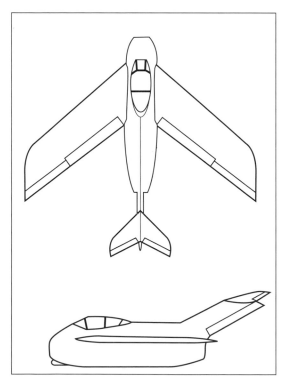

The design of the Ta 183 Hückebein was developed by the Soviet Union after the war and led to the successful MiG 15 jet fighter.

Argentinian air force. He opted for a slightly modified version of the Huckebein and a number of prototypes were constructed. These flew without mishap but failed to impress the test pilots with their performance, and the type was never placed into full-scale production. The Mig 15, on the other hand, was produced in the thousands and flew combat missions in Korea.

HORTEN HO 229

Manufactured by the Gotha aircraft works (previously manufacturers of gliders) from a design by brothers Reimar and Walter Horten, this was another futuristic design which greatly influenced post-war aircraft. The Gotha firm made a number of recommendations to the Air Ministry which they felt would improve the adaptability of the basic design and allow alternative power-plants and manufacturing methods to be used in future developments. This was accepted and led to the new designation of Go P 60.

The aircraft was effectively a 'flying wing' with engines mounted in the wing roots, where they merged with the 'fuselage'. There was no tail fin and no tailplane. Two BMW turbojet engines would provide the thrust. The pilot of the aircraft sat in a pressurised armoured cockpit. Typically, as with most jets, a tricycle undercarriage was featured. Armament would be four 30mm cannon.

Unlike many of the Luftwaffe's proposed jet fighter designs, this one made it past the drawing board and a prototype was constructed, though no volume production was ever achieved. The aircraft first flew in December 1944 and achieved speeds of up to 800kph. The prototype crashed in February 1945 but had already convinced the Luftwaffe of the viability of the design.

Volume production was ordered but the factory was overrun by the advancing Allies before any aircraft could be completed. This influential design was of great interest to the Americans, who subsequently produced their own 'flying wing' types, such as the B-2 bomber.

Reimar Horten was also involved in the design of a gigantic jet-engined bomber, the Ho 18, known as the Amerika bomber. This six-engined flying wing was intended to drop an atomic bomb on New York or Washington but was never anything more than a theoretical concept.

LIPPISCH LI P13A

Designed by Dr Alexander Lippisch, this advanced interceptor fighter featured sharply swept-back wings reaching to the tail of the aircraft, and an extremely large, triangular tail fin, the cockpit being located in the forward edge of this fin. The aircraft looked rather like the chopped-off tail section of a more conventional aircraft. The ramjet engine was fed via a circular air intake in the nose.

An unpowered prototype was built for wind tunnel speed testing and was found to be extremely stable. In its intended form with its ramjet engine it was designed to be capable of speeds in excess of twice the speed of sound.

MESSERSCHMITT P1101

This aircraft was to have been a single-engine, swept-wing jet fighter. Prototypes were completed but the war ended before the aircraft could enter production. The Allies were impressed with the design, however, and the P1101 led directly to the American Bell X-5 and to the Swedish Saab J29. The P1102 was to have been a swing-wing jet, a concept adopted in postwar

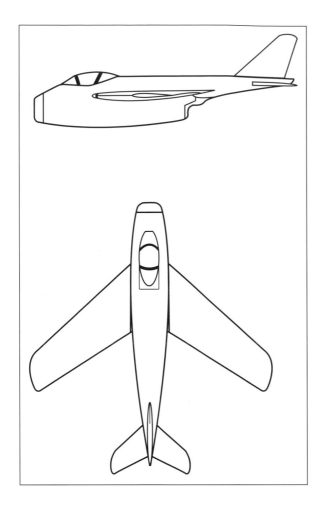

The Messerschmitt P1101 was a sound concept intended as a swing-wing jet fighter, and prototypes were constructed. Many of its concepts were used in the postwar Saab J29 and the American Bell X-5.

designs such as the US F-111 or the Anglo-German-Italian 'Tornado'.

Junkers were in the process of developing the EF09, a vertical-take-off jet, while Focke Wulf were developing the Triebflugel, a fighter with multi-directional jets, a concept later taken up by the British for the famous Harrier vertical-take-off aircraft.

The Focke Wulf vertical-take-off fighter was designed in autumn 1944. It had three wings with a ramjet engine at the end of each wing. These wings would rotate around the fuselage like a large propeller. The aircraft would have sat vertically on its tail for its rocket-assisted take-off. Intended armament was two 30mm cannon plus two

20mm cannon. Although the Triebflugel was not constructed, a wind tunnel prototype was tested.

Other advanced designs included the Ju 287 heavy-bomber project. This aircraft, with unusual swept-forward wings and six engines was to have had a top speed of over 800kph, faster than any Allied fighter interceptors.

While the impact of this developmental work on the war was negligible (apart from, it can be argued, from diverting essential resource away from existing conventional aircraft manufacture), the influence on postwar aircraft design was substantial.

CHAPTER EIGHT

THE PARATROOP UNITS

Although the parachute was first utilised in 1785, its use as a piece of military equipment did not occur until the First World War, when it was issued to crews of observation balloons. As a method of delivering troops to the battlefield, as opposed to a safety device, the parachute was first used by the Italians in the First World War, and indeed the Italians were enthusiastic pioneers of the concept. The Soviet Union, too, was quick to develop a paratroop force and was the first country to make large-scale combat drops of paratroops, during the 1939/40 winter war with Finland.

The Germans were swift to see the potential of such troops and in 1936 set up a paratroop school at Stendal. Initially, the German Army also fielded paratroops, but these were ultimately absorbed into the Fallschirmjäger under Luftwaffe control.

Initial successes were stunning, with paratroopers scoring impressive successes at Eben Emael in Belgium and at Narvik in Norway. The airborne invasion of Crete saw the Fallschirmjäger at their zenith. Although victory was theirs, it was gained at such a high cost in lives that future large-scale operations of this type were prohibited. Thereafter, the paratroops were to be used as elite infantry, fighting on the ground on every front from the frozen wastes of Russia, through Italy, and in Normandy. On many occasions the Fallschirmjäger covered themselves in glory, such as with their heroic defence of Monte Cassino, but as regular ground troops. A medium-scale airborne drop was made during the Ardennes offensive of December 1944 but was of very limited value to the operation.

THE PARACHUTE CORPS

I FALLSCHIRMKORPS

I Fallschirmkorps was responsible for Fallschirmjäger units operating in Italy. In addition to the divisions it controlled, its own order of battle included an assault gun brigade, an artillery regiment and a flak regiment.

Commanding Officers
General der Fallschirmtruppe Alfred Schlemm   1 Jan 1944–1 Nov 1944

General der Fallschirmtruppe Richard Heidrich	1 Nov 1944–23 Jan 1945
Generalleutnant Hellmuth Böhlke	23 Jan 1945–7 Feb 1945
General der Fallschirmtruppe Richard Heidrich	7 Feb 1945–8 May 1945

II FALLSCHIRMKORPS

II Fallschirmkorps operated solely in western Europe, seeing action in France, Holland and Germany. As well as controlling a number of Fallschirm divisions, it, too, fielded its own assault gun brigade, flak regiment and artillery regiment.

Commanding Officers

| General der Fallschirmtruppe Eugen Meindl | 5 Nov 1943–8 May 1945 |

THE PARACHUTE DIVISIONS

1 FALLSCHIRM DIVISION

Formed in France in May 1943, this division was sent into action in the battle for Sicily from July to September of that year, before pulling back to the Italian mainland, where it fought out the remainder of the war.

Divisional Commanders

General der Fallschirmtruppe Richard Heidrich	May 1943–Dec 1944
Generalmajor Hans Korte	Jan 1944–Feb 1944
General der Fallschirmtruppe Richard Heidrich	Feb 1944–Nov 1944
Generalmajor Karl-Lothar Schulz	Nov 1944–May 1945

Hermann Bernhard Ramcke was one of Germany's most distinguished airborne soldiers. Ramcke took part in the battle for Crete, where he was awarded the Knight's Cross. He then saw action in North Africa, winning the Oakleaves. In September 1944 he was awarded the Oakleaves with Swords, and, at the same time, the Oakleaves with Swords and Diamonds to the Knight's Cross for his steadfast defence of the port of Brest.

2 FALLSCHIRM DIVISION

Raised in France in the early part of 1943, the division was first committed to action in Italy in July of that year. In November it was moved eastwards and served on the central sector of the Eastern Front. It retreated into Germany towards the end of the war.

Divisional Commanders

General der Fallschirmtruppe Bernhard Ramcke	Feb 1943–Sep 1943
Oberstleutnant Kurt Meder-Eggebert	Sep 1943
Generalmajor Walter Barenthin	Sep 1943–Nov 1943
Generalleutnant Gustav Wilke	Nov 1943–Mar 1944
Generalmajor Hans Kroh	Mar 1944–Jun 1944
General der Fallschirmtruppe Bernhard Ramcke	Jun 1944–Nov 1944
Generalmajor Hans Kroh	Nov 1944
Generalleutnant Walter Lackner	Nov 1944–Apr 1945

3 FALLSCHIRM DIVISION

Raised in France in October 1943, this division saw action in the battle for Normandy and suffered heavy casualties during the escape from the Falaise pocket. It subsequently fought in Belgium and Holland before withdrawing into Germany, where it fought around Aachen. The division surrendered in the Ruhr pocket in April 1945.

Divisional Commanders

Generalmajor Walter Barenthin	Oct 1943–Feb 1944
Generalleutnant Richard Schimpf	Feb 1944–Aug 1944
General der Fallschirmtruppe Eugen Meindl	Aug 1944
Generalmajor Walter Wadehn	Aug 1944–Jan 1945
Generalleutnant Richard Schimpf	Jan 1945–Mar 1945
Oberst Helmut Hoffmann	Mar 1945
Oberst Karl-Heinz Becker	Mar 1945–Apr 1945

4 FALLSCHIRM DIVISION

Raised in Italy in late 1943, this division saw its first major action on the Nettuno front in January 1944. It put up stiff resistance to the Allies in the retreat up through the Italian mainland. Among its personnel were many volunteers from the Italian Folgore and Demgo parachute divisions.

Divisional Commanders

Generalleutnant Heinrich Trettner	Oct 1943–May 1945

Dr Heinrich Neumann was one of a rare breed, a technically non-combatant medical officer awarded one of Germany's highest decorations for combat gallantry. Neumann served with the Fallschirmjäger Sturm Regiment during the assault on Crete, where, after all other officers had been killed or wounded, he led an assault on enemy-held positions overlooking Maleme airfield, driving them out and securing the positions.

5 FALLSCHIRM DIVISION

Raised in France in March 1944, the division saw action during the battle for Normandy and the retreat through Avranches, Mortain and Argentan. Badly battered, it had to be re-formed in October and went back into action during the Ardennes offensive. The division was trapped in the Ruhr pocket in April 1945 and surrendered to US forces.

Divisional Commanders

Generalleutnant Gustav Wilke	Apr 1944–Sep 1944
Generalmajor Sebastian-Ludwig Heilmann	Sep 1944–Mar 1945
Oberst Kurt Gröschke	Mar 1945–Apr 1945

6 FALLSCHIRM DIVISION

Raised in France in the area around Amiens in June 1944, the division saw very heavy fighting in the area to the north-west of Paris and was virtually destroyed. The remnants fought in the retreat through Belgium and Holland, around Arnhem and Xanten. The survivors surrendered to US forces in April 1945 in Holland.

Divisional Commanders

Generalleutnant Rüdiger von Heyking	May 1944–Sep 1944
Oberst Harry Herrmann	Sep 1944–Oct 1944
Generalleutnant Hermann Plocher	Oct 1944–May 1945

7 FALLSCHIRM DIVISION

Raised in Elsass in September 1944, this division took part in the fighting withdrawal through Belgium and Holland, and saw action around Arnhem and Nijmegen before being pushed back over the Rhine into Germany. It fought in the battles for the Reichswald and by the closing days of the war was located around Oldenburg, where it eventually surrendered to US forces in May 1945.

Divisional Commanders

Generalleutnant Wolfgang Erdmann	Oct 1944–May 1945

8 FALLSCHIRM DIVISION

Raised in Cologne in December 1944, the division saw action in Holland, where it fought at Arnhem and Nijmegen before withdrawing over the Rhine into Germany. It ended up in the Ruhr pocket, near Werl, where it surrendered to US troops in April 1945.

Divisional Commanders

Generalmajor Walter Wadehn	Jan 1945–Apr 1945

9 FALLSCHIRM DIVISION

Established in December 1944, the division went into action in January 1945 in Pomerania. It fought through Stettin and the Küstrin bridgehead, eventually being drawn into the fighting around Berlin, where most of the survivors went into Soviet captivity.

Divisional Commanders

Generalleutnant Gustav Wilke	Dec 1944–Mar 1945
General der Fallschirmtruppe Bruno Bräuer	Mar 1945–Apr 1945
Oberst Harry Herrmann	Apr 1945–May 1945

10 FALLSCHIRM DIVISION

Established in Austria in March 1945, this short-lived unit was still working up when it was overrun by the Russians before it saw any major actions.

Divisional Commanders

Generalleutnant Gustav Wilke	Mar 1945–Apr 1945
Oberst Karl-Heinz von Hoffmann	Apr 1945–May 1945

11 FALLSCHIRM DIVISION

This unit was still forming up in the area around Oldenburg when the war ended.

Divisional Commanders

Oberst Walter Gericke	Mar 1945–Apr 1945

By the second half of the war, German paratroopers were rarely involved in parachute drops but were instead used as elite infantry. This shot shows Fallschirmjäger during the battle for Normandy in the summer of 1944, in a heavily camouflaged Horch field car, the NCO sitting on the hood, keeping a watchful eye for the enemy fighter-bombers that ruled the skies, making daylight movement of vehicles extremely risky. (*Josef Charita*)

20 FALLSCHIRM DIVISION

A division on paper only, it was created in Holland in April 1945 but saw no action as a coherent fighting force.

Divisional Commanders
Generalmajor Walter Barenthin   Apr 1945–May 1945

21 FALLSCHIRM DIVISION

Another of Germany's many 'paper' divisions whose lifetime was measured in weeks. The war ended well before it could be formed.

Divisional Commanders
Oberst Walter Gericke   Apr 1945–May 1945

FALLSCHIRM DIVISION ERDMANN

Brought together in late August 1944, in order to resist the Allied push on Arnhem. It was disbanded in October.

Divisional Commanders
Generalleutnant Wolfgang Erdmann   Aug 1944–Oct 1944

FALLSCHIRM-AUSBILDUNGS UND ERSATZ DIVISION

Divisional Commanders
Generalmajor Walter Barenthin   Dec 1944–Apr 1945

CHAPTER NINE

GROUND UNITS

THE FLAK UNITS

As well as the traditional role of providing anti-aircraft defences to the nation's cities and industrial and military complexes, Flak units served on every front. These units could consist of large-calibre, heavy anti-aircraft guns working in close coordination with searchlight units, and based in mammoth concrete flak towers like those in Berlin, Hamburg and Vienna, through smaller-calibre, light anti-aircraft weapons providing airfield defence 'in the field', to the highly mobile mounted flak with light or medium weapons, affixed to half-track prime movers or even flatbed trucks that could provide travelling defensive cover to units on the move.

Many Luftwaffe Flak units also found themselves pressed into service in the ground role, where their famed 8.8cm guns proved to be equally devastating when used against enemy armour. These units were particularly successful in the early part of the campaign in the east, when the light armament carried by many German tanks was ineffectual against the heavy armour of Soviet tanks. The 8.8cm gun was, however, perfectly capable of knocking out even the heaviest enemy tanks of the day, and doing so at a long range.

By the middle of the war, it is estimated that somewhere in the region of 15,000 of the excellent 8.8cm flak formed the mainstay of Germany's anti-aircraft defences. In addition to these, innumerable smaller 3.7cm and 2cm guns contributed to the nation's defence.

The larger weapons fired shells that were preset to explode at a specific altitude, filling the sky with metal shrapnel. When groups of anything up to forty heavy flak pieces fired into a particular area of the sky through which enemy aircraft were passing, the effect could be devastating. Any aircraft within 30m of the exploding shell would be likely to suffer fatal damage, and any within 200m would still be likely to suffer damage to some degree.

By early 1944, well over 20,000 flak guns were defending German home territory, of which around one-third were heavy calibre. In addition, approximately 10,000 more were in action in areas occupied by Germany. Within six months, the number of heavy-calibre flak weapons would have increased to well over 11,000, the majority of which were the dependable 8.8cm.

During 1944, in excess of 3,500 enemy aircraft were shot down by flak, while during the same period, less than 1,000 were downed by the Luftwaffe's fighters, thus giving the lie to claims that devoting huge resources to the nation's flak defences was wasteful.

One of the most effective weapons available to the Flakartillerie was the quad 2cm anti-aircraft gun or Flakvierling. This weapon was capable of putting up a rate of fire of up to 1,800 rounds per minute and could also be used to devastating effect against ground targets. As well as being operated from a fixed position, it could be mounted on a wheeled carriage, or on a truck or half-track, making it an extremely versatile weapon. (*Josef Charita*)

While the 8.8cm gun was a highly effective weapon, perhaps one of the best weapons of any type produced by Germany during this period, it was later to be backed up by even heavier weapons such as the 10.5cm and 12.8cm flak. The 12.8cm Flak 40 was a particularly awesome weapon, consisting of twin barrels in a single mount. Normally such weapons were grouped in batteries of four, each controlled by a single predictor unit, meaning that the phenomenal weight of fire of eight 12.8cm barrels could be directed at a single aircraft. On the night of 24 March 1944, an attacking force of some 72 RAF bombers targeted Berlin and were met by defensive fire from the city's 12.8cm flak batteries. The British force was heavily

mauled, with fifty of the seventy-two aircraft shot down. Daylight raids in the face of such firepower were equally punished. In November of that same year, fifty-six B-17 bombers were shot down in a single raid over Merseburg.

It is interesting to note that many of the flak batteries on home defence were crewed by young boys, volunteers from the Hitler Youth, old men unfit for front-line duty, and female auxiliaries. Several functions worked in close cooperation with each other. First, a sound location unit would detect the approximate position of the enemy aircraft. This would be passed to a searchlight unit that would sweep that sector of the sky until the enemy aircraft were illuminated. The predictor unit would work out the position at which the guns should fire, taking into consideration altitude, speed, etc. of the enemy aircraft, and finally the guns would unleash their deadly projectiles. During daylight hours, the predictors were guided by telescopic optical rangefinders.

Though estimates vary, depending on the level of auxiliary helpers included, there were certainly well over a million flak personnel involved in the defence of the Reich, and by the end of 1944 the flak guns were expending over 3 million shells per month (a huge increase from the figure of around 500,000 per month in 1942). Measuring the expenditure of shells against the number of enemy bombers shot down, it has been estimated that the cost to Germany of downing each enemy bomber was in the region of a quarter of a million RM (over £650,000 in today's money).

Although it is rarely given much coverage in military literature, the importance of the Flakartillerie to Germany during an Allied bombing campaign in which well over a million tons of bombs were dropped is difficult to overstate.

THE FLAKKORPS

These corps commands were headquarter units which commanded a number of subordinate regiments or divisions. The exact composition of each corps changed often, and individual divisions could move from one corps to another.

Luftwaffe ground troops manoeuvre an 8.8cm flak gun into position. This weapon was to develop into one of the best of the war, being used as an effective anti-aircraft weapon, but ultimately as an even more effective tank killer. So ineffective were the small-calibre guns fitted to many German tanks in the first half of the war that the 'eighty-eight' became the principal weapon against medium or heavy enemy armour. (*Josef Charita*)

I FLAKKORPS

Formed in October 1939, and consisting of three Flak regiments (101, 102 and 104), a signals regiment and a searchlight detachment, I Flakkorps was originally based in Germany, but moved to France after the successful conclusion of the campaign in the west. It returned to Germany in September 1940. In March 1941 it was redesignated Luftwaffenbefehlshaber Mitte. In the summer of 1941, the corps moved to Russia, where it was further renamed Luftwaffen Kommando Kaukasus in November 1942. At this time it controlled 9, 10, 12 and 15 Flak Divisions. It remained in Russia until October 1944, at which time it withdrew from the northern Ukraine into Poland and finally, in February 1945, back to Germany. In its final form it controlled 10, 11 and 17 Flak Divisions. The corps surrendered to the Soviets near Königgrätz in May 1945.

Corps Commanders

Generaloberst Hubert Weise	Oct 1939–Mar 1941
General der Flakartillerie Walter von Axthelm	Mar 1941–Dec 1941
General der Flakartillerie Richard Reimann	Dec 1941–Apr 1942
Generaloberst Otto Dessloch	Apr 1942–Nov 1942
Generaloberst Otto Dessloch	Feb 1943–Jun 1943
General der Flakartillerie Richard Reimann	Jun 1943–May 1945
General der Flakartillerie Walter von Axthelm	May 1945

II FLAKKORPS

Formed in Germany in October 1939 and comprising Flak Regiments 103, 201 and 202, as well as a signals regiment, this corps moved to France in May 1940, and was earmarked for participation in the invasion of Great Britain. In March 1941, it moved to Heeresgruppe Süd, taking part in the invasion of Russia. After September 1941, it operated predominantly under Heeresgruppe Mitte. It was disbanded in April 1942 and re-formed in November 1943, with command of 10, 12 and 18 Flak Divisions. It remained operational in Russia until August 1944, after which it was gradually withdrawn westwards through Poland and into Germany. In January 1945, it controlled 12, 18, 23 and 27 Flak Divisions. By the closing weeks of the war it was on the Oder front with 19 Armee. In its penultimate form it controlled 6 and 15 Flak Brigades and 27 Flak Division under 3 Panzer Armee. The corps took part in the final defence of Berlin with 1 Flak Division and surrendered to the Soviets at the end of the war.

Corps Commanders

Generaloberst Otto Dessloch	Oct 1939–Mar 1942
General der Flakartillerie Job Odebrecht	Nov 1943–May 1945

Flak units operated in close cooperation with searchlight units and barrage balloons and this photograph gives an idea of how large these balloons were. They presented a serious hazard to aircraft, particularly at night. Unwitting aircraft that flew into the steel cables tethering these balloons to the ground could suffer serious or fatal damage. Barrage balloons were usually controlled by the same units that operated the searchlights. (*Josef Charita*)

III FLAKKORPS

Formed in France in early 1944, this corps moved back to Germany in the autumn of that year, after seeing action in Normandy. It took part in the Ardennes offensive and was finally pushed back into Germany where it ended the war in the Ruhr pocket, in control of 2, 7 and 16 Flak Divisions and 1, 18 and 19 Flak Brigades.

Corps Commanders

Generalleutnant Johannes Hintz	Feb 1944–May 1944
General der Flakartillerie Wolfgang Pickert	May 1944–Jul 1944
Oberst Werner von Kistowski	Jul 1944–Aug 1944
General der Flakartillerie Wolfgang Pickert	Aug 1944–Mar 1945
Generalleutnant Heino von Rantzau	Mar 1945–Apr 1945

IV FLAKKORPS

Formed in the summer of 1944, the corps spent its operational life within Germany. Units passing under its control included 9, 13, 21, 26 and 28 Flak Divisions and 1, 5 and 12 Flak Brigades.

Corps Commanders
General der Flakartillerie Otto-Wilhelm von Renz Jul 1944–Aug 1944
General der Flieger Rudolf Bogatsch Aug 1944–May 1945

V FLAKKORPS

This corps was formed in November 1944 for operational use in Hungary. It served in the retreat through Yugoslavia, Slovakia and into Austria. During its short life it controlled 15, 19, 20 and 24 Flak Divisions and 7 and 17 Flak Brigades.

Corps Commanders
General der Flakartillerie Otto-Wilhelm von Renz Nov 1944–May 1945

VI FLAKKORPS

This short-lived corps was only formed in February 1945 and ended the war fighting on German soil in the northern sector of the Western Front. It controlled 3, 4 and 8 Flak Divisions and 9 and 18 Flak Brigades

Corps Commanders
Generalleutnant Ludwig Schilffarth Feb 1945–May 1945

FLAK DIVISIONS

1 FLAK DIVISION

Formed in September 1941 under the control of Luftverteidigungskommando 1 (Berlin), this division spent the greatest part of the war tasked with defending the German capital. In the closing days of the war, however, elements of the division saw action on the Oder front. Its principal components were 22, 53 and 140 Flak Regiments and 82 Searchlight Regiment.

Divisional Commanders
Generalleutnant Ludwig Schilffarth Sep 1941–Jan 1943
Generalmajor Max Schaller Jan 1943–Apr 1944
Generalleutnant Erich Kressmann Apr 1944–Nov 1944
Generalmajor Kurt von Ludwig Nov 1944
Generalmajor Otto Sydow Nov 1944–May 1945

2 FLAK DIVISION

Formed in September 1941 under Luftverteidigungskommando 2 in Leipzig, this unit served initially in Germany before being committed to the Eastern Front in January 1942, where it served with Heeresgruppe Nord until September 1944. It also took part in the Ardennes offensive before being pushed back into Germany, where it was eventually overrun in the Ruhr pocket in April 1945. Its principal components were Flak Regiments 18, 41, 43, 136, 151, 164 and 183.

Divisional Commanders
Generalleutnant Oskar Bertram	Sep 1941–Jan 1942
Generalleutnant Walter Feyerabend	Jan 1942–Feb 1942
Generalleutnant Heino von Rantzau	Feb 1942–Sep 1943
Generalleutnant Alfons Luczny	Sep 1943–Nov 1944
Oberst Fritz Laicher	Nov 1944–Apr 1945

3 FLAK DIVISION

Formed in September 1941 under the control of Luftverteidigungskommando 3 in Hamburg, this unit spent the entire war in Germany on home defence duties. Its principal components were Flak Regiments 61 and 123 and Searchlight Regiments 160 and 161.

Divisional Commanders
Generalleutnant Theodor Spiess	Sep 1941–Jun 1942
Generalleutnant Walter von Hippel	Jun 1942–Apr 1944
Generalmajor Alwin Wolz	Apr 1944–Apr 1945
Generalmajor Otto Stange	Apr 1945–May 1945

As discussed in the accompanying text, the effect of a direct hit or near miss by heavy flak could be devastating. This B-24 Liberator bomber has sustained a hit to its starboard wing, just at the mount for the outer engine, and is peeling off from the formation, fatally damaged.

4 FLAK DIVISION

Formed in September 1941 under Luftverteidigungskommando 4 in Düsseldorf, it was a home defence unit tasked with the defence of the Ruhr region. It spent the whole war in Germany, eventually surrendering at Duisburg in April 1945. Principal components were Flak Regiments 24, 44, 46, 94, 124 and Searchlight Regiments 73 and 74.

Divisional Commanders

General der Flakartillerie Gerhard Hoffmann	Sep 1941–Feb 1942
Generalleutnant Johannes Hintz	Feb 1942–Feb 1944
Generalleutnant Ludwig Schilffarth	Feb 1944–Oct 1944
Oberst Max Hecht	Oct 1944–Apr 1945

5 FLAK DIVISION

Formed in September 1941 under Luftverteidigungskommando 5 in Frankfurt am Main. It remained in Germany until 1942, when it was sent to the Balkans. In 1943 it was relocated to Italy and in 1944 was tasked with defending the Romanian oilfields at Ploesti and took part in the defence of Bucharest. It was all but destroyed on the Eastern Front but re-formed in November 1944 and was given the task of defending the V1 launching sites. In the closing stages of the war it withdrew into the area around Hamburg. Principal components were Flak Regiments 202, 229 and Searchlight Regiment 188.

Divisional Commanders

Generalleutnant Kurt Menzel	Sep 1941–Apr 1942
Generalleutnant Georg Neuffes	Apr 1942–Nov 1942
Generalmajor Julius Kudema	Nov 1942–Aug 1944

6 FLAK DIVISION

Formed in September 1941 under Luftverteidigungskommando 6, covering Belgium and northern France. In 1942 it was sent to the Eastern Front, where it served under Heeresgruppe Mitte. It ended the war cut off in the Kurland pocket. Principal components were Flak Regiments 18, 41, 43, 64, 111, 151 and 164.

Divisional Commanders

General der Flakartillerie Job Odebrecht	Sep 1941–Sep 1942
Generalleutnant Werner Anton	Sep 1942–May 1945

7 FLAK DIVISION

Formed in September 1941 under Luftverteidigungskommando 7 in Cologne. It spent the entire war on home defence duties covering the area around Cologne, Aachen and Bonn.

Several of the largest cities in the Reich were protected by enormous concrete flak towers. Ammunition supplies were contained inside, and on the roof were mounted batteries of 8.8cm flak guns. The sheer difficulty of demolishing them after the war means that several still survive today, such as this tower in Hamburg.

Divisional Commanders

General der Flakartillerie Heinrich Burchard	Sep 1941–Feb 1942
Generalleutnant Rudolf Eibenstein	Feb 1942–Feb 1943
General der Flakartillerie Heinrich Burchard	Feb 1943–Jul 1944
Generalmajor Alfred Ehrhard	Jul 1944–Apr 1945

8 FLAK DIVISION

Formed in September 1941 under Luftverteidigungskommando 8 in Bremen, this unit spent the entire war tasked with the defence of the area around Bremen and the Rivers Weser and Ems. The only positively identified component of this corps was Flak Regiment 26, though others certainly came under its control.

Divisional Commanders

Generalleutnant Kurt Wagner	Sep 1941–Dec 1944
Generalmajor Max Schaller	Dec 1944–May 1945

9 FLAK DIVISION

Formed in 1941 under Luftverteidigungskommando 9, covering west France with Flak Regiments 30, 59 and 169. In 1942 it was sent to the Eastern Front, serving under Heeresgruppe Süd, where it controlled 11, 37 and 91 Flak Regiments. It became encircled at Stalingrad, where it was destroyed at the beginning of 1943. Within weeks, it had been re-formed with control of 27, 42 and 77 Flak Regiments and served in the defence of the Crimea, where it was destroyed for a second time in April 1944. In August of that year it was re-formed yet again and took part in the retreat through Poland and into Germany, ending the war in Bavaria.

Divisional Commanders

General der Flakartillerie Otto-Wilhelm von Renz	Sep 1941–Jun 1942
General der Flakartillerie Wolfgang Pickert	Jun 1942–Jan 1943
Oberst Wilhelm Wolff	Jan 1943
General der Flakartillerie Wolfgang Pickert	Feb 1943–Apr 1944
Generalleutnant Adolf Pirmann	Apr 1944–May 1945

10 FLAK DIVISION

Formed in September 1941 under Luftverteidigungskommando 10, based in Romania around the Ploesti oilfields. In February 1942 it was sent to the Eastern Front, where it served under Heeresgruppe Süd in the Crimea, Sevastopol and the Caucasus. It was driven back into Poland in 1944 and finally destroyed there in mid-February 1945. Known components included Flak Regiments 124 and 153.

Divisional Commanders

Generalleutnant Johann Seifert	Sep 1941–Jun 1943
Generalmajor Franz Engel	Jun 1943–Feb 1945
Oberst Oskar Vorbrugg	Feb 1945
Generalmajor Franz Engel	Feb 1945

11 FLAK DIVISION

Formed in September 1941 under Luftverteidigungskommando 11, covering southwest France as far as the Spanish border. In January 1944 it was disbanded and used to form III Flakkorps. Subsequently re-formed in September 1944, it served in the defence of Silesia. Known components included Flak Regiments 45, 69, 71, 85, 100, 145, 150 and 653.

Divisional Commanders

General der Flakartillerie Helmut Richter	Sep 1941–Oct 1943
Generalleutnant Erich Kressmann	Nov 1943–Feb 1944

An 8.8cm flak gun at maximum elevation, with its Luftwaffe crew. A rudimentary attempt at camouflaging the weapon with foliage has been made.

12 FLAK DIVISION

Formed in France in September 1941, it was committed to the Eastern Front in February 1942 and remained there until 1945, when it gradually retreated through Poland and eventually took part in the defence of Berlin. Known components included Flak Regiments 6, 10, 16, 21, 34, 35, 101, 125, 133 and 136.

Divisional Commanders

Generalleutnant Rudolf Eibenstein	Sep 1941–Dec 1941
Generalleutnant Gotthard Frantz	Dec 1941–Dec 1943
Generalleutnant Ernst Buffa	Dec 1943–Apr 1944
Generalleutnant Werner Prellberg	Apr 1944–May 1945

13 FLAK DIVISION

Formed in France in February 1942, the division was tasked with the defence of Brittany. By late 1944 the Allied advance had driven it back into Germany, where it took part in the defence of the upper Rhine around Freiburg. It ended the war in the area around Pilsen. Known components included Flak Regiments 15, 18, 30, 45, 59, 100, 117, 130 and 134.

Divisional Commanders

Generalleutnant Gaston von Chaulin-Egersberg	Feb 1942–Jul 1942
Generalleutnant Theodor Spiess	Jul 1942–Mar 1944
Generalmajor Max Schaller	Mar 1944–Oct 1944
Generalmajor Adolf Wolff	Oct 1944–May 1945

14 FLAK DIVISION

Formed in January 1942, this division was tasked with the defence of the industrial heartland of central Germany, remaining here throughout the war. It was a huge organisation, with over 60,000 troops, including almost 4,000 volunteers from captured Russian troops. Only around half of its strength consisted of actual Luftwaffe soldiers. Components included Flak Regiment 97 and Searchlight Regiment 73.

Divisional Commanders

Generalleutnant Walter Feyerabend	Feb 1942–Nov 1942
Generalleutnant Rudolf Schulze	Nov 1942–May 1944
Generalmajor Adolf Gerlach	May 1944
Oberst Max Hecht	May 1944
Generalmajor Adolf Gerlach	May 1944–May 1945

15 FLAK DIVISION

Formed in March 1942 from III Flak Brigade, this division spent its first three months in the defence of the Ploesti oilfields before being sent to Russia, where it remained until September 1944. Pushed back into Hungary, it fought around Siebenbürgen, where it was finally destroyed in May 1945. Known components included Flak Regiments 4, 12, 17, 37, 42, 180, 202 and 229.

Divisional Commanders

General der Flakartillerie Gerhard Hoffmann	Mar 1942–Nov 1942
Generalleutnant Eduard Muhr	Nov 1942–Apr 1944
Oberst Hans Simon	Apr 1944–Aug 1944
Oberst Ernst Jansa	Aug 1944–Sep 1944
Generalmajor Theodor Herbert	Sep 1944–Jan 1945
Oberst Theodor Peters	Jan 1945
Generalmajor Hans-Wilhelm Döring-Manteuffel	Jan 1945–May 1945

16 FLAK DIVISION

Formed in March 1942 for the air defence of Belgium and northern France. After the Allied invasion in June 1944, it was pushed back into Holland as part of III Flakkorps and took part in the battle for Arnhem. In February 1945 it became the nucleus for IV Flakkorps. Known components included Flak Regiments 112 and 132.

Divisional Commanders

Generalleutnant Kurt Steudemann	Jun 1942–Feb 1943
Generalleutnant Rudolf Eibenstein	Feb 1943–Apr 1944
Generalmajor Friedrich-Wilhelm Deutsch	Apr 1944–Feb 1945

17 FLAK DIVISION

Formed in March 1942 on the southern sector of the Eastern Front, it saw action in the Stalino area, in the Caucasus, in Galicia and later in the retreat through Poland and into eastern Saxony, where it ended the war. Known components included Flak Regiments 12, 17, 42, 48 and 99.

Divisional Commanders

Generalleutnant Karl Veith	Apr 1942–Mar 1944
Oberst Hans Simon	Mar 1944–Apr 1944
Generalleutnant Karl Veith	Apr 1944–May 1944
Generalmajor Wilhelm Köppen	May 1944–May 1945

18 FLAK DIVISION

Formed in April 1942 for operations on the Eastern Front, it operated as part of Heeresgruppe Mitte until June 1944, when it was pushed back into east Prussia. It ended the war in the area around Hela, near Danzig. Constituent units included Flak Regiments 6, 10, 15, 16, 21, 34, 35, 77, 87, 101, 102, 116, 125, 133 and 136.

Divisional Commanders

General der Flakartillerie Richard Reimann	Apr 1942–Mar 1943
Generalleutnant Prinz Heinrich Reuss	Mar 1943–Apr 1944
Generalmajor Adolf Wolf	Apr 1944–Oct 1944
Generalmajor Günther Sachs	Oct 1944–May 1945

19 FLAK DIVISION

Raised in June 1942 in Sicily from VII Flak Brigade, this division was committed to action in North Africa and took part in all major operations through to the German surrender there in May 1943. It was re-formed in November of that year and served in Greece until late 1944, when it moved to Yugoslavia, where it was largely destroyed. Known components included Flak Regiments 40, 58, 66, 102, 114, 131, 135 and 201.

Divisional Commanders

General der Flakartillerie Heinrich Burchard	Aug 1942–Nov 1942
Generalleutnant Gotthard Frantz	Nov 1942–May 1943
Generalmajor Paul Pavel	Nov 1943–May 1945

20 FLAK DIVISION

Formed in November 1942 for service in North Africa, this division served in Tunisia through to the German surrender in May 1943. It was re-formed in October and served in the Balkans, where it saw action in anti-partisan operations. Towards the end of the war it was in Hungary, before retreating back on to German soil at the war's end. Components included Flak Regiments 40, 52, 66, 78 and 80.

Divisional Commanders

Generalleutnant George Neuffes	Nov 1942–May 1943
Generalmajor Otto Sydow	Oct 1943–Oct 1944
Oberst Hermann Rudhardt	Oct 1944
Generalmajor Johann-Wilhelm Döring-Manteuffel	Oct 1944–Jan 1945
Generalmajor Theodor Herbert	Jan 1945–Mar 1945
Oberst Ernst Schluchtmann	Mar 1945–May 1945

21 FLAK DIVISION

Formed in March 1943 from Flak Brigade VI, this unit spent its entire life on home defence duties within Germany, covering in particular the Rhine–Main area. It ended the war in upper Bavaria.

Divisional Commanders

Generalleutnant Kurt Steudemann	Mar 1943–Jun 1944
Generalleutnant Ernst Buffa	Jun 1944–Nov 1944
Oberst Erich Gröpler	Nov 1941–May 1945

22 FLAK DIVISION

Formed in January 1943 for home defence duties, it covered the eastern part of the Ruhr, where it was finally destroyed in the Ruhr pocket in April 1945 and its remnants disbanded.

Divisional Commanders

Generalmajor Friedrich Römer	May 1943–Apr 1945

23 FLAK DIVISION

Formed in December 1943 from the remnants of 22 Luftwaffen Feld-Division, this unit provided air defences for the rearward areas of Heeresgruppe Mitte on the central sector of the Eastern Front. In the retreat of 1944/5 it was pushed back through Poland into Germany and eventually took part in the defence of Berlin. Components included Flak Regiments 7, 23, 34, 35, 53 and 182.

Divisional Commanders

Oberst Hans-Wilhelm Fichter	Oct 1943–Aug 1944
Generalleutnant Walter Kathmann	Aug 1944–Oct 1944
Oberst Oskar Vorbrugg	Oct 1944–Jan 1945
Generalmajor Karl Andersen	Jan 1945–May 1945

24 FLAK DIVISION

Formed in January 1944 around elements of 16 Flak Brigade, this unit was used to provide air defences for Vienna and the lower Danube.

Divisional Commanders

Generalmajor Fritz Greishammer	Jan 1944–May 1945

25 FLAK DIVISION

Formed in April 1944 to provide air defences for northern Italy.

Divisional Commanders

Generalleutnant Walter von Hippel	Apr 1944–Feb 1945
Oberst Oskar Vorbrugg	Feb 1945–Mar 1945
Oberst Alfred Thomas	Mar 1945
Oberst Oskar Vorbrugg	Mar 1945–May 1945

A battery of four 8.8cm flak guns during a night action, captured at the exact moment of firing. A significant amount of destructive power could be delivered by a salvo from such a battery.

26 FLAK DIVISION

Formed in May 1944 around elements of 4 Flak Brigade, this unit provided air defence for the area around Munich and upper Bavaria. It surrendered in April 1945.

Known components included Flak Regiments 19, 55, 93, 114, 115 and 118 and Searchlight Regiments 2 and 8.

Divisional Commanders

Oberst Ernst Uhl	May 1944–Jul 1944
Generalleutnant Rudolf Eibenstein	Jul 1944–Apr 1945

27 FLAK DIVISION

Formed in September 1944 around elements of 11 Flak Brigade, this unit provided air defence for east and south-east Prussia.

Known components included Flak Regiments 21, 87, 116 and 171 and Searchlight Regiment 171.

Divisional Commanders

Generalleutnant Walter Kathmann	Oct 1944–Jan 1945
Generalleutnant Walter von Hippel	Feb 1945–May 1945
Generalmajor Oskar Vorbrugg	May 1945

28 FLAK DIVISION

Formed in October 1944 around elements of 9 Flak Brigade, this unit was tasked with the air defence of Baden-Württemberg and the upper Rhine. It surrendered to US forces in Bavaria in 1945. Known components included Flak Regiments 45, 68 and 86 and Searchlight Regiment 56.

Divisional Commanders

Oberst Hans-Jürgen Heckmanns	Oct 1944–Nov 1944
Generalmajor Kurt von Ludwig	Nov 1944–May 1945

29 FLAK DIVISION

Formed in Norway in February 1945 around elements of 14 Flak Brigade, it remained in Norway for the duration of its rather short life. Known components included Flak Regiments 83, 92, 142, 152 and 162.

Divisional Commanders

Oberst Alexander Nieper	Feb 1945–May 1945

30 FLAK DIVISION

Formed in February 1945 in Berlin around elements of 5 Flak Brigade, it operated in Bavaria, where it surrendered in May 1945.

Divisional Commanders

Oberst Egon Bauer   Feb 1945–May 1945

31 FLAK DIVISION

Little is known about this unit, other than it operated in the northern part of Germany during its brief life.

Divisional Commanders

Generalmajor Herbert Giese   Jan 1945–Apr 1945
Oberst Herbert Röhler   Apr 1945–May 1945

THE FIELD DIVISIONS

The Luftwaffe's field divisions were one of the least successful elements of that branch of the armed forces. A total of twenty-two divisions were formed and a review of their history reveals a depressing litany of ill-trained units being thrown into the maelstrom of the Eastern Front, where they were almost all completely annihilated within months of their arrival.

As Prussian Minister of the Interior, Göring had formed the politically reliable Landespolizeigruppe General Göring, which had, as will be seen elsewhere, evolved into the Luftwaffe's Regiment General Göring, so that the control of ground combat forces by the Luftwaffe was already well established before the outbreak of war. The Reichsmarschall had initially been content to build up his own 'private' regiment and enjoy its share of the glory in several campaigns. With the opening of the campaign in the east against the Soviet Union, however, battlefield losses became a cause for concern. As a result the Army sought to make up some of these losses by transferring up to 10,000 non-essential personnel from the Kriegsmarine and up to 50,000 from the Luftwaffe into the Army.

Göring, knowing that Hitler considered the Army as 'reactionary', successfully argued that the 'national socialist' fervour of the Luftwaffe personnel would be diluted by their transfer to the Army. Hitler agreed to Göring's alternative proposal that the Luftwaffe would form its own field units. In early 1942, a call went out for volunteers to serve in these units and sufficient people answered the call to allow a number of field regiments to be formed, each of four battalions. These saw service, usually independently, though occasionally with several grouped together, on the Eastern Front in a variety of locations, including some fiercely fought actions such as the siege at Demjansk and at Cholm, fighting alongside units of the Army and Waffen-SS. In the process, they earned several compliments for their combat performance, especially the unit comprising Luftwaffe Field Regiments 1 to 4 grouped together under paratrooper general Eugen Meindl. Given the highly satisfactory performance of the regiments, Göring issued a call for more volunteers, planning an initial establishment of ten field divisions, later increased to twenty-two.

The field divisions typically featured three Jäger regiments, an artillery regiment, and support battalions of engineers, signals, fusiliers, transport and supply troops, etc.

These divisions were grouped under the various newly formed field corps, as follows:

I LUFTWAFFEN-FELDKORPS

Formed in October 1942 under General der Fallschirmtruppe Eugen Meindl, this corps operated on the southern sector of the Eastern Front until June 1943, when it was absorbed into XIII Fliegerkorps.

II LUFTWAFFEN-FELDKORPS

Formed under the command of General der Fallschirmtruppe Alfred Schlemm in October 1942, this corps operated in the central region of the Eastern Front until November 1943, after which it transferred to Italy. In June 1943, it was absorbed into I Fallschirmkorps.

III LUFTWAFFEN-FELDKORPS

From its creation in November 1942, this corps operated on the northern sector of the Eastern Front under the command of General der Flakartillerie Job Odebrecht, until November 1943 when it was absorbed into II Flakkorps.

IV LUFTWAFFEN-FELDKORPS

Initially formed up under the command of General der Flakartillerie Gerhard Hoffmann in November 1942, this corps operated on the southern sector of the Eastern Front. In August 1943, command passed to General der Flieger Erich Petersen. In November 1943, the corps moved to France and in November 1944 it was redesignated XC Armeekorps.

FELDDIVISIONEN

Typical components of a Luftwaffe feld division would include two Jäger (rifle) regiments, each of three battalions, an artillery regiment, a heavy motorised flak battalion, a fusilier battalion, a pioneer battalion, an anti-tank battalion, a signals battalion and a medical battalion.

As the sub-unit designations were similar to those used in the Army, Luftwaffe units were identified by the letter (L), thus Jäger Regiment 1 (L), Panzerjäger Abteilung 1 (L), etc. These Luftwaffe field units were originally intended for use, on Göring's orders, for 'defensive missions', and then only on quieter parts of the front. Göring was well aware that the levels of competency of these units was low as a result of lack of training and experience, many of the volunteers being former cooks, clerks, admin staff and even barbers. When in the field, these divisions came under the tactical control of the Army, although the Luftwaffe remained in administrative control. This was much the same as the situation that existed for the soldiers of the Waffen-SS.

In real terms, these divisions were more comparable to an average Army brigade-sized unit, some fielding only around 8,000 men, where some of the better full-strength Army divisions could field around 20,000. There were no tanks allocated to the Luftwaffe's field divisions though there was generally a battery of Sturmgeschütze self-propelled guns in the artillery regiment. An additional problem was that much of the equipment and armament issued to these divisions was captured enemy material of a lower standard of quality than the German equivalent.

Unfortunately, Göring's order that his divisions be used only on defensive missions was completely ignored and, on arrival at the front, many were thrown, unprepared, directly into combat in an attempt to counter Soviet offensives and, not surprisingly, were torn to pieces. There were subsequent suggestions that a number of the divisions be combined to form a smaller

Luftwaffe ground units did not have a particularly good record as far as combat reliability was concerned, primarily through lack of sufficient training. Some of the better field divisions, however, were just as good as their Army counterparts. Here, a single-barrelled 2cm flak gun covers the progress of an Army horse-drawn column. The soldier at right has the sleeve badge of a Luftwaffe flak specialist. (*Josef Charita*)

number of new, full-strength 'Luftlande' assault divisions to work in close cooperation with Army panzer units, but nothing came of the idea.

In November 1943 responsibility for the Luftwaffen-Feld-Divisionen passed from the Luftwaffe to the Army. By this time these units ranged in strength from just over 5,000 men to well over 16,000. The Army retitled these units Feld-Division (Luftwaffe) and replaced much of their officer cadres with experienced Army officers. The retention of many specialist soldiers and much of the high-quality flak elements by the Luftwaffe did nothing to improve general morale of those transferred to the Army.

Of the twenty-two Luftwaffe-Feld-Divisionen, one, 14, saw no action. Of the other twenty-one, only three, 11, 12 and 21, were still in existence by the closing days of the war, and then only as battered remnants of their original form.

1 LUFTWAFFEN-FELD-DIVISION

Formed in Germany in July 1942, this division was allocated to the northern sector of the Eastern Front and went into action once it was fully trained and worked up, in the early part of 1943. The division suffered badly, taking heavy losses, particularly during the late part of 1943 and early 1944 and was disbanded in February 1944. The remnants were allocated to the Army's 28 Jäger Division. Main components were Jäger Regiments 1 and 2, Artillerie Regiment 1 and Panzerjäger Abteilung 1.

Unit Commanders

Generalleutnant Gustav Wilke	30 Sep 1942–17 Jan 1943
Generalmajor Werner Zech	17 Jan 1943–14 Apr 1943
Generalleutnant Gustav Wilke	14 Apr 1943–1 Nov 1943
Generalmajor Rudolf Petrauschke	1 Nov 1943–10 Feb 1944

2 LUFTWAFFEN-FELD-DIVISION

Formed in Germany around the same time as 1 Feld-Division, this unit was committed to the central sector of the Eastern Front. It saw action near Rzhev with 9 Armee. Its inexperienced troops were no match for the Soviets and it was severely reduced in fighting around Belvy. It subsequently took part in some moderately effective anti-partisan operations near Vitebsk. A massive Soviet offensive which struck the area between Heeresgruppe Nord and Heeresgruppe Mitte at Nevel in October 1943 saw the division completely smashed. Remnants were distributed to 3 and 4 Feld-Divisions and the unit was disbanded in November 1943. Main components were Jäger Regiments 3 and 4 and Artillerie Regiment 2.

Unit Commanders

Oberst Hellmuth Petzold	30 Sep 1942–1 Nov 1943

3 LUFTWAFFEN-FELD-DIVISION

Also formed in Germany in September 1942, this division was allocated to Heeresgruppe Mitte in the central sector of the Eastern Front. It was disbanded in January 1944 and its remnants allocated to 4 and 6 Feld-Divisions. Main components were Jäger Regiments 5 and 6 and Artillerie Regiment 3.

Unit Commanders

Generalleutnant Robert Pistorious	30 Sep 1942–17 Jan 1943

4 LUFTWAFFEN-FELD-DIVISION

Allocated to the central sector of the Eastern Front, this division formed part of LIII Armeekorps and was destroyed when the corps was encircled and virtually annihilated at Vitebsk in the summer of 1944. Main components were Jäger Regiments 7 and 8 and Artillerie Regiment 4.

Unit Commanders

Generalleutnant Rainer Stachel	25 Sep 1942–22 Nov 1942
Generalmajor Hans-Georg Schreder	22 Nov 1942–8 Apr 1943
Generalmajor Wilhelm Völk	8 Apr 1943–5 Nov 1943
Generalmajor Hans Saubrey	5 Nov 1943–20 Nov 1943
Generalmajor Wilhelm Völk	20 Nov 1943–Dec 1943
Generalmajor Heinrich Geerkens	Dec 1943–24 Jan 1944
Generalleutnant Robert Pistorious	24 Jan 1944–27 Jun 1944

5 LUFTWAFFEN-FELD-DIVISION

Allocated to the southern sector of the Eastern Front at the beginning of 1943, this division was virtually destroyed during the Soviet winter offensive of 1943/4 and the retreat from the Kuban, and was eventually disbanded in June 1944, by which time it had in any case virtually ceased to exist as a cohesive fighting unit. Main components were Jäger Regiments 9 and 10 and Artillerie Regiment 5.

Unit Commanders

Generalmajor Hans-Joachim von Arnim	Oct 1943–10 Mar 1944
Generalleutnant Botho, Graf von Hülsen	10 Mar 1944–1 Jun 1944

6 LUFTWAFFEN-FELD-DIVISION

Allocated to the central sector of the Eastern Front in January 1943, this unit also served as part of LIII Armeekorps and, like 4 Feld-Division, was virtually destroyed at Vitebsk in the summer of 1944, resulting in the disbandment of the remnants. Main components were Jäger Regiments 11 and 12 and Artillerie Regiment 6.

Unit Commanders

Generalmajor Ernst Weber	Sep 1942–25 Nov 1942
Generalleutnant Rudiger von Heyking	25 Nov 1942–5 Nov 1943
Generalmajor Rudolf Peschel	5 Nov 1943–30 Jun 1944

7 LUFTWAFFEN-FELD-DIVISION

Assigned to Heeresgruppe Don under Generalfeldmarschall Manstein, along with 8 Feld-Division, this unit took part in the attempt to relieve Stalingrad. It fought along the upper Chir river, where it suffered massive casualties and was disbanded in March 1943. Most of its remnants were posted to 15 Feld-Division. Main components were Jäger Regiments 13 and 14 and Artillerie Regiment 7.

Unit Commanders

Generalmajor Wolf Freiherr von Biedermann	Sep 1942–9 Jan 1943
Generalleutnant Willibald Spang	9 Jan 1943–11 Feb 1943
Generalmajor Wolf Freiherr von Biedermann	11 Feb 1943–Mar 1943

8 LUFTWAFFEN-FELD-DIVISION

Allocated to Heeresgruppe Don at the end of 1942, it took part in the drive to attempt the relief of the German 6 Armee at Stalingrad. It was torn to pieces by Red Army units and by March 1943 had suffered such heavy losses that it was disbanded. Main components were Jäger Regiments 15 and 16 and Artillerie Regiment 8.

Unit Commanders

Oberst Hans Heidemeyer	Oct 1942–1 Jan 1943
Generalleutnant Willibald Spang	1 Jan 1943–14 Feb 1943
Oberst Kurt Hahling	14 Feb 1943–Mar 1943

9 LUFTWAFFEN-FELD-DIVISION

Allocated to the northern sector of the Eastern Front at the end of 1942, this division fought around Leningrad and suffered heavily during the retreat in the winter of 1943/4. A massive Soviet offensive in January 1944 hit the division near Oranienbaum and it was literally smashed to pieces. At this point it was serving as part of the III SS-Panzerkorps. It was formally disbanded in February 1944 and its Panzerjäger Abteilung taken over by the Army. Main components were Jäger Regiments 17 and 18 and Artillerie Regiment 9.

A soldier from a Luftwaffe Feld Division, carrying the MP40 machine pistol and wearing the camouflaged shelter quarter, several of which could be buttoned together to make a tent, in poncho form. This photograph was taken on the Eastern Front, where most of these divisions served. Note the heavy, fleece-lined gloves. (*Josef Charita*)

Unit Commanders

Generalmajor Hans Erdmann	8 Oct 1942–11 Aug 1943
Generalmajor Anton-Carl Longin	11 Aug 1943–5 Nov 1943
Generalleutnant Paul Winter	5 Nov 1943–25 Nov 1943
Generalmajor Ernst Michael	25 Nov 1943–22 Jan 1944

10 LUFTWAFFEN-FELD-DIVISION

Arriving on the Eastern Front at the start of 1943, this unit fought as part of Heeresgruppe Nord. It suffered badly during the retreat from the Leningrad front and was virtually devastated at Narva in January 1944, along with 9 Feld-Division. Its remnants, after fighting in a small Kampfgruppen for a short time, were eventually absorbed into the Army's 170 Infanterie Division and the unit formally disbanded in mid-1944. Its artillery regiment was taken over by the Army Coastal Artillery. Main components were Jäger Regiments 19 and 20 and Artillerie Regiment 10.

Unit Commanders

Generalmajor Walter Wadehn	25 Sep 1942–5 Nov 1943
Generalleutnant Hermann von Wedel	5 Nov 1943–29 Jan 1944

11 LUFTWAFFEN-FELD-DIVISION

This division spent its entire life in the Balkans, first seeing action in Greece in January 1943, predominantly on security and anti-partisan duties. It did, however, take part in the capture of the island of Leros in November 1943. In October 1944 it moved into Yugoslavia, where it remained until the end of the war, spending much of its time combating enemy partisan units. Its losses reduced it to a fraction of its strength and its remnants were absorbed into the Army's 22 Infanterie Division. Main components were Jäger Regiments 21 and 22 and Artillerie Regiment 10.

Unit Commanders

General der Flieger Karl Drum	1 Oct 1942–1 Feb 1943
Generalleutnant Wilhelm Kohler	1 Feb 1943–10 Nov 1943
Generalleutnant Alexander Bourquin	10 Nov 1943–1 Dec 1943
Generalleutnant Wilhelm Kohler	1 Dec 1943–1 Nov 1944
Generalmajor Gerhard Henke	1 Nov 1944–8 May 1945

12 LUFTWAFFEN-FELD-DIVISION

The combat career of this unit mirrored that of 21 Feld-Division. It fought on the Leningrad front and, along with 13 Feld-Division, was in defensive positions along the Volkov when it was hit by a fresh enemy offensive. It then took part in the long retreat into Latvia and encirclement in the Kurland pocket. It was one of the few that survived operations on the Eastern Front until the end of the war. Main components were Jäger Regiments 23 and 24 and Artillerie Regiment 12.

Unit Commanders

Generalleutnant Herbert Kettner	1 Dec 1942–15 Nov 1943
Generalleutnant Gottfried Weber	15 Nov 1943–10 Apr 1945
Generalmajor Franz Schlieper	10 Apr 1945–8 May 1945

13 LUFTWAFFEN-FELD-DIVISION

Another unit which suffered horrendous losses on the northern sector of the Eastern Front, this division held positions along the Volkov river when it was hit by the Soviet January offensive and brutally mauled during the retreat towards the Estonian/Latvian border. Its remnants were absorbed into 12 Feld-Division and the unit disbanded in April 1944. Main components were Jäger Regiments 25 and 26 and Artillerie Regiment 13.

Unit Commanders

Generalleutnant Herbert Olbrich	10 Nov 1942–1 Dec 1942
Generalmajor Hans Korte	1 Dec 1942–1 Oct 1943
Generalleutnant Hellmuth Reymann	1 Oct 1943–1 Apr 1944

14 LUFTWAFFEN-FELD-DIVISION

Sent to Norway in January 1943 after forming up in Germany, it also carried out occupation duties in Denmark in June/July 1944 before returning to Norway, where it remained for the rest of the war. The division never saw combat. Main components were Jäger Regiments 27 and 28 and Artillerie Regiment 14.

Unit Commanders

Generalleutnant Günther Lohmann	28 Nov 1942–8 May 1945

15 LUFTWAFFEN-FELD-DIVISION

Committed to the southern sector of the Eastern Front in December 1942, this unit suffered very heavy casualties. Its numbers were then made up by the remnants of 7 Feld-Division, but its future operations saw it badly battered in the fighting around Rostov and at Taganrog in early 1943. It was, however, commended for the fighting spirit it displayed. During the Soviet counter-attack that followed the calling-off of the German offensive at Kursk in July 1943, the division, now dug in in defensive positions, was very nearly cut off by the enemy advance and only broke out with severe losses. Its remnants were disbanded in November 1943. Main components were Jäger Regiments 29 and 30 and Artillerie Regiment 15.

Unit Commanders

General der Flieger Alfred Mahnke	1 Nov 1942–1 Jan 1943
Oberst Heinrich Comrody	1 Jan 1943–15 Feb 1943
Generalleutnant Willibald Spang	15 Feb 1943–6 Nov 1943

16 LUFTWAFFEN-FELD-DIVISION

Formed in Germany in late 1942, this unit, equipped with three Jäger regiments, went into action in Holland on occupation duty in early 1943. Following the Allied landings in Normandy it went into battle against Anglo-American forces and was hit by an Allied offensive the day after it arrived at the front. It was destroyed in combat around Caen. The remnants were absorbed into the Army's 21 Panzer Division and 346 Infanterie Division. Main components were Jäger Regiments 31 and 32 and Artillerie Regiment 16.

Unit Commanders

Oberst Otto Lachemair	1 Dec 1942–5 Nov 1943
Generalleutnant Karl Sievers	5 Nov 1943–30 July 1944

17 LUFTWAFFEN-FELD-DIVISION

Another three-regiment unit, the 17th was used on occupation duty on the French coast until the Allied invasion, after which it took part in the defence of the approaches to Paris. Understrength, short of vehicular transport and equipped with First World War artillery, almost from the moment it was thrown into the line it was on the retreat. It was disbanded in October 1944 after suffering crippling losses in action against US forces, and the remnants absorbed into 167 Volksgrenadier Division. The unit included two battalions of Russian volunteer troops. In May 1944, Jäger Regiment 34 was transferred to the Nordkaukasischen Legion. Main components were Jäger Regiments 33 and 34 and Artillerie Regiment 17.

Unit Commanders

Generalleutnant Herbert Olbrich	25 Jan 1943–30 Oct 1943
Oberst Hans Korte	30 October 1943–5 Nov 1943
Generalleutnant Hans-Kurt Höcker	5 Nov 1943–Oct 1944

18 LUFTWAFFEN-FELD-DIVISION

This was another unit which began life on occupation duties in France, where it defended part of the coast between Dieppe and Calais. It, too, was short of transport, moving mostly on foot or by horse. It actually succeeded in halting the enemy advance near Mantes and even recaptured some territory. Thereafter facing increasing enemy pressure, it carried out a remarkably disciplined and orderly retreat, pursued by enemy armoured units. Withdrawing into Belgium, it was surrounded near Mons. After heavy fighting, a small number of troops, led by the divisional commander, Joachim von Tresckow, succeeded in breaking out and eventually reached the safety of German-held territory seventeen days later, having crossed over 250km of enemy-held territory. Tresckow was decorated with the Knight's Cross of the Iron Cross for this achievement. The division was formally disbanded in October 1944 and its remnants absorbed into 18 Volksgrenadier Division. Main components were Jäger Regiments 35 and 36 and Artillerie Regiment 18.

Unit Commanders

Generalmajor Ferdinand Frhr. von Stein-Liebenstein	Dec 1942–1 Apr 1943
Generalleutnant Wolfgang Erdmann	1 Apr 1943–26 Aug 1943
Generalmajor Fritz Reinshagen	26 Aug 1943–27 Oct 1943
Generalleutnant Wilhelm Rupprecht	27 Oct 1943–1 Feb 1944
Generalleutnant Joachim von Tresckow	1 Feb 1944–Oct 1944

19 LUFTWAFFEN-FELD-DIVISION

This unit spent its life on occupation duties, variously in France, Holland and Belgium. Heavy losses in Italy in the autumn of 1944 led to most of its remnants being absorbed into 20 Feld-Division, and those not so transferred being used to form the cadre for 19 Volksgrenadier Division. Main components were Jäger Regiments 37 and 38 and Artillerie Regiment 19.

Unit Commanders

Generalmajor Gerhard Bassenge	1 Dec 1942–1 Feb 1943
General der Flakartillerie Hermann Plocher	1 Feb 1943–30 Jun 1943
Generalleutnant Erich Bässler	30 Jun 1943–1 Jun 1944

20 LUFTWAFFEN-FELD-DIVISION

This unit spent its operational life on occupation duties in Denmark before being redesignated 20 Luftwaffe Sturm Division in June 1944. It then served in Italy, where it saw action at Roccostrada fighting alongside the Army's 90 Panzergrenadier Division. Gradually forced to withdraw up the 'leg' of the Italian mainland, it spent some time in the corps reserve and saw action against Italian partisans near the Gothic Line defences. It was disbanded in December 1944. An indication of just how short the unit was of transport may be had from the fact that, despite being designated as a fast motorised assault unit, most of its troops had, at best, bicycles as their mode of transport. Main components were Jäger Regiments 39 and 40 and Artillerie Regiment 20.

The Fliegerbluse was not only worn by flight personnel, but was equally popular with ground crew, paratroops, flak personnel and members of the Luftwaffe Field Divisions. This Fliegerbluse, on display in a European museum, shows the Fliegerbluse as worn by a Feldwebel for ground combat, with belts, ammunition pouches, straps and an MP40 machine pistol.

Unit Commanders

Generalleutnant Wolfgang Erdmann	1 Apr 1943–5 Apr 1943
Oberst Hermann Vaue	5 Apr 1943–Aug 1943
Generalmajor Robert Fuchs	Aug 1943–31 Oct 1943
Generalmajor Wilhelm Crisoli	31 Oct 1943–1 Jun 1944

21 LUFTWAFFEN-FELD-DIVISION

Generally considered to be one of the best of the Luftwaffe field divisions, this unit was sent to the northern sector of the Eastern Front in early 1943 under Heeresgruppe Nord. It fought in the Leningrad area, although it suffered heavy casualties in the retreat from that sector and especially in the fighting around Lake Ilmen. The division also helped cover the extraction of German troops cut off in the Demjansk pocket, combating both Red Army units and partisans. It continued fighting, eventually ending up in the Kurland pocket, where it held out until the end of the war, eventually surrendering on 8 May. Main components were Jäger Regiments 41 and 42 and Artillerie Regiment 21.

Unit Commanders

Generalleutnant Richard Schimpf	Dec 1942–12 Oct 1943
Generalleutnant Rudolf-Eduard Licht	12 Oct 1943–1 Apr 1944
Generalmajor Rudolf Goltzsch	1 Apr 1944–Aug 1944
Generalleutnant Albert Henze	Aug 1944–28 Jan 1945
Generalmajor Otto Barth	28 Jan 1945–8 May 1945

22 LUFTWAFFEN-FELD-DIVISION

This unit began working up in 1943 but work on the new division was never completed.

Unit Commanders

Generalmajor Robert Fuchs	1943

FALLSCHIRM-PANZERKORPS HERMANN GÖRING

This, the premiere elite unit of the Luftwaffe, began its life in early 1933 as a police formation, the Polizei Abteilung z.b.V. Wecke, commanded by Major der Schutzpolizei Wecke. It was used against communist agitators in Berlin. A few months later it was renamed first Landespolizeigruppe Wecke, and then, shortly afterwards, Landespolizeigruppe General Göring. At this point in time, Göring held the post of chief of the Prussian police. It was subsequently expanded to regimental status as Regiment General Göring in April 1935 under the command of Oberstleutnant der Polizei Friedrich Wilhelm Jakoby, but just six months later was transferred into the Luftwaffe. Göring wished to ensure that he would retain control over 'his' unit, since his position as chief of the police was soon

Major Constantin Hahm, commander of II./Fallschirm-Panzer-Regiment 'Hermann Göring'. Hahm was decorated with the Knight's Cross of the Iron Cross on 9 June 1944 for his command of his battalion during particularly difficult battles on the Eastern Front. (*Josef Charita*)

to be taken by Reichsführer-SS Heinrich Himmler. A few months later, part of the regiment was detached to form the nucleus of the Fallschirmtruppe.

Göring was exceptionally proud of his unit, which wore distinctive white uniform piping and collar patches and a cuffband with his name. Under his personal patronage it flourished, being provided with the best of equipment and modern accommodation with state of the art facilities, and, unlike regiments in the Army, which recruited locally, was permitted to recruit from across the entire nation, with only the highest standard of applicant being accepted. This effectively put the regiment on a par with Infanterie Regiment Grossdeutschland, the premiere elite unit of the Wehrmacht, which was also permitted to recruit nationally, to ensure it was manned by volunteers of the highest calibre.

The regiment was used during the so-called 'Flower Wars' of 1938 – the annexation of Austria, the occupation of the Sudetenland and the seizure of Prague. Only a small number of personnel saw action during the Polish campaign, while the bulk of the regiment was committed to the defence of Berlin and to guarding Göring's headquarters. It did see action, however, during the campaign in the west, where various detachments took part in the occupation of Denmark, the invasion of Norway and the attack on France and the Low Countries. The regiment's 8.8cm flak guns, used in the ground role took a heavy toll of enemy tanks, and in reward for its performance and contribution to the victory, it was given a place in the ceremonial guard for the armistice ceremony at Compiègne in June 1940. After spending some time on duty in the defences around

Paris and on the Atlantic coast, the regiment returned to its home in Berlin in the latter part of 1940.

During the Balkan campaign it saw little action, forming part of the reserve, although some elements were used to provide air defences for the Romanian oilfields at Ploesti. The regiment took part in the opening phases of Operation Barbarossa, the attack on the Soviet Union, with Panzergruppe Kleist, and once again excelled in the tank-killing role with its 8.8cm guns. Towards the end of 1941, it was withdrawn for rest and refitting and was allocated to the aerial defence first of Munich, and then Paris. In July 1942 the regiment was expanded to brigade strength.

Regimental Commanders

Oberstleutnant Friedrich Wilhelm Jakoby	24 Sep 1935–12 Aug 1936
Major Walther von Axthelm	13 Aug 1936–31 May 1940
Oberst Paul Conrath	1 Jun 1940–14 Jul 1940

As Brigade Hermann Göring, the unit was still being worked up under Generalmajor Conrath when the decision was taken to expand it even further, to divisional status.

Brigade Commanders

Generalmajor Paul Conrath	15 Jul 1942–15 Oct 1942

Not long after its formation, in November 1942, elements of the new division, numerous components of which were being worked up in various locations, were used in the occupation of Vichy France. A Kampfgruppe of around 10,000 men from Division Hermann Göring was sent to North Africa under Generalmajor Josef 'Beppo' Schmid, where it served as Kampfgruppe Schmid and fought with distinction in Tunisia. Most of its personnel went into captivity when the German forces in North Africa surrendered and, during the necessary rebuilding of the unit, it was upgraded to an armoured division in May 1943 as Panzer Division Hermann Göring.

Divisional Commanders

Generalmajor Paul Conrath	16 Oct 1942–20 May 1943

The powerful new armoured unit was committed to action in the defence of Sicily, where it enhanced its already fine reputation as a combat formation acting as a rearguard for the withdrawal of German forces over the Straits of Messina to the Italian mainland. US combat units which had engaged the 'HG' troops commented that they were among the toughest opponents they had ever faced.

Over on the Italian mainland, the 'HG' Division found itself in fierce combat once again, in the defence of the approaches to Rome. It was in Italy that the division found itself embroiled in controversy. At Monte Cassino, the ancient Benedictine monastery was in imminent danger of destruction by Allied bombing raids aimed at dislodging German forces that the Allies believed to be ensconced there. In fact, no German units were yet in occupation of the monastery or its immediate surroundings. 'HG' troops under the command of Oberstleutnant Schlegel unofficially offered to provide

The Musikzug of the Hermann Göring Division. The band was renowned throughout Germany for the quality of its performances. With the onset of war, however, the opportunities for it to play were drastically reduced. The bulk of its members were therefore drafted into the Military Police company of the division for the duration of the war.

mayed at the propaganda coup any looting of the abbey would provide for the Allies and unaware of what was really going on, despatched Waffen-SS Feldgendarmerie (military police) to arrest the culprits. It took some persuading from the monks that they were being assisted, not robbed. Schlegel, now with the full backing of his divisional commander, continued his rescue mission and was presented with a large hand-illuminated scroll by the monks in thanks for his assistance. Nevertheless, after the war, Schlegel was arrested by the Allies on charges of looting and was held in prison for seven months before being released.

The division was further redesignated Fallschirm-Panzer-Division Hermann Göring in May 1944 and remained in Italy until July 1944, fighting on the Gustav Line, at Anzio and Nettuno, until it was withdrawn and transferred to the crumbling Eastern Front. Sent into action in the central sector of the Eastern Front, it once again enhanced its reputation as a first-class combat unit. It went into action to the north of Warsaw where, in concert with both Army and Waffen-SS units, it was instrumental in smashing the Soviet 3rd Tank Corps. The unit was praised by Generalfeldmarschall Model, who claimed it was because of the efforts of the 'HG' Division that Warsaw had been held. Following the defence of Warsaw, the division fought on the Vistula front alongside IV SS-Panzerkorps.

In October 1944, the Hermann Göring units were expanded to corps status, with the original division, now known as Fallschirm-Panzer-Division Hermann Göring 1, to be joined by a sister unit, Fallschirm-Panzer-grenadier-Division Hermann Göring 2. Before the corps could be formed into a cohesive unit, the original division was sent northwards to defend the approaches to, first, Memel, then Königsberg. It was gradually driven back into east Prussia though it

transportation for the abbey's priceless treasure to the safety of the Vatican. The Allies reported this humanitarian mission as 'looting' and the German authorities, discontinued to inflict heavy losses on the pursuing enemy and destroyed a Polish division at Köningsbrück. In the closing days of the war it was in action around Dresden, trying to withdraw westwards to surrender to US forces, but was surrounded and captured by the Soviets.

Divisional Commanders
Fallschirm-Panzer-Division Hermann Göring

Generalmajor Wilhelm Schmalz	1 May 1944–30 Sep 1944
Generalmajor Horst von Necker	1 Oct 1944–8 Feb 1945
Generalmajor Max Lemke	9 Feb 1945–8 May 1945

The Panzergrenadier-Division also saw intensive fighting in east Prussia, where it was cut off, but was evacuated by sea to Swinemünde in Germany. From there it made its way eastwards again, via Berlin, and joined with the Panzer-Division to help inflict the crushing defeat on Polish troops at Köningsbrück. It suffered the same ultimate fate as its sister division.

Although most of the elite German units were fully mechanised, it was often found that in the difficult terrain of Russia, horses were a far more effective mode of transport. Here we see an NCO of the Feldgendarmerie unit of the Hermann Göring Division on mounted patrol, passing through a Russian village. Note the chained Military Police gorget plate worn on the chest. Partisan units were often based in heavily forested or swampy regions where motorised transport was of no great benefit.

Divisional Commanders
Fallschirm-Panzergrenadier-Division
Hermann Göring 2

Generalmajor Erich Walther	24 Sep 1944–Nov 1944
Oberst Wilhelm Söth	Nov 1944–Jan 1945
Oberst Georg Seegers	Feb 1945–Mar 1945
Oberst Helmuth Hufenbach	Mar 1945
Generalmajor Erich Walther	Mar 1945–8 May 1945

Fallschirm-Panzerkorps Hermann Göring became operational in October 1944 as the overall command structure for Fallschirm-Panzer-Division Hermann Göring 1 and Fallschirm-Panzergrenadier-Division Hermann Göring 2. As well as being a higher command formation, it did have a number of combat units on its own strength, such as Fallschirm-Flakregiment Hermann Göring, Fallschirm-Panzersturmbataillon Hermann Göring and Fallschirm-Panzerkorpspionier-bataillon Hermann Göring. The corps commander from 4 October 1944 through to 8 May 1945 was Generalleutnant Wilhelm Schmalz.

The Hermann Göring formations also included some smaller subsidiary units, including:

WACHBATAILLON REGIMENT HERMAN GÖRING

A special guard unit from the original regiment served at Göring's personal private estate at Karinhall, near Berlin, providing security for the considerable number of German and foreign dignitaries who visited. This guard unit was maintained at Karinhall until the very end, and in the closing days of the war blew up the luxurious buildings to prevent their falling into Russian hands.

WACHREGIMENT HERMANN GÖRING

Formed over the winter of 1942/3 from the original Wachbataillon. In April 1944 it was renamed as Begleit Regiment Herman Göring.

BEGLEIT REGIMENT HERMANN GÖRING

Formed in April 1944, this escort unit consisted of a battalion of panzergrenadiers, a flak battalion and an anti-aircraft battery mounted on railway carriages. It fought on the Eastern Front from July to September 1944, after which it was withdrawn and disbanded, its personnel allocated to other units in the corps. A final, very short-lived escort formation, the Begleit-Bataillon Reichsmarschall Göring, was formed in January 1945 and disbanded in March 1945.

ERSATZ UND AUSBILDUNGS REGIMENT HERMANN GÖRING

The training and replacement unit of the Hermann Göring Division was based at Utrecht in occupied Holland. Elements of the unit took part in the battles at Arnhem that resulted in the defeat of the British airborne landings there. As the 'HG' formations grew from divisional to corps strength, so the training and replacement unit itself expanded from regimental to brigade size. It is estimated that these replacement units in Holland contained as many as 12,000 troops. In the later stages of the war, elements of these units fought on both Western and Eastern Fronts.

MUSIKKORPS HERMANN GÖRING

The Regiment General Göring boasted its own music corps, comprising the finest musicians to serve in military bands, and gained a reputation second to none for the quality of its performances in pre-war Germany. After the start of the war, the music corps also visited the troops at the front to provide morale-boosting concerts. As the fortunes of war turned against Germany, however, such luxuries could no longer be afforded and the bulk of the music corps was absorbed into the Feldgendarmerie of the Hermann Göring Division.

Although the majority of the Luftwaffe's ground formations were shown to be of limited military value, achieving little on the field of battle and suffering horrendous losses, the Fallschirmpanzerkorps Hermann Göring was an exception to this, gaining a very high reputation for combat achievements, this being reflected by the fact that eighty-two soldiers who had served with one of its units at some point were decorated with the Knight's Cross of the Iron Cross (thirteen of them subsequently gaining the oakleaves and three the oakleaves with swords).

CHAPTER TEN

SPECIALIST UNITS

As well as the main command and combat units already listed, the Luftwaffe possessed a number of smaller formations that are worthy of mention. These included:

PROPAGANDAKOMPANIEN

At the outbreak of war, four war correspondent companies existed. Each company comprised around 120 men, and were designated Luftwaffen-Propagandakompanien.

They were based as follows:

LUFTWAFFEN-PROPAGANDAKOMPANIE 1 – BERNAU

Initially assigned to Luftflotte 1, this unit saw service in Poland, Norway, the Battle of Britain, and on the Eastern Front.

LUFTWAFFEN-PROPAGANDAKOMPANIE 2 – BRAUNSCHWEIG

Initially assigned to Luftflotte 2, this unit saw service first on the Western Front during the Battle of Britain, but served most of its lifetime in the east.

LUFTWAFFEN-PROPAGANDAKOMPANIE 3 – MÜNCHEN

Initially assigned to Luftflotte 3, this unit saw service in the west during the Battle of Britain, in the Balkan campaign and on the Eastern Front.

LUFTWAFFEN-PROPAGANDAKOMPANIE 4 – WIEN

Initially assigned to Luftflotte 4, this unit saw some service on the Western Front but was predominantly employed in the northern sector of the Eastern Front.

During the war, four more units were added, and the designation changed from Propagandakompanien to Kriegsberichterkompanien.

The new units were based as follows:

LUFTWAFFEN-KRIEGSBERICHTERKOMPANIE 5 – JÜTERBOG

Initially assigned to Luftflotte 5, it saw action in the campaign in the west against France and the Low Countries, the Battle of Britain and on the central sector of the Eastern Front, where among other actions it covered the Kursk offensive.

LUFTWAFFEN-KRIEGSBERICHTERKOMPANIE 6 – DRESDEN-LOSCHWITZ

This unit saw action on the Western Front during the campaign against France, in the Balkans, on the southern sector of the Eastern Front and also in Sicily and Italy.

LUFTWAFFEN-KRIEGSBERICHTERKOMPANIE 7 – BERLIN-ADLERSHOF

Covered the actions of Rommel's Afrikakorps in North Africa.

LUFTWAFFEN-KRIEGSBERICHTERKOMPANIE 8 – BERLIN-REINICKERNDORF

This unit first saw service in the Balkan campaign before moving east, where it saw service in the northern, central and southern sectors.

FALLSCHIRMJÄGER-KRIEGSBERICHTER-KOMPANIE

This unit was formed to cover the airborne invasion of Crete in February 1941, where it came under the control of XI Fliegerkorps.

It subsequently also served on the Eastern Front, in North Africa and in Italy.

The fact that so much superb photographic material on the Luftwaffe exists is thanks to the efforts of these war correspondents, of whom some 250 lost their lives in action, representing a death rate of fully 50 per cent, some indication of the dangerous nature of their profession.

KURIER STAFFELN

A number of small communications or 'courier' squadrons were created for general communication and reconnaissance work. The types of aircraft used varied from the diminutive Fieseler Fi 156 Storch to massive four-engine types like the Fw 200 Condor.

The following units existed:

Squadron	Deployment
Kurier Staffel 1	Central sector, Eastern Front. Armee Oberkommando 3.
Kurier Staffel 2	Assigned to Armee Oberkommando 4.
Kurier Staffel 3	Northern sector, Eastern Front. Heeresgruppe Nord.
Kurier Staffel 4	Southern sector, Eastern Front. Heeresgruppe Süd.
Kurier Staffel 5	Southern sector, Eastern Front. Armee Oberkommando 10.
Kurier Staffel 6	Southern sector, Eastern Front. Armee Oberkommando 1.
Kurier Staffel 7	Southern sector, Eastern Front. Armee Oberkommando 5.
Kurier Staffel 8	Central sector, Eastern Front. Armee Oberkommando 7.
Kurier Staffel 9	Northern sector, Eastern Front. Heeresgruppe C.
Kurier Staffel 10	Southern sector, Eastern Front. Armee Oberkommando 14.
Kurier Staffel 11	Central sector, Eastern Front. Armee Oberkommando 8.
Kurier Staffel 13	South-eastern sector. Eastern Front.
Kurier Staffel 14	Balkan Front. Heeresgruppe F.
Kurier Staffel 40	Southern sector, Eastern Front.
Kurier Staffel A	Assigned to Heeresgruppe A, Küstenstab Asow.
Kurier Staffel F	Assigned to Heeresgruppe F.
Kurier Staffel	Assigned to Südost Heeresgruppe E in the Balkans.

WETTERERKUNDUNGSSTAFFELN

These squadrons (abbreviated as 'Wekusta') were tasked with providing meteorological information and operated on all fronts.

Eleven such Staffeln were created and used a variety of specially adapted aircraft, including Do 17, Ju 52, Ju 88, Ju 188, He 111 and He 177. Areas of responsibility were as follows:

Squadron	Deployment
Wekusta 1./Ob.d.L.	Poland, Norway, England, Scotland, France. Equipped with He 111 and Ju 188.
Wekusta 2./Ob.d.L.	France, Bay of Biscay, Portugal.
Wekusta 1	East Prussia and the northern sector of the Eastern Front.
Wekusta 5	Norway, North Sea.
Wekusta 6	Northern sector, Eastern Front.
Wekusta 26	Served on all fronts.
Wekusta 27	Eastern Mediterranean, Balkans.
Wekusta 51	France, English coast, Irish Sea.
Wekusta 76	Eastern Front.
Wekusta 76/1	Southern sector of the Eastern Front, Black Sea.
Wekusta 76/2	Southern sector, Eastern Front.

A Junkers Ju 52 from a Wettererkundungsstaffel. Note the legend 'Wetterflug Visvenow', indicating that this aircraft most likely belonged to Wekusta 6 or Wekusta 76, both of which served exclusively on the Eastern Front. The cold-weather clothing certainly suggests that this shot was taken during the winter months. Although high-altitude flying would require warm clothing at any time of year, it is unlikely that the Ju 52 would have been used for such missions. (*Josef Charita*)

The same officer shown in the accompanying photograph of the Wekusta Ju 52 is seen here tending to some of the meteorological measuring equipment attached under the starboard wing of the aircraft. The corrugated surface of the Ju 52 wing is clearly evident. (*Josef Charita*)

SEEAUFKLÄRERGRUPPEN

Maritime reconnaissance units were classed as Küstenflieger or Seeaufklärer, the former being concerned with coastal reconnaissance and anti-shipping operations, air-sea rescue, etc., and the latter with longer-range maritime reconnaissance. These units were predominantly equipped with floatplanes.

KÜSTENFLIEGERGRUPPE 106

Took part in the occupation of Norway and the campaign in the west, and operated in the North Sea and English Channel. Equipped with He 60, Do 18, He 59 and He 118.

KÜSTENFLIEGERGRUPPE 306

Operated over the North Sea and English Channel. Equipped with He 60 and Do 18.

KÜSTENFLIEGERGRUPPE 406

Operated over the North Sea and the English Channel against enemy shipping. Some elements also operated in the Mediterranean. Equipped with the He 59, He 114, He 115, Do 18 and the Blohm and Voss Bv 138.

KÜSTENFLIEGERGRUPPE 506

Initially operated in the Baltic during the Polish campaign, then in the invasion of Norway. Equipped at first with He 59, He 60 and Do 18. Subsequently operated in both the Mediterranean and Atlantic on anti-shipping strikes, equipped with Ju 88 and He 115.

KÜSTENFLIEGERGRUPPE 606

Operated in the Baltic. Equipped with Do 18.

KÜSTENFLIEGERGRUPPE 706

Initially operated in the Baltic during the Polish campaign, then over the North Sea, the English Channel and Italian waters. Aircraft operated included He 59, He 60, He 114, Arado 196 and Blohm & Voss Bv 138.

KÜSTENFLIEGERGRUPPE 806

Formed in late 1939 and equipped with He 111. A short-lived unit which was subsequently redesignated as a Kampfgruppe.

KÜSTENFLIEGERGRUPPE 906

Formed in late 1939, this unit took part in the invasion of Norway before being allocated to anti-shipping duties over the Atlantic, in the Mediterranean and the Black Sea. Equipped with the Do 18, He 115, Blohm & Voss Bv 138, Arado 196 and latterly Ju 88.

SEEAUFKLÄRUNGSGRUPPE 125

Formed in 1941 and used initially over the Baltic. Subsequently, elements saw service in the Mediterranean, Norwegian waters and the Black Sea. Aircraft operated included He 60, He 114, Arado Ar 95, and Blohm & Voss Bv 138.

SEEAUFKLÄRUNGSGRUPPE 126

Formed in 1941. Operated in the Mediterranean using the Arado Ar 196.

SEEAUFKLÄRUNGSGRUPPE 127

Formed in 1942 and operated in Baltic waters, equipped primarily with captured enemy aircraft.

SEEAUFKLÄRUNGSGRUPPE 128

Formed in 1943 and operated over the Atlantic. Equipped with the Arado Ar 196.

SEEAUFKLÄRUNGSGRUPPE 129

Formed in March 1943, operating the huge Blohm & Voss Bv 222 flying boat. Disbanded August 1944.

SEEAUFKLÄRUNGSGRUPPE 130

Formed in mid-1943. Operated from bases in Norway equipped with the He 115.

SEEAUFKLÄRUNGSGRUPPE 131

Formed in August 1943. Disbanded in late 1944.

AUFKLÄRUNGSGRUPPEN

Reconnaissance units were classed as either Nahaufklärungsgruppen (short-range reconnaissance groups) or Fernaufklärungsgruppen (long-range reconnaissance groups).

SHORT-RANGE RECONNAISSANCE GROUPS

Aufklärungsgruppe 10 'Tannenberg'
Operated during the Polish campaign, the campaign in the west, the Balkan campaign and on the Eastern Front. Aircraft operated included Me 109, Hs 126, Fw 189, Do 17 and Ju 88.

Aufklärungsgeschwader 11
This wing comprised four Aufklärungsgruppen: 11, 21, 31 and 41. It operated during the Polish campaign, the campaign

in the west, the Blitz on Great Britain, the Balkan campaign and on the Eastern Front.

Aufklärungsgeschwader 12

This wing comprised two Aufklärungs-gruppen: 12 and 22. It operated during the Polish campaign, the campaign in the west and on the Eastern Front. Some elements also operated in Italy and North Africa.

Cornelius Noell was originally a civil pilot with Lufthansa and saw service prior to the Second World War with the Condor Legion in Spain. After seeing service in the campaign in the west, in Norway, during the Battle of Britain and over Crete, he moved to the Eastern Front, where in July 1941 he became the first pilot to overfly and produce complete aerial-photograph cover of Moscow. He was decorated with the Knight's Cross on 22 October 1941 as an Oberleutnant serving with 4./(F) Aufklärungsgruppe. (*Josef Charita*)

Aufklärungsgruppe 32

Formed in 1940, this Gruppe operated in the latter phases of the campaign in the west, in the Balkans and in the northern, central and southern sectors of the Eastern Front. One element, the 4th Staffel, was also used on air-sea rescue missions over the English Channel.

Aufklärungsgeschwader 13

Formed in 1939, this Geschwader comprised two Aufklärungsgruppen: 13 and 23. It operated during the Polish campaign and the campaign in the west. Aufklärungsgruppe 13 operated in the central and southern sectors of the Eastern Front, and Aufklärungsgruppe 23 on all three sectors.

Aufklärungsgruppe 33

Formed in early 1941, this Gruppe was initially equipped with twin-engine types (Me 110 and Ju 88) and utilised on the Eastern Front. It later transferred to the Western Front, and in 1944 some elements were re-equipped with the Me 109.

Aufklärungsgruppe 14

This Gruppe saw action in the Polish campaign, the campaign in the west, in North Africa, Italy and in the central and southern sectors of the Eastern Front.

Aufklärungsgruppe Nacht

This Gruppe, comprising four Staffeln, was formed in 1941 for night reconnaissance operations on the Eastern Front. It operated the He 111, Do 17 and Do 217.

LONG-RANGE RECONNAISSANCE

Aufklärungsgruppe (F) /Ob.d.L.

A long-range reconnaissance Gruppe which operated on the Eastern Front and also undertook maritime reconnaissance searching for Allied convoys on behalf of the U-boats. Aircraft operated included the Do 215, Ju 290 and the Arado Ar 234 jet.

Aufklärungsgruppe (F) 121

Operated during the Polish campaign, the campaign in the west, the attack on Norway, the Blitz on Great Britain, in Italy, North Africa, the Balkan campaign and in the central and southern sectors of the Eastern Front.

Aufklärungsgruppe (F) 122

Operated over the North Sea and English Channel, during the campaign in the west, the Blitz on Great Britain, in Italy, North Africa and on the Eastern Front.

Aufklärungsgruppe (F) 123

Operated on the Western Front, in the attack on Great Britain, in Italy and North Africa. It also carried out maritime reconnaissance over the Atlantic.

Aufklärungsgruppe (F) 124

Operated during the Polish campaign. Later based in Norway before being transferred to the Eastern Front, where it served in the northern sector.

A ground crewman retrieves the camera from a Junkers Ju 88 which has just completed a photo-reconnaissance mission. The effort clearly being expended in this shot gives some idea of how large and heavy these cameras were. (*Josef Charita*)

CHAPTER ELEVEN

AUXILIARIES

Prior to the Second World War, there was no precedence for the large-scale use of female personnel in the German military. In the Luftwaffe, however, women had served since its creation. To begin with, they fulfilled traditional female roles such as clerical workers, telephonists, canteen staff, etc. As time went on, however, wartime needs saw them employed in more important roles, including the following:

Flugmeldedienstpersonal (Auxiliary Aircraft Reporting Service)
Luftnachrichtenhelferinnen (Air Force Signals Auxiliaries)
Luftschutz Warndienst Helferinnen (Air Raid Warning Service Auxiliaries)
Flakhelferinnen (Anti-Aircraft Auxiliaries)
Stabshelferinnen (Staff Auxiliaries)

If fact, although Hitler had never seen a role for women in the military, all Germany was doing was bringing itself in line with what was happening in other nations, and roles similar to those above were also carried out by women in the British forces.

FLUGMELDEDIENSTPERSONAL

These female auxiliaries crewed listening posts, radar stations and reporting stations. The role was absorbed into the Luftnachrichtenhelferinnen in February 1941. In mid-1940, Flugmeldedienst person-

A member of the Luftwaffe's Nachrichtenhelferinnen wearing the regulation female auxiliary uniform. Note that the cap, with brown piping to the flap, does not feature the national cockade. Note also the Luftwaffe 'Zivilabzeichen' worn as a tie pin rather than on the lapel. (*Otto Spronk*)

nel were authorised their own uniform, comprising a cap, jacket, skirt, smock, greatcoat and blouse. Unfortunately for the auxiliaries, however, they were obliged to pay for their uniforms using their own civilian clothing ration coupons.

LUFTNACHRICHTENHELFERINNEN

This branch was established in February 1941 and absorbed the earlier Flugmeldedienst. As well as carrying out the duties previously specified, these auxiliaries also acted as telephonists, teletype and teleprinter operators, radio operators and enciphering and deciphering personnel. The uniforms of the Flugmeldedienst were retained, but with new insignia, introduced in July 1941.

LUFTSCHUTZ WARNDIENST HELFERINNEN (AIR RAID WARNING SERVICE)

These auxiliaries wore the same uniforms as already described for other Luftwaffe auxiliaries, but with their own special insignia.

FLAKHELFERINNEN (ANTI-AIRCRAFT AUXILIARIES)

Although Flak auxiliaries supplied by the Reichsarbeitsdienst had been employed by the Luftwaffe for some time, it was only after October 1943 that a Flak auxiliary branch was officially constituted, and all existing volunteers absorbed into it. The primary function of these personnel was to crew searchlights and barrage balloons, and serve on fire-control equipment, etc. Their use as actual gun crews was only approved in the closing months of the war. Once again, existing uniforms as used by other Luftwaffe auxiliary branches were used.

STABSHELFERINNEN (STAFF AUXILIARIES)

These auxiliaries worked as telephonists, signallers, secretaries and a number of general roles.

Once again, staff auxiliaries of the Luftwaffe wore exactly the same range of uniform items as previously described for other auxiliaries.

The only specific item of insignia which identified these auxiliaries was a diamond shaped blue grey cloth patch worn on the upper left sleeve. It had a silver grey border and in the centre the text Stabs/Helferin in two lines, over a Luftwaffe-style national emblem.

In general terms, period photographs of auxiliaries often show non-regulation garments being worn, in particular protective clothing such as one-piece boiler-suit-type coveralls and so the information provided above should be taken only as a general guide to official regulation uniforms and clothing.

Male clothing was also widely issued where the official garments were unavailable.

CHAPTER TWELVE

PERSONALITIES

HERMANN WILHELM GÖRING

Hermann Göring was born in Marienbad on 12 January 1893, the son of a Protestant governor for German South West Africa. He attended the cadet school at Berlin-Lichterfelde and graduated as one of the top in his class, subsequently joining Infanterie Regiment 4 as a leutnant in 1914.

At the end of the First World War in 1918, Oberleutnant Göring was an accomplished 'ace', with twenty-two kills to his credit, and was commander of the legendary 'Richthofen's Flying Circus'. Göring's decorations included both classes of the Iron Cross, the 'Pour le Merite' (colloquially known as the 'Blue Max') and the Hohenzollern House Order with swords.

Following the end of the war, Göring spent time in Denmark and Sweden working in aviation as a test pilot, and also, like Udet, did some stunt flying. Back in Germany in 1921, he studied economics and history at university in Munich. In 1923 he married Swedish divorcee Carin von Kantzow,

Hermann Göring in a portrait study as Reichsmarschall des Grossdeutschen Reiches, with the final-pattern insignia for that rank. Note the crossed field marshal's batons on the collar patches, the Grand Cross of the Iron Cross worn at the neck along with the Knight's Cross, and the 'Pour le Mérite' he won in the First World War. Göring had a great liking for fancy uniforms and many of those he wore were unique to him. In the late part of the war, with the Luftwaffe's fortunes on the wane and Germany suffering from the Allied air offensive, Göring would often appear without his numerous glittering orders and decorations.

Baronesse von Fock. He also met Adolf Hitler for the first time in 1923. Hitler saw the advantage of having a highly decorated war hero as one of the main figures in his movement and made Göring head of the SA 'Stormtroopers'.

Göring marched with Hitler in the abortive Munich 'Putsch' of 1923 and afterwards fled the country. He had been wounded during the attempted coup and became addicted to the morphine used to kill the pain of his wound.

In 1926 Göring returned to Germany, where he worked in the aircraft industry as a salesman. He remained a member of the Nazi Party, however, and maintained his close links with Hitler. Elected as a member of the Reichstag, he eventually became its president in July 1932. As the 'respectable' face of Nazism, he and his wife played a vital role in bringing together members of the military, the aristocracy, industrialists and other influential elements and using their fear of communism and anarchy to encourage support of the Nazis.

On the Nazi accession to power in January 1933, Göring was appointed as head of the Prussian police and was instrumental in the creation of the secret state police (Gestapo). One of his earliest moves was to create the first concentration camp, at Sachsenhausen, though at this point political enemies were the prime victims, rather than Jews. Göring is regarded as one of the prime suspects for orchestrating the Reichstag fire that allowed him to promulgate numerous 'emergency decrees' which led to the total suppression of any political opposition, before handing over control of Germany's police apparatus to Heinrich Himmler. On 5 May 1934, Göring was appointed Minister of Aviation and in October 1936 became General Plenipotentiary for the Four Year Plan, giving him huge power and influence over Germany's economy.

In April 1938, Hitler elevated Göring to the status of Generalfeldmarschall, and on the outbreak of war, Göring was nominated as Hitler's official successor, both as head of state and as supreme commander of the armed forces. For a time at least, Göring had become, next to Hitler, the most powerful man in Germany.

After the rapid successes against, first, Poland and then France and the Low Countries, in which his Luftwaffe had played a key role, Göring had a new rank created especially for him. He would henceforth be Reichsmarschall des Grossdeutschen Reiches, and he became the only person in the Second World War to be awarded the Grand Cross of the Iron Cross. It was to be the zenith of his power, however, and thereafter, as the Luftwaffe began to struggle against the combined strength of the Allied countries, his influence would wane.

While Göring's lavish lifestyle and eccentric and excessive behaviour were tolerated with a degree of good humour when Germany was triumphant, it reduced him to a figure of ridicule once Germany faced losing the war. First, the failure of the Luftwaffe to subjugate the RAF during the Battle of Britain, then its failure to keep the 6 Armee supplied at Stalingrad despite his boasts, and most of all its failure to protect German soil from ever-increasing punishment from incessant Allied heavy bombing raids, saw Göring's influence with Hitler almost completely disappear.

Hitler retained a good deal of trust in those who had been faithful supporters in the early days of the Nazi movement and took no action against the Reichsmarschall despite the machinations of others to have Göring replaced as head of the Luftwaffe. Only in April 1945, with Hitler in his Berlin bunker surrounded by Soviet forces, when Göring delivered an ultimatum to Hitler demanding a free hand to act as Hitler's successor in the original terms of his appointment, did Hitler relent to the pressure from others in his inner circle and order Göring's arrest.

However, Göring, surrounded by a contingent of loyal Luftwaffe troops, escaped the clutches of the SS and was eventually taken prisoner by US forces in Fischhorn in May 1945. The bloated, drug-addled Reichsmarschall was placed on a strict health regime by his captors, so that by the time he was placed on trial during the Nuremberg Process of 1946, he had regained much of his old flair and sharp wit and performed impressively in verbal jousting with prosecuting council. The result was a foregone conclusion for someone who had served as part of the innermost circle of such an evil regime and he was found guilty and sentenced to death. Göring seemed prepared for death, had he been given the opportunity to face a firing squad like a soldier, something he saw as an honourable death. But he was not prepared to face the gallows like a criminal and, with the collusion of some of his guards, cheated the hangman by taking poison on 15 October 1946.

Erhard Milch, shown here with the rank of General der Flieger in the double-breasted full-dress tunic for officers of General rank. Milch ultimately reached the rank of Generalfeldmarschall. Note that on his left breast he wears the gold Nazi Party badge. As well as being awarded to early members of the party, it was also bestowed by Hitler on those deemed deserving, as a special honour, indicating the high standing of Milch among the Nazi hierarchy.

ERHARD MILCH

Born in Wilhelmshaven on 30 March 1892, Erhard Milch began his military career when he joined the Imperial German Army as a cadet, eventually gaining his commission and becoming an officer in the artillery. He served initially on the Western Front until transferring to the Air Corps, in which he was an observer. He ended the war as a squadron commander with the rank of Hauptmann. Milch was initially retained by the Army of the Weimar Republic but resigned in 1921 to take up a career in aviation. He joined the Junkers company, with which he served until 1926, at which point he was appointed as a director of Lufthansa, the German national airline.

Milch was a close acquaintance of his fellow wartime flier, Hermann Göring, and in 1933 joined the Air Ministry as one of Göring's deputies. Milch was responsible for managing armament production for the Luftwaffe. He was rather unusual in becoming a senior member of the Nazi hierarchy, as it was believed by many that he was part Jewish. His family is said to have been investigated by the Gestapo, which was at that time of course under the command of Göring. Göring's solution to the problem was reputedly simple. He persuaded Milch's mother to sign a statement to the effect that her Jewish husband was not the true biological father of Erhard Milch. Milch was then allegedly certified as Aryan.

By 1938 Milch had risen rapidly through the senior ranks of the new Luftwaffe to reach the rank of Generaloberst. He commanded Luftflotte V during the campaign against Norway, and after the successful conclusion of the campaign in the west, which ultimately resulted in the surrender of France in June 1940, Milch, together with his colleagues Albert Kesselring and Hugo Sperrle, was elevated to the status of General-feldmarschall. In 1941, Milch became Generalluftzeugmeister, the Quartermaster General of the Luftwaffe.

Milch repaid the protection he had received from Göring by conspiring with others, including the Reichsführer-SS, Heinrich Himmler, to persuade Hitler to replace Göring as head of the Luftwaffe. Hitler, still harbouring some loyalty to his old comrade, refused. Milch was now seriously out of favour with the commander-in-chief of the Luftwaffe and in June 1944 Göring forced him to resign as director of air armament. Milch then moved to work with the Reich Minister of Armaments, Albert Speer, remaining with Speer until the end of the war.

Milch was arrested on 4 May 1945 and indicted during the war crimes trials in Nuremberg in 1946. The use of significant levels of slave labour, including concentration camp inmates, in the armaments industry was his undoing and he was sentenced to life imprisonment. Released in June 1954, Milch lived quietly in retirement, during which he penned his book *The Rise and Fall of the Luftwaffe*. He died on 25 January 1972.

First World War fighter ace Ernst Udet was hugely popular in Germany, not only as a decorated war hero – here he wears the coveted 'Pour le Mérite' – but as a skilled stunt flier who often appeared at air displays. Recruiting him into the higher echelons of the new Luftwaffe was a shrewd tactical move for Göring. Udet had in fact at one time tried to have Göring ejected from the veterans' association of the Richthofen Geschwader for allegedly falsifying his victory claims.

ERNST UDET

Born in Frankfurt on 26 April 1896, Ernst Udet was fascinated by aviation from an early stage, beginning with flying model aircraft. Initially taken into the Army as a motorcycle despatch rider, he paid for his own flying lessons in order to be eligible for service as a flier. He joined the Air Corps in 1915. As an NCO fighter pilot flying the Fokker triplane, he scored his first victory on 18 March 1916 during a solo attack on a large formation of French planes, reported to have exceeded twenty in number. Udet became a highly accomplished fighter ace, serving under Manfred von Richthofen and commanding the squadron briefly after Richthofen's death, before being replaced by Hermann Göring. By the end of hostilities he had risen to the rank of Oberleutnant, earned the coveted 'Pour le Mérite' ('Blue Max') and amassed a score of sixty-two victories, ranking him second only to the Red Baron. He was the highest-scoring ace to survive the war.

After the war, with Germany forbidden to possess military aircraft and opportunities for civil flying greatly restricted, Udet formed his own aircraft design company in Munich, secretly supported by the military. Udet flew as much as he could, appearing in extremely successful films such as *Die weiße Hölle von Piz Palü* (1929), *Stürme über dem Mont Blanc* (1930) and *SOS Eisberg* (1933). He also became internationally famous as a stunt flier. Udet took an active part in the veterans' association for the Richthofen squadron and in fact campaigned to have his future commander-in-chief Hermann Göring ejected on the grounds of having falsified his claims of aerial victories during the war. When the Nazis came to power, Udet, though not much of a political animal, was drawn into the Nazi Party partly by Göring bribing him with two aircraft for his own use. The appearance of a much-loved war hero in their ranks was a propaganda coup for the Nazis.

In 1935, Udet was taken into the new Luftwaffe with the rank of Oberst. During the following year he was appointed head of the Technical Office of the Air Ministry, and was in charge of the development of fighter and dive-bomber aircraft. It was largely Udet who was responsible for the introduction of aircraft such as the Messerschmitt Me 109 and the Junkers Ju 87 Stuka. Still flying, he set a new speed record in 1938, in the Heinkel He 100.

Udet as a Generaloberst of the Luftwaffe, now wearing the Knight's Cross of the Iron Cross alongside his 'Pour le Mérite'. Göring would eventually turn on Udet, using him as a scapegoat for the Luftwaffe's failure to subjugate Great Britain. Udet eventually committed suicide in November 1941, convinced that Germany could no longer win the war.

After the successful conclusion of the campaign in the west and the fall of France, Udet was decorated with the Knight's Cross of the Iron Cross for the part he played in the successful development of the fighter and dive-bomber arms of the Luftwaffe. The Battle of Britain, however, would show serious deficiencies in Luftwaffe planning. The Germans had no heavy bombers capable of delivering a significant payload, and as Göring looked for a scapegoat on which to pin responsibility for the Luftwaffe's failure to subjugate Britain during the Blitz, Udet would take the blame.

Udet sank into depression and took to drinking excessively, and his health inevitably suffered. Things were made worse when Milch blocked Udet's proposals for prioritising the development of the excellent Focke Wulf Fw 190 fighter and, convinced that Germany could not win the war following the attack on the Soviet Union, on 17 November 1941 Udet shot himself in the head. His suicide was hushed up by the Nazis, who claimed that he had been killed while personally testing a new aircraft. He was given a state funeral.

WOLFRAM FREIHERR VON RICHTHOFEN

Born in Gut Barzdorf in 1895, Wolfram von Richthofen was a cousin of the famous First World War ace Manfred von Richthofen. His military career began in 1913, when he joined the Imperial German Army, and the young von Richthofen saw extensive combat service on both the Western and Eastern Fronts. He only transferred to flying duties in March 1918 after qualifying as a pilot.

In postwar Germany, von Richthofen studied engineering for a few years before re-entering military service in 1922. He remained with the Army until the formation of the new air force, which he joined in

Wolfram von Richthofen was a cousin of the famous First World War flying ace. Although he, too, transferred to the Flying Corps, this was not until late in the war, and most of his service was with the Army. Von Richthofen nevertheless had a very successful career in the new Luftwaffe, eventually becoming the youngest field marshal in the Wehrmacht. He died of cancer just before the end of the Second World War. In this shot, one that he would often autograph for admirers, he is seen at the controls of his personal aircraft. (*Josef Charita*)

1933 before its 'official' creation. In 1936, von Richthofen enlisted in the Condor Legion and served in Spain under Hugo Sperrle as his chief of staff. During the course of his service in Spain, he was elevated to Generalmajor and, in May 1939, took overall command of the Condor Legion.

On the outbreak of war in 1939, von Richthofen commanded Luftflotte 8, which took part in the attack on Poland and in particular the devastation of Warsaw. Von

Richthofen played an active and important part in the campaign in the west in command of VIII Fliegerkorps and was a keen exponent of the tactics of Blitzkrieg, with his Ju 87 Stuka dive-bombers giving tremendous support to the 8 Armee under General von Reichenau during the drive through Belgium, and again in France. In recognition of the important part he had played in achieving victory in the west, he was awarded the Knight's Cross of the Iron Cross on 17 May 1940.

He had less success in the next stage of the war when, during the Battle of Britain, his forces were unable to gain the air superiority that was essential for any attempt at the invasion of the British Isles. In April 1941, however, he achieved success once again when his forces supplied air cover for the airborne invasion of Crete. The success of this battle brought von Richthofen the award of the Oakleaves to his Knight's Cross on 17 July 1941.

After a spell based in Italy in command of Luftflotte 2, von Richthofen and his forces moved eastwards into Russia, where they operated in support of Heeresgruppe Süd in the drive towards the Don and the eventual debacle at Stalingrad. The supply of General von Paulus and 6 Armee at Stalingrad was to be one of von Richthofen's greatest challenges, and was brought about by Göring's boasts that he could keep the troops in the pocket fully supplied from the air. In the event, von Richthofen's forces dropped over 8,000 tons of supplies over a two-month period for the loss of nearly 500 aircraft and over 1,000 airmen. Despite his best efforts, it was nowhere near enough to save the doomed 6 Armee.

On 17 February 1943 von Richthofen reached the pinnacle of his career when Hitler elevated him to the rank of Generalfeldmarschall. He was Germany's youngest field marshal. By 1944, von Richthofen's health had deteriorated and he was diagnosed as having a cancerous brain tumour. He was forced to retire from active duty because of his ill health and died on 12 July 1945, shortly after the end of the war.

ADOLF GALLAND

Born in Westerholt on 19 March 1912, Adolf Galland developed an early interest in flying and as a 19-year-old was already setting local records for endurance in glider flying. Galland began training as a commercial pilot in powered aircraft in 1932 and for a time was employed by Lufthansa. His official military career, however, like that of many early Luftwaffe personalities, began with the Army. He joined the Army in February 1934 and was assigned to Infanterie Regiment 10. One year later, however, with the official announcement of the existence of the new Luftwaffe, Galland transferred and was assigned as an instructor to the Jagdfliegerschule, where he served for two years before joining Jagdgeschwader Richthofen as a fighter pilot flying the Me 109.

In 1937, Galland volunteered for service with the Condor Legion in Spain and was appointed Staffelkapitän of 3./J88. He proved himself a first-class pilot, flying the obsolescent He 51 biplane in 280 combat missions in the ground support role. In reward for his performance in Spain he was awarded the Spanish Cross in Gold with Diamonds.

On the outbreak of war, Galland, by now an Oberleutnant, was flying the Hs 123 biplane with Lehrgeschwader 2 and earned the Iron Cross Second Class for his actions in the ground support role during the Polish campaign. He was promoted to Hauptmann on 1 October 1940.

In February 1940 he succeeded in gaining a transfer to fighters and was posted to Jagdgeschwader 27, where he became the

Adolf Galland was one of Germany's finest, and most charismatic, leaders. Seen here with the rank of Oberst and General der Jagdflieger, just after his promotion from Kommodore of Jagdgeschwader 26 'Schlageter', he wears the Knight's Cross with Oakleaves, Swords and Diamonds, the Spanish Cross in Gold with Diamonds, and the Pilot/Observer Badge with Diamonds. Galland eventually reached the rank of Generalleutnant and commanded the famous 'Squadron of Experts', flying the Me 262 jet fighter.

Geschwader Adjutant. On 12 May 1940, he scored his first victory, shooting down an RAF Hurricane fighter, the first of three he shot down that day. By the end of the short campaign in the west, Galland had achieved a total score of fourteen kills.

On 6 June 1940, he was assigned as Gruppenkommandeur of III./Jagdgeschwader 26 'Schlageter', a post which one month later brought with it promotion to Major. By 1 August his score had risen to seventeen victories and at this point he was awarded the Knight's Cross of the Iron Cross. Victories then began to come faster and several well-known British aces were among his victims. By 24 September his score had risen to forty and on the following day he was awarded the Oakleaves to his Knight's Cross. On 1 November 1940, Galland was promoted to Oberstleutnant and posted as Geschwaderkommodore of Jagdgeschwader 26.

His tally of victories continued to grow steadily over the months to come, but on 21 June 1941 he in turn was shot down by a Polish pilot flying with the RAF and, wounded, was forced to bale out. Fortunately for Galland he landed safely and, unperturbed by his experience, is reported to have happily puffed away on one of his trademark cigars while receiving treatment on the operating table.

Galland was a chivalrous airman and when the legless British ace Douglas Bader was shot down by an aircraft of his unit, he had Bader invited to visit his airfield, where he was allowed to sit in the cockpit of an Me 109. Bader had been obliged to remove his prosthetic legs when he baled out of his stricken aircraft and Galland arranged to grant safe passage for a British aircraft to fly over and drop a replacement set. This was done, though the British, rather unsportingly in the circumstances, dropped some bombs as well as the replacement legs.

On 26 June, Galland was awarded the Swords to his Oakleaves. At this point he was ordered by both Hitler and Göring to desist from flying further combat missions but cheerfully ignored these orders and continued to rack up further victories. On 22 November 1941, following the death of his friend Werner Mölders in an air crash, Galland was appointed to succeed him as General der Jagdflieger and on 4 December he was promoted to Oberst. On 28 January 1942, with his score at ninety-four kills, he was awarded the Oakleaves with Swords and Diamonds to his Knight's Cross.

On 11 February 1942, the battle cruisers *Scharnhorst* and *Gneisenau*, together with the heavy cruiser *Prinz Eugen* and numerous smaller ships, broke out from the port of Brest and passed through the narrows of the English Channel to reach safe home ports in Germany. It was an audacious attempt which succeeded brilliantly, giving the Germans a great propaganda victory. Air cover was provided by fighter forces under the command of Adolf Galland.

In December 1942, Galland was promoted to Generalmajor. He himself, however, would not score any further personal victories until 1944, when he took advantage of the occasional opportunity, despite orders to the contrary, to fly some combat missions and downed two B-17 bombers, flying the Focke Wulf Fw 190. His blatant disregard of orders was disguised by crediting these two kills not to him personally, but to the 'Staff' of the squadron. He was promoted to General-leutnant in December 1944.

Galland in fact became somewhat of a thorn in the flesh of the Nazi hierarchy, often arguing quite determinedly with Göring and speaking to Hitler with a level of frankness to which the Führer was not accustomed. Galland stressed that more fighters would be needed if Germany was to challenge the Allied bombing campaign effectively. The majority of senior Luftwaffe pilots had lost all confidence in Göring, who had now, in turn, unfairly taken to accusing the fighter pilots of cowardice for failing to halt the enemy bombers. The fighter pilots were determined to seek support from Hitler in forcing the commander-in-chief of

the Luftwaffe to resign. Galland was not directly involved in this 'plot', although he could not have been unaware of it. When a showdown meeting between representatives of the fighter pilots and Göring was arranged in January 1945, Göring reacted furiously, accusing them of mutiny and threatening to have them shot. Göring blamed Galland, dismissed him from his position as General der Jagdflieger and began to make arrangements for his court martial.

Galland had always reacted rather bluntly to Göring. When, during the Battle of Britain, Göring asked him what equipment he needed to win the battle, he replied, much to Göring's discomfiture, 'A squadron of Spitfires.' On another occasion, when Göring sounded him out about how he would react if given orders to shoot at enemy pilots who had baled out, Galland told him quite emphatically that he would refuse to obey such orders. Now, fortunately for Galland, Hitler intervened to prevent the vindictive Reichsmarschall from prosecuting Galland, and ordered the former fighter ace to be given a combat command.

Galland had been a great champion of the Me 262 jet fighter, and had been dismayed that a weapon with such potential should be used as a bomber on Hitler's orders. Now, Galland would be given command of Jagdverband 44, a combat unit flying the Me 262 as originally intended, as a fighter-interceptor. Galland shot down seven additional enemy aircraft while flying the Me 262, one of the few combat pilots to qualify as an ace flying jets.

On 26 April 1945, Galland was flying an Me 262 intercepting a US bomber formation. He shot down two B-26 Marauder bombers but was hit by return fire from the bombers. On turning away from the bombers, he was attacked by a P-47 Thunderbolt escort fighter, causing more damage to his aircraft and resulting in a leg wound for Galland. He succeeded in nursing his damaged fighter back to his home airstrip and landing safely, but came under attack again from enemy fighters which had followed him back. He was able to run from his plane into cover but the wounds he had received were sufficient to end his combat flying for good.

Galland surrendered to US troops on 5 May 1945 and spent two years as a prisoner of war. In 1948, Galland moved to Argentina where he worked as an aviation consultant and helped to design Argentina's first combat jet fighter. He returned to Germany in the mid-1950s and settled in Bonn, where he started his own aviation consultancy and became a very prosperous businessman. He died on 9 February 1996 after a heart attack.

Adolf Galland had achieved a victory tally of 104 over the course of more than 700 combat missions. His victims included 31 Hurricanes and 53 Spitfires.

WERNER MÖLDERS

Werner Mölders was born in Gelsenkirchen on 18 March 1913. His military career began in the Army when he joined the infantry in 1931, serving as an officer cadet. In 1934 he applied for training as a pilot. His first application was rejected, as he had been declared unfit for flying duty because of a tendency to suffer from airsickness. Mölders was nothing if not determined, however; by sheer willpower, he managed to overcome his airsickness and reapplied. This time he was successful and was accepted into the new Luftwaffe, and in July 1935, a freshly commissioned Leutnant Mölders joined Fliegergruppe Schwerin.

By April 1936 he had moved to Jagdgeschwader 134 to undertake instructing duties with its training squadron. He served as a flying instructor for around two years. With

the outbreak of the Spanish Civil War, Mölders volunteered for service with the Condor Legion and duly arrived in Spain on 14 April of that year.

In Spain, Mölders took over from Adolf Galland as Staffelkapitän of 3./J88. Service during the Spanish Civil War gave Mölders the opportunity to show his considerable skills as a pilot, shooting down a total of fourteen enemy aircraft. He was in fact the highest-scoring pilot of the Condor Legion. Equally importantly, he proved himself a first-class tactician and leader of men. On his return to Germany, Mölders was one of a small number of soldiers to be honoured with the Spanish Cross in Gold with Diamonds.

By the outbreak of war in 1939, Mölders was serving as Staffelkapitän of 1./JG53, the 'Pik As', or Ace of Spades Geschwader. Despite his age (just 26), his maturity brought him the affectionate nickname 'Vati' (Daddy).

Mölders's first victory of the Second World War came on 21 September 1939, when he shot down a French fighter. In November, now an Oberleutnant, he was appointed Gruppenkommandeur of III./JG53, based at Wiesbaden. Victories continued to mount and by May 1940, he had downed twenty additional enemy aircraft, bringing his overall total, including the Spanish victories, to thirty-four. This achievement brought him the Knight's Cross of the Iron Cross and a well-deserved promotion to Hauptmann.

Mölders's luck ran out on 5 June 1940, when he was shot down during a dogfight with a French fighter piloted by René Pommier Layragues, himself an ace with 6 kills. With a total of 39 kills and 128 combat missions to his credit, it looked as if Mölders's career might be over. The French capitulation just two weeks later, however, brought his early release from captivity and

Galland's close friend and rival in the victory stakes during the first part of the war, Werner Mölders, is seen here as an Oberst, wearing the Knight's Cross with Oakleaves, Swords and Diamonds. Mölders was one of only a very small number of senior military figures of the Third Reich period who were so highly respected that, even in the politically correct world of postwar Germany, ships, fighter squadrons and military barracks were named in their honour.

the award of the Oakleaves to his Knight's Cross. He was only the second to win this coveted award (the first was Mountain Troop General Eduard Dietl), just beating his rival, Adolf Galland. Within a month, he had added a further ten kills to his tally to bring his score to fifty, and by the end of the year had amassed a total of fifty-four kills (sixty-eight including those obtained in Spain).

JG51 remained on the Channel front into the summer of 1941, by which time his score had risen to sixty-seven. In June 1941, Germany invaded the Soviet Union and Mölders's unit was one of those assigned to the attack force. On the very first day of the offensive, 22 June, Mölders shot down four Soviet aircraft to bring his score to seventy-two. This achievement brought him the award of the Swords to his Oakleaves. This time, however, his friendly rival Galland beat him to it as the first to receive the award, Mölders being the second.

On 30 June, Mölders shot down five Soviet bombers to bring his total to eighty-two, making him the first pilot to exceed the record score of eighty set by Baron Manfred von Richthofen in the First World War. Victories continued to accumulate, and on 15 July he became the first-ever pilot to achieve 100 aerial victories. This record-breaking achievement brought him the award of Germany's highest military decoration, the Oakleaves with Swords and

he was soon back with his Geschwader. Promoted to Major, he was appointed Geschwader Kommodore of JG51.

Disaster almost struck once again, on 28 July 1940. This was Mölders's first combat flight with his command and started well when he downed an RAF Spitfire. However, the stricken enemy aircraft hit Mölders's own plane and his legs were badly injured. He was able to make an emergency landing at Wissant but was out of action for a full month while his injuries healed. On his return to combat he began building his score once again and by 20 September had logged his fortieth kill of the Second World War, another Spitfire, shot down over Dungeness. This achievement brought him

Diamonds to the Knight's Cross of the Iron Cross. He was the first of only twenty-seven servicemen to receive this newly created award.

The downside of this success for Mölders was that he was then forbidden to fly any more combat missions. Further honours came with his appointment as General der Jagdflieger. Somewhat confusingly, this role did not bring with it General's rank. The title referred to the post of Inspector General rather than the military rank of General, though Mölders was promoted to Oberst (full colonel), still a very respectable rank for a man of just 28 years.

On 22 November 1941, Mölders was on his way back to Germany to attend the state funeral of Ernst Udet. During a violent thunderstorm the He 111 in which he was a passenger crashed while landing at Breslau and both Mölders and the pilot of the Heinkel were killed.

Werner Mölders had flown 430 combat missions (including 100 in Spain) and had downed a total of 115 enemy aircraft. Unlike many of the later aces who were greatly to surpass his score, the majority of Mölders's victories were scored on the Western Front, where, as a general rule, victories were harder to achieve than in the east. On 20 December 1941, Jagdgeschwader 51 was granted the title Jagdgeschwader Mölders in his honour, and its personnel given the right to wear a sleeveband bearing this title.

Despite his antipathy to the Nazi regime and his outspokenness in criticising it, Mölders was held in high regard by Hitler. Indeed, when Hitler became aware that some of his cronies were agitating against Mölders and trying to cause problems for the highly decorated ace, Hitler warned them not to harass Mölders, whom he referred to as a 'thoroughly decent man'.

Mölders was one of a small number of soldiers of the Wehrmacht whose reputation was such that it was considered acceptable to honour him within the new, postwar Bundeswehr. Fighter wing JG74 of the Bundesluftwaffe was named Geschwader 'Mölders' in his honour and a destroyer of the Bundesmarine was likewise named *Zerstörer Mölders* to commemorate one of Germany's most honoured and honourable servicemen.

HANS-ULRICH RUDEL

Hans-Ulrich Rudel was born in Konradswaldau on 2 July 1916, the son of a church minister. He was not academically gifted but was an accomplished sportsman. Thanks to his membership of the Hitler Youth, Rudel was fully indoctrinated as a Nazi at an early age. He joined the Luftwaffe in 1936 and had no problems in completing his flying training and qualifying as a pilot. He specifically requested a posting to a dive-bomber unit but was turned down and instead allocated to a reconnaissance squadron. It was in this role that Leutnant Rudel performed during the Polish campaign, winning himself the Iron Cross Second Class.

Continued efforts on his behalf to push for a transfer to dive-bombers finally succeeded in the spring of 1940 and Rudel, now an Oberleutnant, missed out on the campaign in the west as he underwent his conversion training for the Ju 87 Stuka. On completing his training he was assigned to Stukageschwader 2 'Immelmann' but was not to fly his first combat mission until after the opening of the attack on the Soviet Union in June 1941.

On 23 September of that year, Rudel's unit was involved on an attack on Soviet naval units in Kronstadt harbour. Rudel made an attack on the Soviet battleship *Marat* and in a chance-in-a-million shot, was able to drop his 1,000kg bomb right down

Stuka ace Hans-Ulrich Rudel is seen here just after his return from another successful mission, still wearing his flight gear and leather pilot's helmet. The Knight's Cross of the Iron Cross with Oakleaves can be seen at his neck.

the funnel of the warship. It exploded in the bowels of the ship, detonated her magazines and caused the ship to break her back. On 25 December 1941, Rudel flew his 500th combat mission, and five days later he was decorated with the German Cross in Gold. This award was usually a cumulative one, given for repeated acts of merit, but his destruction of the *Marat* had not been overlooked and on 15 January 1942, he was decorated with the Knight's Cross of the Iron Cross. By this point, Rudel had been removed from combat duty and sent to the Stuka training school in Graz as an instructor, passing on the benefits of his already considerable experience to trainee pilots.

Rudel did not enjoy being away from the action, however, and badgered his superiors

for a return to combat duty. In June 1942 he was permitted to return to the Eastern Front, where he took command of 1./ Stukageschwader 2 as Staffelkapitän. At this point the unit was operating in support of the German forces around Stalingrad. Here the Stukas were being employed against tank formations as well as against enemy positions. High-explosive bombs were not particularly effective against armour unless a direct hit was achieved.

In February 1943, after flying his 1,000th combat mission, Rudel was removed from combat duty again, not as an instructor this time, but to help develop a special 'tank-buster' version of the Stuka as a member of the Luftwaffe's Panzerjagdkommando Weiss. The new version of the Stuka carried two 3.7cm anti-tank cannon, one under each wing. The first prototypes were tested not against tanks, but against Soviet landing craft operating in the Black Sea and in just over three weeks of operations here, Rudel had destroyed seventy such craft. Operations against tanks came next, and in early spring 1943 Rudel destroyed his first enemy armoured vehicles with the new Stuka.

On 14 April 1943, Rudel was awarded the Oakleaves to his Knight's Cross. Shortly afterwards, his Staffel of Ju 87s was assigned to support 3 SS-Panzer Division 'Totenkopf' during the attack on the Kursk salient, which was to develop into the biggest tank battle in history. On the first mission of the first day of the offensive, Rudel knocked out four enemy tanks, quite an amazing feat considering that each cannon only carried six rounds of ammunition. By the end of the first day, Rudel's score had risen to thirteen, and this was to be only the beginning of a phenomenal run of successes for him against Soviet tank forces.

On 25 October 1943 Rudel was awarded the Swords to his Oakleaves. It is a testament to Rudel's respect for the contribution to his successes made by his rear-gunner, Erwin Hentschel, that he took him along to the formal investiture for the Swords. Here, Rudel promptly refused to accept the decoration unless an immediate award of the Knight's Cross was made to Hentschel for his part in Rudel's victories. His demands were granted.

By March 1944 Rudel had flown 1,500 combat missions. His luck ran out, however, one day in late March when his squadron was attacked by enemy fighters and a Stuka was shot down behind enemy lines. Rudel insisted on landing to pick up the survivors, but because of the extremely soft ground he was unable to take off again. All four airmen then had to make the trek through enemy-occupied territory, pursued by Soviet troops. The airmen finally reached the Dniester river and were forced to swim across its 600m width in freezing cold water. Tragically, just before he reached the opposite shore, Rudel's crewmate Hentschel slipped below the waters and was drowned. The two airmen that Rudel had landed to save were killed by enemy fire and only Rudel himself reached the safety of German lines. His gallant attempt to rescue his comrades had ended in tragedy, but the bravery of his attempt was not overlooked. Coming on top of his phenomenal achievements in battle, it earned him the Oakleaves with Swords and Diamonds to his Knight's Cross, awarded on 29 March 1944.

Shortly after returning to his unit, Rudel received a bullet-wound to the thigh. Undaunted, he insisted on returning to flying duties while his leg was still encased in plaster. He had by now earned every gallantry award the Reich had to offer. On setting a new record of over 2,000 combat missions flown, Rudel was awarded a special version of the Flight Clasp for ground attack units in real gold, with a platinum central motif and with a small pendant with the number 2,000 picked out in diamonds. More was to follow. On 1 January 1945 the one-man army was awarded a completely new decoration, the Golden Oakleaves with Swords and Diamonds, an award which in the event, Rudel would be the only soldier ever to receive.

Rudel's good luck finally ran out in February 1945 when his aircraft took a hit from enemy flak guns during operations on the Oder front and his left leg was shattered. He managed to bring his aircraft back over German-held territory and land safely. Rushed immediately to a field hospital, his injuries were of such severity that his leg had to be amputated. Not one to let the mere loss of a limb deter him, as soon as he had been fitted with an artificial leg, he insisted on returning to his unit and flew combat missions through to the very last day of the war.

Rudel was a true fanatic, offering to fly suicide missions at one point and then requesting permission to fly into Berlin in the last days of the war to rescue Hitler. Operating in Bohemia up to the end of hostilities, Rudel was able to surrender to US forces and thus avoid Soviet captivity.

Rudel's final list of combat achievements was quite awesome. He was responsible for destroying a number of bridges and sinking an enemy battleship and an enemy destroyer, as well as 70 landing craft. He destroyed 519 enemy tanks, 150 artillery positions and around 1,000 other assorted military vehicles. As well as his beloved Stuka, Rudel had also flown around 400 missions with the Fw 190, and in this aircraft had shot down 11 enemy aircraft. These feats were achieved in over 2,530 combat missions, during which he is reckoned to have dropped over 1 million kilograms of bombs, expended 1 million rounds of machine-gun ammunition, 155,000 rounds of cannon ammunition and 5 million litres of aircraft fuel, and flown over 600,000km. So great was the damage that Rudel had wrought, that the Soviets placed a 100,000 roubles reward on his head.

There can be little doubt that Hans-Ulrich Rudel was an extremely skilled and brave flier who richly deserves his place in the record books. It is also undeniable that he was an unrepentant National Socialist. In fact the US officers who interrogated him after his capture labelled him as a 'typical Nazi'.

In 1948 he moved to Argentina, where he worked in the aircraft industry and was involved in a self-help organisation for escaped Nazis. He published a number of works, in which those who had conspired against Hitler were castigated as traitors and criticised for not recognising Hitler's 'genius'. He returned to Germany in 1953 and was briefly involved in politics as a member of the ultra-right-wing Deutsche Reichspartei. Hans-Ulrich Rudel died in retirement in 1982.

HERMANN GRAF

Hermann Graf was born in Engen on 24 October 1912. From a modest family background, he was the son of a simple blacksmith and this, combined with his own poor achievements at school, made a future as a career soldier look unlikely. Graf took up an apprenticeship as a locksmith but this was not successful and he eventually moved into clerical work within local government. Although his academic achievements had been mediocre, Graf was a very keen sportsman and, as well as being a skilled football player, had a keen interest in flying. He first

A later photograph of Rudel shows him as an Oberst, wearing the Knight's Cross with Golden Oakleaves, Swords and Diamonds. He also wears the Pilot/Observer Badge with Diamonds, and of particular note is his Ground Assault Flight Clasp, made from gold and platinum and having the central wreath and the numeral 2,000 on the pendant picked out in diamonds. Rudel was a brave soldier but also a committed Nazi. Even after the war, his political views remained the same, rendering him somewhat *persona non grata* in postwar Germany, where many of his peers achieved rank and status in the new Bundesluftwaffe.

Major Hermann Graf is seen here in the cockpit of his Me 109 fighter. Graf was another winner of the rare Oakleaves, Swords and Diamonds to the Knight's Cross. This shot also shows to good advantage the campaign shield on his left sleeve, earned for participation in the air battle over the Crimea. (*Josef Charita*)

qualified as a glider pilot in 1932 and then took up training in powered aircraft.

In 1935, Graf applied to join the Luftwaffe and, his flying experience standing him in good stead, was accepted for training as an NCO pilot. In 1936 he completed his basic flying training, and in 1938 his advanced flight training. In the spring of 1939, with the rank of Unteroffizier, he was posted to 2./Jagdgeschwader 51, flying the Me 109. Promoted Feldwebel at the outbreak of war, his first missions involved reconnaissance patrols over the border with France, and after over twenty missions, he had still to encounter the enemy.

In January 1940, Graf was posted to Ergänzungs-Jagdgruppe Merseburg as an instructor and, on 1 May of that year, was finally given his commission as a Leutnant. By October of that same year, he had been posted to an active service unit once again, joining Jagdgeschwader 52 just before his Staffel transferred to Romania with the task of training Romanian pilots. In May 1941, elements of Jagdgeschwader 52 were assigned to the attack on Crete, and Graf flew several missions in support of the German invasion of the island.

Only after the invasion of the Soviet Union did Graf finally shoot down an enemy aircraft. His first victory came on 4 August 1941 when he shot down a Soviet I-16 fighter during the course of a mission designated as support for a Ju 87 dive-bomber attack on the city of Kiev. By October his score had moved into double figures and continued to grow rapidly. By January 1942 he had reached a tally of forty-five kills, and on the 24th of that month was awarded the Knight's Cross of the Iron Cross. Two months later, with his score standing at fifty victories, he was appointed Staffelkapitän of 9./Jagdgeschwader 52.

Graf's score was by now rocketing, and in a period of just three weeks at the end of April, he downed forty-eight enemy aircraft. On 17 May 1942, Graf was awarded the Oakleaves to his Knight's Cross after raising his score to 104 victories. He was only the seventh fighter ace to exceed 100 kills. So rapid had been his accumulation of kills, however, that just two days later, on 19 May, the Swords were added to his Oakleaves, and with the award came a promotion to Oberleutnant. By early September, operating in support of German forces attempting to secure Stalingrad, Graf had raised his score to over 150 kills, and on the 26th of that month, he became the first fighter pilot in history to achieve a score of 200 aerial victories. This achievement also brought him promotion to Hauptmann.

On 16 September 1942 Graf received what was at that time the ultimate accolade for a combat soldier, the award of the coveted Oakleaves with Swords and Diamonds. He was only the fifth recipient of this award. As was common practice at the time, after having been decorated with the 'Diamonds', Graf was considered too valuable an asset to risk losing and was ordered not to fly any more combat missions. Recipients of such high military awards were fêted in the German press and Graf became a famous personality. This was enhanced even further by his being selected to play as a goalkeeper for the Luftwaffe's own football team, the so-called 'Roten Jäger', or Red Hunters.

Graf was subsequently posted to command Ergänzungs-Jagdgruppe Ost in occupied France. Based near Bordeaux, this was a fighter pilot advanced training school. In August 1943 Graf, now a Major, was given command of Jagdgeschwader 50, a high-altitude interceptor unit formed with the intent of countering reconnaissance missions by RAF Mosquito twin-engine fighters. He remained with the unit until October of that year, adding a further three victories to his tally, two of which were not Mosquitos but B-17 four-engine heavy bombers. In November 1943 Graf was appointed Kommodore of Jagdgeschwader 11 with the rank of Oberst. And over the weeks and months to come, despite being officially prohibited from flying combat missions, Graf managed to shoot down six more enemy aircraft.

Graf certainly had no fear of becoming embroiled in the most vicious of dogfights. On one occasion in late March 1944, after

an attack on US bombers, he was engaged by their escorting fighters. After shooting down one P-51 Mustang fighter, having expended his ammunition he promptly rammed another. On 1 October 1944 Graf was appointed Kommodore of his old unit, Jagdgeschwader 52, on the Eastern Front and commanded the Geschwader through the most difficult days of the closing months of the war. He surrendered to American forces at Pisek on 8 May 1945 but was quickly handed over to the Soviets.

Regrettably, after the war, Graf was rather shabbily treated by many of his former comrades in the fighter pilot fraternity. During his captivity in Russia, Graf had taken a pragmatic view, reasoning that the war was over and that there was little point in trying to antagonise his captors. Unlike many of his peers, Graf had witnessed at first hand some Nazi atrocities on the Eastern Front and was badly affected by what he had seen. Having experience of the reality of what the Third Reich stood for, Graf was adamant in his belief that the war had been wrong. Unfortunately, many of his erstwhile comrades equated Graf's behaviour to 'defeatism', and even accused him of being a 'collaborator' and of spying for the Soviets. The reality was somewhat different, as Graf had in fact rejected all advances by the Soviets to try to persuade him to take up a position in the air force of the new, communist East Germany, despite offers of high rank, status and early release from captivity.

After his release in 1949, Graf went into the electronics business, initially as a salesman and later in management, where he built a very successful career. He even returned to sport flying and was a member of the Swiss Aeroclub. Tragically, Graf developed Parkinson's disease in later life. He died on 4 November 1988 in Engen. He had flown well over 830 combat missions and downed a total of 212 enemy aircraft.

HANS-JOACHIM MARSEILLE

Generally regarded as one of the finest fighter pilots Germany produced, Hans-Joachim Marseille was born in Berlin in 1920, of French Huguenot ancestry. He had a less than spectacular beginning to the career which would see him become one of the greatest-ever fighter aces. He missed the opening stages of the war and only joined JG52 during the closing stages of the Battle of Britain. Nevertheless he did manage to score seven victories during that conflict, achieving 'ace' status but only at the expense of being shot down himself four times.

Marseille developed a reputation for indiscipline, with a taste for 'wine, women and song', and is reputed to have been too 'tired' to fly on the morning after some of his wilder excesses. He was also considered 'politically incorrect', growing his hair longer than was the norm in those days, and with a liking for 'degenerate' music, such as jazz and swing. Marseille was also an incorrigible practical joker. To keep him out of trouble, he was posted to JG27, designated for service in North Africa, far from the temptations of occupied France.

His new commanding officer, Edu Neumann, could see great potential in the troublesome ace and gradually encouraged him to train rigorously, improving his flying skills and his marksmanship. Neumann even managed to persuade Marseille to stop drinking alcohol and drink milk instead. He also gradually cut down on the use of sunglasses, allowing his eyes to become accustomed to the bright skies over the Western Desert. He started a vigorous physical fitness regime, intended to give him greater ability to withstand the tremendous 'G' forces experienced by pilots when executing turns at high speed during dogfights. Marseille developed incredible skills as a marksman, using high-angle-deflection firing at very short range while turning sharply. Instead of using his aircraft's gun sight he would wait until the moment when the propeller of the enemy aircraft disappeared from sight behind the nose of his own aircraft and at that moment fire a short burst. He calculated correctly that from this position his rounds would hit the enemy's engine and cockpit area. Constant training perfected his marksmanship.

All Marseille's efforts paid off. On 24 September 1941 he shot down five enemy aircraft. The first victim to his guns came when he spotted a bomber that no one else had noticed and left formation to bag his first 'kill' of the day. Later, when his formation, totalling six Me 109s, intercepted a more powerful force of sixteen Hurricanes, he shot down two with a single burst, turned and attacked again to shoot down a third, and then after the two formations had disengaged, pursued the fleeing British and shot down another.

When attacked, Allied aircraft formed into a defensive circle so that each fighter would cover the tail of the fighter in front. Marseille developed a tactic for breaking this circle which involved diving from well above the enemy, building up tremendous speed, to a point below the enemy, then swooping up and firing from below at his victim. He would then deliberately stall his aircraft, putting it into a spin that the enemy could not follow. Cool nerves and superb flying skills were required, both of which Marseille had in abundance. Other Luftwaffe aces tried to emulate him, but none came near the astonishing level of success that he achieved.

On 22 February 1942 he was decorated with the Knight's Cross, following his fiftieth victory. His most incredible achievement came on 6 June 1942 when he attacked a formation of sixteen Curtiss P-40 fighters. Marseille had been on an escort mission

Oberleutnant Hans-Joachim Marseille had an early reputation as an ill-disciplined joker, but with training and guidance developed into the finest marksman the Luftwaffe ever produced. His accuracy and the low number of rounds fired for each enemy aircraft shot down have never been bettered. Known as the 'Star of Africa', he is seen here, appropriately enough, in the Luftwaffe's tropical service uniform in a portrait shot taken just after the award of the Oakleaves with Swords to the Knight's Cross. (*Josef Charita*)

providing cover for a German bomber formation and at first ignored the fighters and remained with the bombers. The temptation was too much for him, however, and a few minutes later, with only his wingman following, he flew off to attack the enemy. At top speed he engaged the enemy formation, hitting his first victim from a distance of just 50m. By the time this first aircraft hit the ground he was already attacking his fourth victim of the day. Within the space of just eleven minutes he had shot down six of them, five scored within the first five minutes of the action and two of these within 15 seconds of each other. The surviving Allied pilots claimed that they had been attacked by a 'superior enemy force'.

His incredible feats on that day earned him the immediate award of the Oakleaves and, just twelve days later, his score now at over 100, the Swords followed. Multiple victories in a single sortie became commonplace for this virtuoso. On 1 September 1942, seventeen aircraft fell to his guns, eight of them within just ten minutes of combat, and during the course of that month, he added fifty-four victories to his score. On 2 September the award of the Oakleaves with Swords and Diamonds was announced. Along with the decorations had come rapid promotion, and now Marseille, holding the rank of Hauptmann, was promoted to become, at 22, the youngest Major in the Luftwaffe.

In late September a new Bf 109G-2 fighter was delivered for Marseille. Strongly attached to his trusted old machine he refused to fly the new one until ordered to accept the new plane by Generalfeldmarschall Kesselring. On 30 September he took off in his new aircraft, tasked with providing cover for a formation of Ju 87 Stuka dive-bombers. On completion of the mission, the escorts were diverted to intercept a formation of enemy fighters that had been reported. No enemy was encountered but on the return flight his aircraft developed technical problems. The cooling system broke down and his engine caught fire. His cockpit filling with acrid smoke, Marseille persisted with his aircraft until he was back over German-held territory. At this point he could stand the conditions no longer and had no option but to bale out. Turning his aircraft upside down to allow gravity to assist with leaving the plane, he ejected himself from the stricken aircraft. As he did so, he was struck by the tailplane. Knocked unconscious, he was unable to pull the ripcord and thus his parachute did not open. He fell to the ground and was killed instantly.

The loss of Marseille was a tragic blow to his squadron. It was doubly ironic that, having survived so many heated combat actions, he should die accidentally during a sortie in which no enemy was encountered. Marseille was buried with full military honours in the German military cemetery at Derna. In 1989, a monument in his memory was erected there.

Marseille had flown 388 combat missions, during which he had shot down 158 enemy aircraft. Although his final score was beaten by several other Luftwaffe aces as the war went on, no other pilot shot down as many enemy aircraft on the Western Front, where 'kills' were generally accepted as being much harder to achieve than on the Eastern Front. Much scepticism has been voiced over Marseille's victory claims, especially the shooting down of seventeen aircraft on a single day on 1 September 1942. Postwar examination of Allied records, however, shows that losses on this day in the area in which Marseille was operating exceeded this number. Multiple kills in a single day were not unheard of, even among Allied pilots. With Marseille, however, rather than an exception, such achievements were regular enough to be commonplace, and in that he was truly unique. Adolf Galland, General der Jagdflieger, and himself one of the most respected of Luftwaffe aces, said of Marseille, 'He was the unrivalled virtuoso among the fighter pilots of World War 2. His achievements were previously considered impossible.' Marseille was never to receive the Diamonds clasp he had been awarded, meeting his tragic death before he could be recalled to Germany for the formal investiture.

HANS SANDROCK

Hans Sandrock was born in Saarbrücken on 20 April 1913, the son of an official in the Air Ministry. Raised and educated in Berlin, where his father was employed, after completing his schooling he went on to undergo an engineering apprenticeship before taking a four-year course in engineering studies at the Berlin Technical High School.

In 1924, Sandrock volunteered for military service with the Army and was posted to the driving instruction unit at Berlin-Zossen. Within a few months, Sandrock had not only obtained his first promotion, to Gefreiter, but had also been earmarked as a potential officer. As the Army expanded rapidly, Sandrock's unit was absorbed into the new Panzer Regiment 5 and, after successfully completing an officer training course at the Kriegsschule, Hannover, he was commissioned as a Leutnant and returned to his unit to become a platoon commander with 2./Panzer Regiment 5.

Sandrock took part in the occupation of the Sudetenland and, just before the outbreak of war, was promoted to Oberleutnant. During the Polish campaign, on 22 October 1939, he was awarded the Iron Cross Second Class, and to this was later added the Panzer Assault Badge for his participation in the 1940 campaign in the west.

Later that year, Panzer Regiment 5 was removed from its parent unit, 3 Panzer Division, and used to form the nucleus of a new division, 5 Leichte Division. This new unit was despatched to North Africa in March 1941 to serve as part of Rommel's Afrikakorps. It took part in the push on Tobruk, during which Sandrock was awarded the Iron Cross First Class. The division suffered heavy casualties and in the summer of that year was re-formed with 21 Panzer Division, and saw further fierce combat action at the capture of Benghazi, the battles around Gazala and the push towards El Alamein. In February 1942, Sandrock was promoted to the rank of Hauptmann. Further distinction came to Sandrock in June of that year, when he was awarded the German Cross in Gold for repeatedly distinguishing himself in these many battles. In November 1942 Sandrock was severely wounded during the Allied offensive code-named 'Supercharge' and

was evacuated to Germany for hospital treatment.

It was not until July 1943 that Sandrock would be fully recovered from his wounds and, at this point, along with a number of experienced panzer officers from the Army, was posted to III (Sturmgeschütz) Abteilung, Fallschirm Panzer Regiment Hermann Göring, at that time serving in the Mediterranean theatre. Sandrock subsequently served in Sicily before the 'HG' troops were evacuated over the Straits of Messina to the Italian mainland. In December 1943 Sandrock qualified for the Panzer Assault badge for twenty-five engagements with the enemy, and in February 1944 was promoted to the rank of Major.

After Rome fell to the Allies, the 'HG' troops were transferred to the Eastern Front, where they would form part of the reinforcements promised to Generalfeldmarschall Model for his summer offensive. The 'HG' troops fought alongside the Army's 19 Panzer Division and the 5 SS Panzer Division 'Wiking' in a counter-attack that mauled the Soviet III Tank Corps on the approaches to Warsaw. By October of that year, Sandrock and his men were near Radom in Poland, where his Abteilung was responsible for destroying a total of 123 Soviet armoured vehicles which had penetrated into the

Hans Sandrock began his career as an Army officer, transferring to the assault gun detachment of the Hermann Göring Division in 1943. He was awarded the Knight's Cross of the Iron Cross and the Luftwaffe Salver of Honour for actions on the Eastern Front during October 1944. Sandrock, seen here with his pet dog, wears a typical mixed form of dress common in armoured units. The black field cap is for tank crews, while the field-grey uniform is the correct dress for the crews of assault guns.

German lines, thus blocking a Soviet attempt at breaking through the German positions. For this achievement, Sandrock was awarded the Knight's Cross of the Iron Cross. The award was bestowed on 21 October 1944, and with it came the Luftwaffe's Salver of Honour, both presented by General Weidlich, commander of XXXI Panzerkorps.

Sandrock was wounded in action again shortly afterwards and was once again evacuated for hospital treatment. On his release, he joined the reserve units of the 'HG' in Oranienburg, where he spent the final part of the war. After the surrender, Sandrock was captured by the Allies but escaped and made his way back to his family in Bonn. After the war, he became the treasurer of the Association of Knight's Cross Bearers.

ALEXANDER UHLIG

Alexander Uhlig was born near Leipzig on 9 February 1919. On completing his schooling, he joined the Reichsarbeitsdienst for the obligatory period of national labour service, and in 1937 joined the Luftwaffe, where in 1938 he became a paratrooper with the first of Germany's Fallschirmjäger units, seeing service in the occupation of the Sudetenland and the remainder of Czechoslovakia. Uhlig also took part in the Polish campaign and in the invasion of Norway. Dropped at Dombas in April 1940, after some fierce fighting he found himself captured by Norwegian troops. Fortunately for Uhlig, the Germans soon gained the upper hand again and he was released. He was quickly back in the thick of the fighting again and subsequently dropped during the first Battle of Narvik in May 1940. His performance in Norway earned him the Iron Cross Second Class and the Narvik Shield.

After the end of the successful campaign in Norway, Uhlig transferred to flying duties, serving as a navigator, and over the next two years took part in over 170 combat missions, including the invasion of Crete. During this period in his career, Uhlig gained the Iron Cross First Class, the Flight Clasp in Gold, and the Kreta cuff-title, before eventually transferring back to the paratroops.

Following the Allied invasion of Normandy on 6 June 1944, Uhlig found himself in action against US troops of 90th Infantry Division. Fighting was extremely fierce and indeed Fallschirmjäger Regiment 6 had seen its entire 1st Battalion wiped out. On 22 July 1944, the defensive positions of the Fallschirmjäger around St Germain sur Seves came under heavy artillery bombardment, a precursor to a major attack. The German positions were bordered by a river and boggy swampland – difficult terrain for the enemy advance. Nevertheless the Americans made good initial progress, albeit at a heavy cost in casualties.

Alexander Uhlig was in command of 16 Kompanie and at around midday on 22 July was ordered to push back the enemy troops, at first thought to be only a reconnaissance force, and capture some prisoners for interrogation. He soon realised that he was facing a much larger force that was first thought, somewhere around 300 men. Nevertheless, he determined to carry out his task and, with the assistance of a few other German troops he had encountered along the way, he stealthily infiltrated the enemy positions. By late afternoon, Uhlig was in position and launched his attack, driving the enemy back several hundred yards and causing heavy casualties. Uhlig then changed his positions and attacked the enemy from the opposite flank. Bolstered by some additional men from a neighbouring unit and three tanks loaned by the Das Reich division of the Waffen-SS, Uhlig prepared to attack once again. Next morning,

A paratrooper who transferred to flight crew before becoming a paratrooper once again, Alexander Uhlig saw action at Narvik and Crete before winning the Knight's Cross of the Iron Cross in Normandy in 1944.

he was relieved to find that low cloud cover was preventing Allied aircraft from supporting their ground troops.

Just after 0700 on 23 July, Uhlig launched his attack. Unfortunately one of the SS tanks broke down and another became trapped in the ruins of a building through which it had tried to break its way. Uhlig's first two assaults were thrown back but the third broke through the enemy positions and the American troops began to fall back in a panic. Some tried to retreat but were cut down by German machine-gun fire. Many simply gave up and Uhlig was soon faced by large numbers of enemy troops with their hands up. A total force of no more than 50 Germans had attacked and routed a US force of several hundred and taken over 200 prisoners.

Uhlig sent his prisoners back in batches of two dozen or so, with a single Falls-chirmjäger guarding each group. Leaving some men to cover the positions he had just recaptured, Uhlig returned to his regimental command post to report to his commander, Baron Friedrich August von der Heydte. He was heartily congratulated by his commander, who recommended him for the Knight's Cross of the Iron Cross for his stunning achievement, and the award was duly bestowed on 24 October 1944. It is also worth noting that after the battle, von der Heydte chivalrously agreed to a three-hour truce to allow the Americans to recover their wounded, and indeed several Falls-chirmjäger assisted with this task.

Uhlig himself was subsequently captured by troops from the same American division he had so brilliantly defeated. He ended the war in an Allied POW camp and ultimately arrived in the UK. Incredibly, in 1947, he succeeded in escaping from the POW camp in England and managed to stow away on a ship bound for Cuxhaven in Germany, from where he eventually made his way home to Leipzig, then in the Russian-occupied zone. Interestingly, Uhlig's POW records falsely show that he was recaptured. It seems that even though the war had ended, the fact that a German prisoner had escaped from a British POW camp was something the authorities wished to cover up.

After the war, Uhlig became an active member of the Fallschirmjäger Veterans' Association and, in fact, was also made an honorary member of the New Zealand Crete Veterans' Association, testament to the respect in which he was held even by his former enemies. At the time of writing, he is still alive.

CHAPTER THIRTEEN

LUFTWAFFE CAREER STRUCTURE

After the introduction of conscription (Wehrpflicht) in 1935, all German males between the ages of 17 and 25 were required by law to register for military service. Prior to the outbreak of war, a temporary deferment could be obtained if the individual was undergoing an apprenticeship or other training. On reporting for registration, the future soldier would be medically examined and his personal details recorded, including any skills which might be particularly useful to a specific branch of the armed services. If determined to be fit to serve, the soldier would first be issued a military ID book (Wehrpass) and sent home to await his call-up. This ID would be his proof that he had registered for service. When he was called up and reported for duty, his Wehrpass would be withdrawn and retained in his unit records office, to be replaced by a pay and ID book (Soldbuch) with his photo in uniform. This book would record all his unit affiliations, promotions, decorations and much other information.

During wartime, military personnel broadly fell into two categories: 'Auf Kriegsdauer' ('For the duration') and 'Berufsoldat' ('Career soldier'). Those who elected for a career in the military, as opposed to serving solely for the duration of the conflict, were required to contract for a specific term of service. Generally, for enlisted men, the minimum service time was one year, later increased to two. For those who wished to serve as NCOs, a twelve-year service contract was required. To meet increased manpower needs, this was later reduced to four and a half years. Officers were required to contract for a period of service of unlimited duration.

Officers commissioned during wartime (Kriegsoffiziere) could be promoted on the basis that their commission would last until the end of hostilities and only then would a decision be made as to whether they would be accepted as career soldiers. This category included those promoted from NCO rank to commissioned officers during wartime. Such officers were designated as 'der Reserve' and carried the suffix 'd.R.' after their rank.

There were five basic career paths for officers in the Luftwaffe:

Line (covering most active front-line service officers, including flying personnel and paratroops)
Medical
Ordnance (abolished in 1944)
Engineers

Special Service Officers – including administrative officers and judicial officers

Officers were classified into different bands:

d.R. (der Reserve). The official body of reserves, prohibited to Germany under the Treaty of Versailles, was re-created in 1935 and its members adopted the 'd.R.' suffix after their rank title.

z.V. (zur Verfügung). Created in 1938, this suffix indicated that the officer was 'at disposal' and liable to be called for duty at any time.

z.D. (zum Dienst). This suffix indicated that the officer 'at disposal' had now been called 'to duty'.

Both the z.V. and z.D. suffixes were dropped in 1939.

a.D. (ausser Dienst). Officers who had retired from active service were classified as 'a.D.' or 'out of service'.

Supplementary Officers. Officers 'a.D.' who were voluntarily called back for active service were classified as supplementary officers.

Wartime commissions. Officers commissioned during wartime were known as Kriegsoffiziere. They had the same status as career officers but did not have the unlimited service time commitment, it being considered they would probably be demobbed at the end of hostilities.

Officials. Officials (or 'Beamte') were generally expected to serve until normal civilian retirement age (i.e. 65 years). Branches considered as officials included the Corps of Engineers and the Navigation Corps.

CHAPTER FOURTEEN

RANKS AND INSIGNIA

The rank system in the Luftwaffe was based upon that of the German Army. Unlike the RAF, where, to an extent, the rank also described the position within the structure (flight lieutenant, wing commander, group captain, etc.,) in the Luftwaffe, a standard military rank was used, followed by, where necessary, the position of that individual (Hauptmann und Staffelkapitän, Major und Geschwader Kommodore, etc.).

The basic rank structure was as follows (with approximate British equivalents where applicable):

Flieger (generally specific to branch, e.g. Jäger for paratroops, Flieger for flight, Kanonier for artillery, etc.)	Aircraftsman 2nd class
Oberjäger, Oberkanonier, etc.	Senior aircraftsman
Gefreiter	Senior aircraftsman
Obergefreiter	Leading aircraftsman
Stabsgefreiter	Leading aircraftsman
Unteroffizier	Corporal
Unterfeldwebel Feldwebel	Sergeant
Oberfeldwebel	Flight sergeant
Stabsfeldwebel	Warrant officer
Leutnant	Pilot officer
Oberleutnant	Flying officer
Hauptmann	Flight lieutenant
Major	Squadron leader
Oberstleutnant	Wing commander
Oberst	Group captain
Generalmajor	Air commodore
Generalleutnant	Air vice marshal

General (specific to branch, e.g.General der Flieger, etc.)	Air marshal
Generaloberst	Air chief marshal
Generalfeldmarschall	Marshal of the Royal Air Force

Luftwaffe rank structure was displayed by a combination of both shoulder straps and collar patches. For ranks below General, the collar patches were in the colour of the wearer's branch of service, with the same colour used as piping or underlay to the shoulder strap. For most Generals, the collar patch and shoulder strap underlay colour was white. Exceptions to this are noted in the text. Collar patch insignia for the most part consisted of small, stylised wings in white metal for enlisted men and NCOs, and in hand-embroidered wire for officers, combined with embroidered oakleaves where appropriate.

Rank combinations were as follows:

Flieger. Collar tab with single metal wing; plain, piped shoulder straps; no sleeve chevron.

Gefreiter. Collar tab with two metal wings; plain, piped shoulder straps; single chevron on left sleeve.

Obergefreiter. Collar tab with three metal wings; plain, piped shoulder straps; double chevron on left sleeve.

Hauptgefreiter. Collar tab with four metal wings; plain, piped shoulder straps; triple chevron on left sleeve.

Unteroffizier. Collar tab with single metal wing; shoulder strap trimmed in braid 'Tresse' around edges, but not across base.

Unterfeldwebel. Collar tab with two metal wings; shoulder strap trimmed all around in braid 'Tresse'.

Feldwebel. Collar tab with three metal wings; shoulder strap trimmed all around with braid 'Tresse', and with single metal rank star.

Oberfeldwebel. Collar tab with four metal wings; shoulder strap as above, but with two metal rank stars.

Luftwaffe enlisted ranks wore plain field-blue shoulder straps piped in their branch colour. Collar tabs were sewn to the tunic collar with no braid surround. Early tunics had the collar piped in branch-of-service colour as here. Note that there were qualified Luftwaffe pilots with a rank as low as Gefreiter. (*François Saez*)

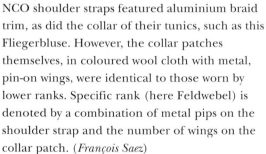

NCO shoulder straps featured aluminium braid trim, as did the collar of their tunics, such as this Fliegerbluse. However, the collar patches themselves, in coloured wool cloth with metal, pin-on wings, were identical to those worn by lower ranks. Specific rank (here Feldwebel) is denoted by a combination of metal pips on the shoulder strap and the number of wings on the collar patch. (*François Saez*)

Officers' collar patches had the rank insignia hand-embroidered in aluminium wire on a cloth base in the branch-of-service colour, and featured a twisted aluminium cord border. Shoulder straps were in bright aluminium braid on a cloth base in branch-of-service colour. The rank illustrated here is Leutnant of Flieger-truppe. (*François Saez*)

Stabsfeldwebel. Collar tab with four metal wings; shoulder strap as above, but with three metal rank stars.

Leutnant. Collar patch with single embroidered wing over small oakleaf cluster; patch trimmed in twisted silver-wire piping; shoulder strap in plain, straight silver-braid cord.

Oberleutnant. Collar patch with two embroidered wings over small oakleaf cluster;

patch trimmed in twisted silver-wire piping; shoulder strap in plain, straight silver-braid cords with single gilt rank star.

Hauptmann. Collar patch with three embroidered wings over small oakleaf cluster; patch trimmed in twisted silver-wire piping; shoulder strap in plain, straight silver-braid cords with two gilt metal rank stars.

Major. Collar patch with single embroidered wing enclosed within oakleaf wreath; patch

This officer wears the special sleeve rank insignia for garments without shoulder straps. A combination of stylised wings and horizontal bars indicates specific rank. Here, the officer is identified as a Hauptmann. (*François Saez*)

trimmed in twisted silver-wire piping; shoulder strap in plaited silver-braid cord.

Oberstleutnant. Collar patch with two embroidered wings enclosed within oakleaf wreath; patch trimmed in twisted silver-wire piping; shoulder strap in plaited silver-braid cord with single gilt metal rank star.

Oberst. Collar patch with three embroidered wings enclosed within oakleaf wreath; patch trimmed in twisted silver-wire piping; shoulder strap in plaited silver-braid cord with two gilt metal rank stars.

Generalmajor. Collar patch with single gold-wire embroidered wing enclosed within oakleaf wreath on white base; patch trimmed in twisted gold-wire piping; shoulder strap in plaited gold/silver braid on white base.

Generalleutnant. Collar patch with two gold-wire embroidered wings enclosed within oakleaf wreath on white base; patch trimmed in twisted gold-wire piping; shoulder strap in plaited gold/silver braid on white base with single large silver rank star.

General. Collar patch with three gold-wire embroidered wings enclosed within oakleaf

This photograph of Generalmajor Ulrich Grauert shows the typical adornments of a General's service tunic. Gold-wire cord surrounds the collar. Collar patches are worked in hand-embroidered gold wire on a white base and the shoulder straps feature intertwined silver and gold braid cord on a white base. Flak Generals would have their insignia embroidered on a red base. Grauert, commanding General of 1 Fliegerkorps, was killed in action on 15 May 1941.

wreath, on white base; patch trimmed in twisted gold-wire piping; shoulder strap in plaited gold/silver braid on white base with two large silver rank stars.

Generaloberst. Collar patch with large gold-wire embroidered Luftwaffe eagle and swastika superimposed on an oakleaf wreath, all on a white base; patch trimmed in twisted gold-wire piping; shoulder strap in plaited gold/silver braid on white base with three silver metal rank stars.

Generalfeldmarschall. Collar patch with large gold-wire embroidered Luftwaffe eagle and swastika superimposed on an oakleaf wreath with crossed marshal's batons, all on white base; patch trimmed in twisted gold-wire piping; shoulder strap in plaited gold/silver braid on white base with metal marshal's batons.

BRANCH OF SERVICE COLOUR (WAFFENFARBE)

The above-noted rank insignia were used in conjunction with a branch-of-service colour. This formed the base for the collar patch and for officers' shoulder straps, and was used as piping on lower ranks' shoulder straps and on lower ranks' headgear.

For conventional Luftwaffe units, these colours were as follows:

Golden yellow	Flight personnel, paratroops
Brown	Signals
Red	Flak artillery
White	Hermann Göring units
Pink	Luftwaffe Engineering Corps
Crimson	General staff
Bordeaux red	Court-martial officials
Dark blue	Medical personnel
Light green	Air traffic control

The Hermann Göring and other field units had their own range of colours based on those used by the Army.

SPECIALISTS

Luftwaffe personnel who had been trained in a particular specialism wore a small, blue-grey cloth patch on their lower left sleeve with a specific insignia embroidered in silver-grey thread as follows:

Flying personnel. A four-bladed propeller with wings emanating from its hub. Worn by flying crew prior to qualification for any of the official qualification badges (pilot, air-gunner, etc.).

Technical personnel. A five-cylinder motor within a wreath of oakleaves, with wings emanating from each side. For those who had achieved an 'outstanding' performance rating, the insignia had a 3mm twisted-gold cord surround.

Medical personnel. A caduceus embroidered on a circular patch.

Ordnance personnel. A silver-grey Gothic letter 'F' (for 'Feuerwerker') on a circular patch.

Admin personnel. A silver-grey 'V' (for 'Verwaltung') on a circular patch.

Equipment administrator. A winged wheel in silver-grey on a circular patch.

Aircraft equipment administrator. A seven-cylinder radial engine with propeller, embroidered on a circular patch.

Searchlight operator. A letter 'T' with a medium-sized ball under either end of the horizontal bar and a larger ball at the base of the vertical bar. A five-fingered ray of light emerges from the right side of the vertical bar.

Air signal equipment operator. A cogwheel, over which is superimposed two crossed lightning bolts.

Air signals personnel. Telephone operators – Two crossed and intertwined lightning bolts.

Teletype operators – Two crossed but not intertwined lightning bolts.

This technical Stabsfeldwebel, another veteran of the Condor Legion as evidenced by the Spanish Cross worn on his right breast, shows the regulation manner for wearing the Luftwaffe trade specialist badge on the left sleeve. (*Jacques Calero*)

oakleaves with swastika below, and with wings emanating from each side of the oakleaf spray.

Rangefinders. A Gothic letter 'E' (for 'Entfernungsmessleute') over a spray of oakleaves sitting atop a swastika, with wings emanating from each side of the spray.

Sound detectors. As above, but with Gothic letter 'H' (for Horcher).

Sound detector insignia could be awarded with a gold-cord border after one year's service if the serviceman had taken part in the successful downing of an enemy aircraft.

Aircraft warning personnel. Two crossed lightning bolts with a small wing superimposed in the centre.

Boat crews. A silver-grey embroidered winged anchor. Worn by crews of, for instance, air-sea rescue launches.

Transport administration. A gothic letter 'S' (for 'Schirrmeister') on a circular patch.

Master radio operator. A vertical lightning bolt, with arrow head at either end, with two similar bolts crossed at its centre at a 45-degree angle.

Radio maintenance personnel. A curved propeller superimposed on a lightning bolt with arrowhead at either end.

Farriers. A silver-grey embroidered horseshoe on a circular patch.

Aerial bomb armourers (light). A small, silver-grey grenade with a six-fingered flame emanating from its top.

Aerial bomb armourers (heavy). As above, but also with an additional five-fingered flame emanating from each side of the grenade.

Radio operators – A serrated horizontal bar with two pairs of crossed lightning bolts.

Directional radio operators – As above, but over the letter 'P' (for 'Peilfunker').

Sound location operators – As above, but over the letter 'H' (for 'Horchfunker').

Signals personnel – Flieger and Flak branches. A single, downward-pointing lightning bolt.

Armourers. Two crossed silver-grey rifles on a circular patch.

Flak armourers. Two crossed cannon barrels on a circular patch.

Drivers. Luftwaffe-style flying eagle superimposed on a vehicle radiator. A twisted gold-cord border was worn for distinguished performance.

Flak artillery. A flak gun with raised barrel pointing to upper right, sitting on a spray of

SHOULDER-STRAP CYPHERS

The following cyphers were either embroidered directly into junior ranks' shoulder straps, or pinned as metal cyphers on to senior NCOs' and officers' straps.

Most relate to various training schools and other, similar establishments. The majority were in a fairly elaborate Latin script, though a few were in Gothic (indicated in the following list by a 'G').

W	Waffenoffiziere	Ordnance officers L)
KS	Kriegsschule	War School (L)
KA	Kriegsakademie	War Academy (L)
L	Lehr	Instructional units(L)
UVS	Unteroffizier Verschule	NCO Preparatory School (L)
US	Unterführerschule	NCO School (L)
TA	Lufttechnisches Akademie	Air Technical Academy (L)
SS	Sportschule	Sports School
KRS	Kraftfahrschule	Motor Transport School
WS	Waffenmeisterschule	Ordnance School
FS	Feuerwerkerschule	Ordnance School
NS	Nachrichtenschule	Signals School
F	Festungsartillerie	Fortress Artillery
FAS	Festungsartillerieschule	Fortress Artillery School
A	Ärztliche Akademie	Medical Academy (G)
Lyre	Musicians	
Caduceus	Medical personnel	
Sword	Justice personnel	
Mercury staff	Admin personnel	

CUFFBANDS

A number of distinctive cuffbands were authorised for Luftwaffe personnel. These tended to fall into three broad categories: honour titles, commemorative titles and branch-of-service titles. Honour titles were bestowed on various units which carried the title to honour an individual, a battle or a formation. Luftwaffe cuff-titles, unless otherwise indicated, were worked on a deep-blue cloth base, in machine-embroidered (or, more rarely, hand-embroidered) silver-grey yarn for lower ranks and hand-embroidered silver wire for officers, with the text in Gothic script.

Those bestowed included:

HONOUR TITLES

Jagdgeschwader Richthofen
Worn by members of Jagdgeschwader 2 to commemorate the memory of Baron Manfred von Richthofen, the famed 'Red Baron' of the First World War. It was introduced in March 1935.

Jagdgeschwader Mölders
Worn by members of Jagdgeschwader 51. The band was introduced in December 1941 when the Geschwader was named in honour of Werner Mölders.

Geschwader Boelcke
Worn by members of Kampfgeschwader 27 to commemorate the memory of First World

Unit cuffbands were worn by Luftwaffe personnel on the lower right sleeve with considerable pride. Shown here are machine-embroidered lower ranks' examples for Jagdgeschwader 3 'Udet', Jagdgeschwader 51 'Mölders' and Zerstörergeschwader 26 'Horst Wessel'.

This Major from Jagdgeschwader 51 wears the Jagdgeschwader Mölders cuffband on the right sleeve. The band on his left sleeve is the commemorative title for those who took part in the campaign in North Africa for a minimum of six months. Note that his Fliegerbluse does not bear officer piping to the collar, a common omission in the second half of the war. (*François Saez*)

War fighter ace Oswald Boelcke. It was introduced in May 1935.

Jagdgeschwader Udet

Worn by members of Jagdgeschwader 3 in honour of Ernst Udet. The band was introduced in December 1941.

Jagdgeschwader Schlageter

Worn by members of Jagdgeschwader 26 in memory of Albert Leo Schlageter, one of the heroes of the early days of the Nazi Party movement. The band was introduced in December 1938.

Geschwader Hindenburg

Worn by members of Kampfgeschwader 1 in memory of Feldmarschall Paul von Hindenburg. It was introduced in April 1936.

Geschwader Horst Wessel

Worn by members of Zerstörergeschwader 26 in memory of Horst Wessel, one of the early 'martyrs' of the Nazi Party, murdered by communists in 1930. It was introduced in March 1936.

Geschwader Immelmann

Introduced in March 1935, this band was worn by members of Schlachtgeschwader 2 to honour the memory of First World War ace Max Immelmann.

Geschwader General Wever

Worn by members of Kampfgeschwader 4 in

Having removed his Fliegerbluse, this junior-ranking observer from Kampfgeschwader 53 'Condor Legion' has neatly laid out the tunic so that his unit cuffband, an item worn with great pride by members of units so distinguished, can be clearly seen. Also of interest is the metal Observer Badge, or Beobachterabzeichen, which can be seen just above the pocket at bottom right. (*François Saez*)

honour of the first chief of staff of the Luftwaffe, who had been killed in a plane crash. It was introduced in June 1936.

Tannenberg

Worn by members of Aufklärungsgruppe 10 to commemorate the victorious Battle of Tannenberg in 1914. It was introduced in September 1939.

Legion Condor

Worn by members of Kampfgeschwader 53, Flak Regiment 9 and Luftnachricht-enregiment 3 to commemorate the achievements of the Condor Legion during the Spanish Civil War. It was introduced in June 1939.

COMMEMORATIVE TITLES

Jagdgeschwader Frhr. v. Richthofen Nr 1. 1917/18

Worn by those who had served in the famed 'Richthofen's Flying Circus' of the First World War.

Jagdstaffel Boelcke Nr 2. 1916/18

Worn by those who had served in Jagdstaffel Nr 2 in the First World War.

BRANCH OF SERVICE/FORMATION TITLES

Afrika

Introduced in February 1942 and worn by those serving with Luftwaffe units in North

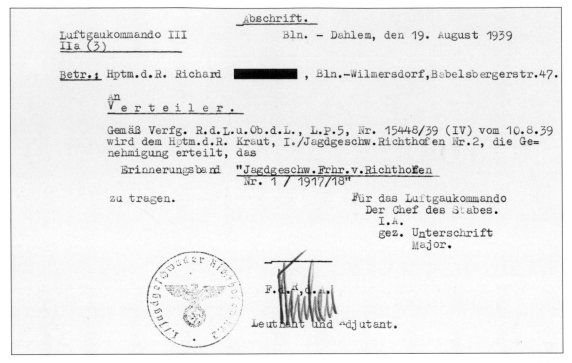

A very rare official document addressed to a Hauptmann der Reserve, and veteran of the First World War, giving authorisation to wear the commemorative cuffband 'Jagdgeschwader Frhr. v. Richthofen Nr.1 1917/18'. (*Thomas Huss*)

Africa. It was only to be worn when the soldier's unit was actually serving in North Africa, and removed when the unit returned to Europe. It could be worn in Europe by soldiers on home leave from a unit serving in North Africa, however. The text was in block Latin script.

Kriegsberichter der Luftwaffe

Introduced in November 1940, this band was worn by members of the Luftwaffe's war correspondent units.

Feldgendarmerie

Worn by members of the Military Police serving with Luftwaffe ground units. Machine-woven with pale-grey Gothic script and edging on a mid-brown band, identical to the pattern worn by Military Police of the Army.

Führerhauptquartier

Worn by Luftwaffe personnel when on attachment at Hitler's headquarters.

General Göring

Introduced in March 1936, this band was in Gothic script, and was worn by members of Regiment General Göring.

Hermann Göring

Introduced in May 1942 in Gothic script for the Brigade Hermann Göring, then in block Latin script, worn by members of Brigade, and later Division, Hermann Göring. Examples also exist on black backing, intended for wear with the black panzer uniform. NCO examples may be found with silver-grey braid edging.

CHAPTER FIFTEEN

UNIFORMS, SPECIALIST CLOTHING AND EQUIPMENT

The Luftwaffe used a huge variety of different uniforms and to cover them in detail would require a massive work in its own right. Only the most common types of uniform that will be encountered in the wartime photos that accompany this text are therefore covered here, with a basic description. For those wishing to study the subject in greater depth, reference to the works listed in the Bibliography is recommended.

The basic service dress uniforms adopted by the Luftwaffe were those of the DLV (Deutsche Luftsport Verband). This organisation had surreptitiously been training future Luftwaffe fliers under the guise of a sporting association prior to the formal creation of the new air force in 1935. The DLV in turn had modelled its uniforms closely on those of the Royal Air Force.

The first regulation service dress for all ranks of the Luftwaffe, though with different adornments according to rank, was the standard four-pocket, open-necked service tunic. It was fastened by four aluminium buttons and had pleated patch pockets on the breast and skirt of the garment, normally with straight-cut flaps. The tunic is seen here worn by Leutnant Hoffmann of Jagdgeschwader 52. (*François Saez*)

The basic service dress consisted of a blue-grey (known as Feldblau, or field blue, as opposed to the Feldgrau, or field grey, of the Army) four-pocket tunic with open collar, worn with a white shirt and black tie.

For shirt-sleeve order during summer months, a blue-grey cotton shirt was provided. This could be worn with or without shoulder straps and, if national insignia were used at all, would most often feature a regular, machine-embroidered, enlisted ranks' breast eagle. It was normally worn open at the neck, but with a decoration such as the Knight's Cross, shown here, it would be fastened. (*François Saez*)

The four-pocket tunic was rapidly superseded in popularity on the introduction of the comfortable Fliegerbluse. The officers' version, usually in finer-quality material, was often worn with a shirt and tie. As seen here, NCOs and lower ranks generally wore their Fliegerbluse without a shirt for normal everyday use. Also note that the officer at centre and NCO at right wear embroidered versions of their qualification badges (for pilot and radio operator respectively). (*François Saez*)

The tunic featured four exterior patch pockets (two breast pockets and two on the skirt) with button-down flaps and four-button front fastening. Buttons were plain pebbled aluminium or zinc. On the right breast was worn the flying eagle and swastika of the Luftwaffe, usually in machine embroidery for lower ranks and hand-embroidered wire for officers.

Officers' tunic collars were piped in twisted silver aluminium wire cord (gold for Generals) and in Waffenfarbe colour for lower ranks. The tunic was worn with blue-grey, straight-legged trousers and black shoes. Blue-grey breeches with jackboots could also be worn by officers.

THE FLIEGERBLUSE

In 1935 a smart new jacket was introduced for flying crew. Known as the Fliegerbluse, or flying blouse, it was a single-breasted jacket with concealed button fastening at the front. No breast pockets were fitted and although early examples were pocketless, later issues from 1940 onwards had internal skirt pockets, with or without an external flap. Cuffs were adjustable by means of a button-down strap and the collar could also be worn fastened up at the neck. Officer versions had twisted-cord wire piping to the collar and early examples for lower ranks often had Waffenfarbe-colour piping. This collar piping was omitted from later examples.

Although designated as a 'flier's blouse', it became so popular that it was widely worn throughout the entire Luftwaffe, not just by flight personnel. It was to have been replaced by the Waffenrock, but although a permitted 'wear-out' period was intended, it remained in production throughout the war.

SUMMER DRESS

A white summer uniform of similar cut and style to the regular blue-grey service dress was also created. In lightweight cotton, all buttons and insignia were removable to facilitate cleaning. This uniform would be worn with the white-top version of the peaked cap described later. Although a full white uniform was produced, photographs show that occasionally the blue-grey jacket was worn with white trousers, and vice versa.

THE WAFFENROCK

In 1938 a Luftwaffe Waffenrock tunic was introduced. This was a four-pocket tunic,

The Fliegerbluse could also, as shown here with an Unteroffizier from IV./Schlachtgeschwader 9, be worn in combination with a woollen pullover in colder weather. Note the Geschwader emblem being worn on the lapel. (*François Saez*)

but unlike the early service dress tunic, it could be buttoned up to the neck. It was intended that this tunic should replace both the earlier four-pocket tunic and the Fliegerbluse. Although the four-pocket tunic was to a great extent replaced by this newer garment, it never did replace the Fliegerbluse, which remained intensely popular right through the war.

FORMAL DRESS UNIFORM

Officers wore, for formal occasions, a uniform consisting of long field-grey trousers, a white shirt, a blue-grey vest or waistcoat, and a short, blue-grey evening jacket. The jacket featured silver piping to the collar (gold for Generals), regulation shoulder straps and a hand-embroidered breast eagle. The jacket had two rows of five purely decorative buttons, and was fastened by a small chain linking to smaller buttons. The waistcoat was grey-blue for regular dress occasions, and fastened by five small aluminium buttons. For more formal occasions, a white waistcoat was worn. The straight-legged trousers featured a strip of aluminium braid over the other leg seam (gold braid for Generals) and were worn with black shoes.

UNDRESS TUNIC FOR GENERALS

A special blue-grey, double-breasted undress tunic for officers of General rank was introduced in 1935. The jacket, based on a design used by the Imperial German forces of the Kaiser's day, had a double row of three gilt aluminium buttons, the top pair of which were purely decorative. The collar was piped in twisted gold cord and the jacket was worn with a gold-wire-embroidered breast eagle and full rank insignia. The facings to the lapels, as well as piping to the front edge of the jacket and

the cuffs, were in branch-of-service colour. For the majority of Generals, this was white, but some other specialists had their own colour (Generals of the Luftwaffe Corps of Engineers wore pink facings and piping). This jacket was worn with straight-legged trousers which carried piping down the outer leg seam, this piping being flanked on either side by broad stripes or 'Lampassen' in the appropriate colour.

GREATCOATS

Luftwaffe personnel were issued with a double-breasted, blue-grey, wool greatcoat. It was provided with two rows of four pebbled aluminium buttons, the top two generally being left unbuttoned with the collar pressed open. To the rear was a half-belt fastened with two buttons, and a long vent, from waist to skirt, could be fastened closed with a further six buttons. Two skirt pockets were provided, with exterior flaps. Rank was displayed predominantly by the shoulder strap, collar patches being equally likely to be omitted as worn.

Generals' greatcoats featured gilt buttons and white facings to the lapels (with some exceptions, e.g. pink facings for engineering Generals, dark blue for medical, dark green for administrative, crimson for judicial and Bordeaux red for court-martial branches).

Leather greatcoats were extremely popular with many Luftwaffe officers, usually in black or blue-grey leather and cut in similar style to the regular greatcoat. Privately purchased greatcoats were often fitted with fur collars at the owner's expense.

TROPICAL UNIFORMS

Luftwaffe personnel in tropical areas such as the Mediterranean countries and North Africa were issued with a lightweight golden-

The Luftwaffe greatcoat is shown here being worn by an Oberfeldwebel of Flakartillerie in command of an 8.8cm flak gun. Note that, unlike those of the Army, Luftwaffe greatcoats were worn with collar patches, in this case complete with NCO braid along the forward and lower edges of the patch. Also of interest in this shot is the (unofficial) use of the edelweiss insignia of the Army's mountain troops as a unit emblem. (*Josef Charita*)

The basic tropical uniform worn by Luftwaffe personnel included a four-pocket, open-neck tunic very similar in styling to that worn with the regular blue uniform. Cut in tan-coloured lightweight cotton, it was usually worn without collar patches, the only insignia being the breast eagle and shoulder straps to indicate rank.

tan-coloured cotton uniform from early 1941. The jacket was in similar cut to the service dress, with four patch pockets, open collar and four-button front fastening. As with the white summer jacket, all buttons were removable, though for lower ranks the machine-embroidered breast eagle was machine-stitched to the tunic. Officers had the option of wearing a pin-on metal breast eagle, though many used the regular other-ranks version. Removable shoulder straps were also worn. Trousers teamed with this jacket were of the same material and of

loose, baggy cut, intended to be worn with ankle boots or shoes.

FLYING CLOTHING

A wide range of different types of flying clothing was produced for flight crews, of which the majority fell into three categories:

Lightweight summer flying suit.
This consisted of a one-piece, 'step-in' combination made from lightweight tan-coloured cotton. It was of a loose, comfort-

The lightweight summer flying suit is being worn here by Leutnant Heinz Fischer, together with the mesh flying helmet of the type with provision for earphones. (*Thomas Huss*)

A Focke Wulf 190 pilot wearing the lightweight flying suit with canvas helmet and oxygen mask. (*Josef Charita*)

These flight crew members wear the lightweight summer flying suit with canvas helmet. The helmet has earphones and also attachments for the oxygen mask. (*François Saez*)

able fit over the blue-grey uniform, and fastened by a diagonal zip running from the neck down to the left hip. Pockets were provided on front of the upper leg. Accompanying the lightweight flying suit was a summerweight flying helmet, made from linen. Two basic lightweight types were manufactured (although there were several variants): one without provision for earphones for crews of aircraft without radio communications (e.g. gliders), and one with provision for earphones and throat microphones. Both types had an attachment to take an oxygen mask. An even-lighter variant, where the body of the helmet was made of simple, lightweight mesh, was produced for use in tropical climates.

Heavy winter flying suit for flying over land.
This suit was made from heavy, fleece-lined, blue-grey material with a black sheepskin fur collar. It was also zip-fastened and featured pockets on the front upper leg. As with the lightweight suit, an appropriate helmet was made to go with this flying suit. It, too, was manufactured both with and without provision for headphones. The winter helmet was usually made from brown goatskin leather with a fleece lining. Both types had provision for the attachment of an oxygen mask.

Heavy winter flying suit for flying over water.
Similar in style to the previous suit, this clothing was also fleece-lined but was made from brown calfskin leather.

The leather flying helmet being worn with oxygen mask. Note that this pattern of helmet has three, rather than two, fittings for the oxygen mask, one at either side and one on the forehead.

One of the most common flight jerkins seen in photographs from the early part of the war is the lightweight, cream-cotton version with knitted collar. Despite the regularity with which it is encountered in period photos, it would seem that very few have survived the war and this is now one of the rarest items of Luftwaffe clothing, with only a small number known to exist. (*François Saez*)

In addition to the winter flying suits, an electrically heated body warmer was provided, worn over the uniform but under the winter flying suit. This body warmer drew its electrical power from the aircraft's own power supply.

Aircrew were also supplied with flying boots. These leather boots were fleece-lined and had a zip fastening to the outside of the shaft and a small, buckled belt fitting to the top.

In some cases, the crews of larger aircraft, such as bombers, wore steel helmets when in action. The regular Luftwaffe-issue steel helmet was often used, sometimes worn back to front, though later in the war a special steel helmet designed specifically for aircrew was developed, with large cut outs at the side to accommodate the headphones on the flying helmet worn under the steel helmet.

One of the most popular forms of clothing was the flier's jerkin. An extremely wide range of patterns was produced and in a variety of colours. Some had fur collars, others plain leather collars. Some were made from lightweight cream fabric, the majority from black leather, though blue-grey and brown leather were also used. Most had zip front fastening and often zip fastenings to pockets. In some cases, insignia (normally only shoulder straps, but sometimes also the Luftwaffe eagle on the right breast) were worn, but as often as not they were omitted.

A two-piece flying suit was also developed sometime in 1943 and known to the Germans as the 'Kanal', or 'Channel', suit.

Left: Flying jerkins in black leather were also extremely popular. They could be worn completely without insignia, as at left here, with shoulder straps showing rank, as at right, and sometimes also with the national emblem on the chest. As can be seen from the flapped versus zipped pockets on the two shown here, there were a number of variants.

The heavyweight, fleece-lined winter flying suit in blue-grey with black sheepskin collar. Note also the fleece-lined flying boots and the fact that a holstered pistol is being worn. (*François Saez*)

Flying jackets in sheepskin were also popular. This example bears the special rank insignia for jackets without shoulder straps and features a dark brown or black fleece collar. The rank shown is Hauptmann and, assuming the aircraft is his own, its markings identify him as on the staff of 1 Gruppe of his Geschwader. (*François Saez*)

This fighter pilot, Horst Oberländer of Jagdgeschwader 5, emerging from the cockpit of his Messerschmitt Me 109, wears the inflatable lifejacket. Note also the flare cartridges strapped to the leg of his 'Kanalhose' trousers. Oberländer was killed in action when his aircraft crashed into the sea in July 1943. (*Josef Charita*)

Paratroops were issued with a one-piece, step-in coverall smock, initially plain but later in splinter-pattern camouflage material. It went over the tunic or Fliegerbluse and is shown here being worn by members of a Fallschirmjäger military police unit in Normandy in the summer of 1944. Note also the Fallschirmjäger-pattern steel helmets. (*Josef Charita*)

In blue-grey wool, it consisted of a jerkin with elasticated, knitted waistband, zip front and a single breast pocket on the left side, together with matching trousers which were visually distinctive in having large bellows-type pockets on the front of each leg and a pistol pocket on the side of the right leg. The inside of each lower leg had a zip fastening so that the trousers could easily be pulled on over the regulation-issue fleece-lined flying boots.

SPECIAL CLOTHING FOR GROUND TROOPS

Not surprisingly given the large number of ground troops which formed part of the Luftwaffe, a wide range of specialist clothing was provided for these soldiers, the most important of which were as follows:

THE PARATROOPER SMOCK

Colloquially known as the 'bone sack', this was a one-piece, 'step-in' garment worn over the regular blue-grey uniform. The original pattern was a simple garment with two long, heavy-duty zips running diagonally from either side of the wearer's throat down to the hem. It had no pockets, but zipped openings either side of the skirt allowed access to the pockets of the tunic worn underneath. A second pattern had a single heavy-duty zip fastening to the front, and was provided with two horizontal skirt pockets and two diagonal breast pockets, all zip-fastened. It was also made from a grey-green gabardine material. A third pattern was produced in so-called 'splinter' camouflage patterns. This version was no longer a step-in garment but had button fastenings on the skirt which allowed it to be gathered between the legs and fastened to form 'legs'. The national emblem was machine-sewn to the right breast and a range of

special insignia comprising a combination of stylised wings and bars machine-sewn to the sleeves in place of the regular collar patches and shoulder straps, which would not have been suitable for wear on such a garment.

Special trousers were produced for wear by paratroopers. These were cut from field-grey wool, with button-down flapped pockets to the side and hips. A pocket was provided to the side of the right knee to accommodate the 'gravity knife' issued to paratroopers.

Paratroops were also issued with special jump boots. The first type was distinctive in being side-lacing with a relatively long shaft. They had leather uppers and moulded rubber soles. A second pattern, introduced in 1940, was more conventional form, front lacing and had a slightly shorter shaft. This type featured leather uppers and leather soles, which were usually set with studs in the same manner as jackboots and ankle boots worn by other troops.

THE CAMOUFLAGED FIELD JACKET

Manufactured for wear by members of the various Luftwaffe field divisions, this was a three-quarter-length jacket cut from camouflaged cotton material and introduced in 1942. It was single-breasted with five-button fastening and had two skirt pockets with button-down flaps. It carried the Luftwaffe eagle machine-sewn to the right breast. Collar patches were not fitted, and although shoulder straps could be worn, these too were often omitted.

Pull-over smocks in camouflage material, complete with matching trousers, were also produced and were intended for wear over the top of the normal wool uniform. These appear only ever to have been issued in very limited numbers, however, the field jacket being much more widely used.

WAFFEN-SS CAMOUFLAGED CLOTHING

The Hermann Göring Division acquired limited stocks of Waffen-SS-issue camouflaged clothing for distribution to its troops in 1942. These were predominantly the SS-pattern smock and the camouflaged helmet cover which were worn by numerous sub-units until the following year, when they were replaced by camouflaged clothing in the regular Wehrmacht 'splinter' patterns.

The smock was a pull-over garment with elasticated cuffs and waist and a lace-up front opening. Two flapped slits at the side of the garment gave access to the uniform worn under the smock. The smock was originally intended to be a loose-fitting garment worn over the belt, ammunition pouches, etc., but was almost exclusively worn over the uniform, with the belt, pouches and any other accoutrements worn over the smock.

The SS-pattern helmet cover was cut from similar material to the smock. It had a 'lip' on the front which hooked over the brim of the helmet and was then held at the sides and rear by spring-loaded alloy clips.

THE ARMOURED VEHICLE UNIFORM

Tank crews from the Hermann Göring Division wore a black wool jacket and trousers almost identical in style to those worn by tank troops of the Army. The principal difference was the Luftwaffe-style eagle machined to the right breast and the use of white for piping to the collar, collar patches and shoulder straps as appropriate, rather than the pink used by the Army. Two main styles of collar patch were used. Either a black rhombus with aluminium skull and white piping, or a plain white patch of the same size and shape as regular Luftwaffe collar patches, but with a white metal skull rather than the typical 'wings'. In some cases the metal death's head was pinned directly to the collar without the use of a collar patch. The earliest Luftwaffe black uniforms were worn along with a leather crash helmet which was covered by a black wool beret bearing a Luftwaffe eagle over the national cockade.

A field-grey version of this uniform was to be worn by crews of armoured vehicles

The Luftwaffe version of the black clothing for armoured personnel was based on the existing Army model, but had the Luftwaffe national emblem on the right breast and white, rather than pink, piping to the collar and collar patches. It is worn here by Oberleutnant Karl Rossmann as commander of 16./Flak-Regiment 'General Göring'. (*Josef Charita*)

The four-pocket M43-style field blouse for Luftwaffe ground forces is seen here being worn by a member of the Feldgendarmerie troop of the Hermann Göring Division serving on the Eastern Front.

other than tanks, and it is believed that some of these were in fact dyed field blue to be more in keeping with their use by Luftwaffe units.

It is known from photographic evidence that, in rare cases, a black leather version of the armoured vehicle uniform was also worn within the Hermann Göring Division. In this case no collar patches were fitted and the metal death's head panzer insignia were simply pinned directly on to the collar.

THE M43-STYLE FIELD BLOUSE

A field blouse styled very closely on the M43 field blouse of the Army was also issued to Luftwaffe ground combat units. It was single-breasted with four patch pockets and could be worn closed at the neck. No collar patches were to be worn with this uniform. The Luftwaffe eagle was machine-sewn over the right breast pocket, and shoulder straps were worn to indicate rank. Similar to late-war M43 tunics of the Army, these were often of field-grey wool with a distinctly brownish shade.

HEADGEAR

The service dress uniform was worn with a peaked cap with blue-grey top, black woven mohair band and shiny black leather or 'Vulkanfiber' peak, the edge of which was bound in leather. On rare occasions it may be encountered with a softer, pliable leather peak. Officer caps had silver aluminium braid piping to crown and band (gold for Generals) while lower ranks' caps were piped in Waffenfarbe colour. Officer caps

had braided chin cords while lower ranks' caps had leather chin-straps.

Insignia consisted of a Luftwaffe flying eagle and swastika on the front of the crown and a national-colours cockade surrounded by a winged oakleaf wreath on the front of the band. The insignia was in metal for lower ranks and hand-embroidered wire for officers. These caps were also produced in a version with a lightweight white cotton top replacing the blue-grey top for summer dress.

In 1935 a new cap, known as the Flieger-mütze, was introduced, analogous to the Feldmütze worn by Army troops. Based on a design used by the DLV, it was cut in blue-grey wool (or in some cases better-quality cloth such as Trikot for officers) and was shaped, when flat, somewhat like an up-turned boat, leading to its common name of 'Schiffchen' (little boat). A national-colours cockade was worn on the front of the flap, with above this a Luftwaffe-style flying eagle

Left: This Leutnant of Fliegertruppe wears an unaltered and rather elegant officer's visored service cap, still retaining its stiffening wire to the brim, as issued. Piping to the crown and band, and all insignia, is in aluminium wire. No branch-of-service colour was used on officers' caps. (*François Saez*)

The officers' version of thc Fliegermütze featured aluminium-braid piping to the edge of the flap. Some had hand-embroidered insignia but many, like the example shown here, used simple enlisted ranks' machine-embroidered cotton insignia. (*François Saez*)

This radio-operator Unteroffizier wears the NCOs' and enlisted ranks' version of the visor cap. Note the stamped metal insignia, leather chin-strap and branch-of-service colour piping to the crown and band. (*François Saez*)

and swastika. Officers' caps were piped along the edge of the flap in woven aluminium braid (gold for Generals). Insignia was machine-embroidered. Although hand-embroidered wire insignia were manufactured for officers, many officer caps used the regular other-ranks machine-embroidered insignia. This cap was also manufactured in black for wear by the crews of Luftwaffe armoured vehicles and in lightweight black cotton for wear by ground crew mechanics, the latter version without a national cockade.

In 1943, a new field cap, the Einheitsfeldmütze, was introduced. This cap, styled after the mountain cap worn by alpine units, featured drop-down side flaps to give protection to the side and back of the head in cold weather, these being fastened by one or two buttons at the front, and a cloth-covered peak. Officer caps were piped around the crown in aluminium braid (gold for Generals). Insignia could consisted of separate eagle and national cockade emblems, or could have these machine-embroidered on to a single trapezoid-shaped piece of cloth. As well as being issued in field blue, this style of cap was also used in black by Luftwaffe tank crews and in field grey by some ground combat units.

TROPICAL HEADGEAR

A number of special items of headgear were produced for wear in tropical climes. These included a version of the Fliegermütze manufactured from golden-tan-coloured lightweight cotton, and a peaked field cap in similar material. This latter piece was very similar in style to the well-known Army

The officer at right in this shot wears the M43-style Einheitsfeldmütze with aluminium-braid officer piping to the crown. Not often seen worn by flying personnel, who seemed to prefer the Fliegermütze, it was, however, extensively used by members of the various ground combat units of the Luftwaffe. (*François Saez*)

The tropical visored field service cap, known to the troops as the 'Hermann Meyer' cap, worn here by members of the Hermann Göring Division in Sicily in 1943. Although it is not shown here, the cap could also be fitted with a neck flap at the rear to protect the wearer's neck from the tropical sun. Original examples of these caps are rare and have been widely copied.

version worn by troops of the Afrikakorps. Officer versions of the former had aluminium braid piping to the flap, and of the latter to the crown.

One of the most distinctive pieces of tropical headgear used by the Luftwaffe was the so-called 'Hermann Meyer' cap. This was a disparaging title aimed at Göring for his boast that if a single enemy bomber ever succeeded in bombing Germany, 'you can call me Meyer'. Similar in basic design to the visor cap, it was made from golden-tan-coloured cotton and came complete with leather chin-strap. It featured insignia also of a similar design to that on the visor cap, with the winged, wreathed cockade on the band, but in machine-woven grey silk on tan. It was also provided with an optional neck flap to give protection to the back of the head, though this seems only rarely to have been fitted. Originals of this cap are extremely rare and highly sought after by collectors, which has of course led to their being widely, and quite accurately, reproduced.

A tropical sun helmet was also produced for the Luftwaffe. Made from cork and covered with canvas panels, it was produced predominantly in a golden tan colour but versions covered in blue-grey canvas and green canvas are also known.

THE STEEL HELMET

Steel helmets issued to regular Luftwaffe units were identical in style and construction to those used by the Army, but were finished in a grey-blue paint finish and bore a Luftwaffe-style flying eagle decal on the left side and a national-colours tricolour shield on the right. The national-colours shield was dropped in 1940, and the eagle emblem around 1943.

Paratrooper units wore their own unique version of the steel helmet, lacking the flared neck protection to the side and rear and having the liner with its much more robust chin-strap system held in place by bolts rather than the small split pins used on the regular helmet. Original paratrooper helmets are extremely rare and have been widely reproduced.

EQUIPMENT

BELTS AND BUCKLES

Lower ranks wore a leather belt (webbing for tropical areas) with a rectangular metal buckle on which was a horizontal oval wreath of laurel enclosing a Luftwaffe flying eagle and swastika. The buckle was normally silver-coloured (and could be natural silver-coloured alloys such as aluminium or nickel) or painted steel but for field use was available with a dull blue-grey painted finish, or a dull olive-coloured paint finish for tropical areas. The leather belt was initially made from brown leather but later changed to black, as for the Army. Accompanying leather equipment such as bayonet frogs, equipment straps, etc. were available in the same materials as the belt, i.e. brown or black leather, or webbing.

For normal everyday use, officer ranks wore a brown leather belt with an open-frame rectangular double-claw buckle. For ceremonial occasions, however, a belt made from woven aluminium brocade was used. This belt was in silver-coloured thread with a narrow, central red stripe flanked by wider black stripes. The buckle in this case was identical to the central design of the lower-ranks buckle, an oval wreath of laurel with a Luftwaffe-style eagle and swastika in the centre. The eagle was manufactured separately from the buckle and attached by one or more rivets or prongs. For officers, the buckle featured a gold eagle on a silver field, for Generals a silver eagle on a gold-coloured buckle.

SIDEARMS

The standard sidearm for lower ranks was the bayonet, or Seitengewehr S 84/98. This was an identical weapon to that used by the other branches of the armed forces. In blued steel, with black bakelite plastic, or brown wooden grip plates, it was worn in a blued-steel scabbard, suspended from a brown leather (or webbing) frog. For formal occasions it was worn with a decorative 'Tassel', or knot, made in a series of colours which indicated the wearer's unit affiliation.

Higher-quality parade bayonets were available as private purchase items. These had nickel-plated blades and hilt fittings. Grip plates were generally in a chequered-finish black plastic but were also available in staghorn. These bayonets were carried in a black-painted scabbard and were available with a range of decorative etchings, all at extra cost.

This Luftwaffe Feldwebel wears two rows of aluminium braid on each sleeve, indicating his status as the senior NCO of his unit, or 'Der Spiess', and carries the first-pattern Luftwaffe dagger, or Fliegerdolch, with portepee.

This Stabsgefreiter wears the winged-propeller sleeve emblem of flying personnel, indicating his position as a member of aircrew. Note that, although he wears the Fliegerdolch, his low rank does not allow the portepee to be worn with it.
(*Jaques Calero*)

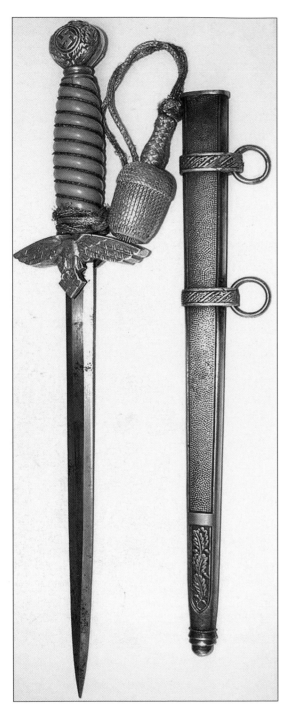

The second-pattern Luftwaffe dagger, introduced in 1938 with stylised Luftwaffe flying eagle as its crossguard. The grips may be encountered in colours ranging from white through yellow to deep orange. (*Detlev Niemann*)

For formal dress wear, a dagger was produced. There are two principal variants, the first of which, known as the Fliegerdolch, was introduced in 1934 and modelled closely on the dagger worn by members of the Luftwaffe's predecessor, the DLV. It had a long (33cm) double-edged blade and a wooden handle wrapped in blue leather with a twisted-silver-wire spiral wrap. The pommel featured a gilt 'sunwheel'-style swastika on a silver disc and the crosspiece a similar swastika on a square silver base with stylised wings emerging. The scabbard was also covered with blue leather and was suspended by plain circular loop chains attached to silvered scabbard fittings. When worn by officers and senior NCOs, a 23cm-long aluminium cord portepee was added. For lower ranks this was omitted.

When the second-pattern dagger was introduced, the wearing of the Fleigerdolch continued to be permitted by junior ranks who had earned one of the Luftwaffe's qualification badges.

A second-pattern dagger was introduced in October 1937. This form had a shorter, narrower blade and a spiralled, white cellulose handle with wire wrap. The alloy pommel was decorated with oakleaves with, in its centre, a gold, anodised swastika. The crosspiece consisted of a finely detailed stylised Luftwaffe-style flying eagle, holding a swastika in its talons. The dagger was contained in an alloy scabbard with a stippled finish and decorated with oakleaves at the lower end. Two scabbard bands held rings, to which the hanging straps, in aluminium brocade, were attached. The buckles and other metal fittings on the straps were initially in silver-coloured alloy for all ranks, but after 1942 were altered to a gilt finish for Generals. As with the previous model, it was worn with a 23cm portepee by officers and senior officer candidates, and without for other NCOs.

A Luftwaffe Feldwebel and veteran of the Condor Legion, wears the second-pattern Luftwaffe dress dagger. Note that his rank entitles him to wear the dagger with portepee in the same fashion as commissioned officers. Note also on his sleeve the trade patch for technical personnel. (*Jaques Calero*)

In both cases, more elaborate, privately purchased examples can be found with decorative blade etchings, or finely hand-crafted damascus-steel blades.

The wearing of all dress daggers was prohibited on 24 December 1944, after which date only pistols were to be carried as sidearms.

SWORDS

The first type of sword carried by Luftwaffe officers was the Fliegerschwert, or flyers' sword. Introduced in 1934, it followed the same basic style as the early dagger, with both handle and scabbard being covered in blue leather. The hilt fittings also closely

This Feldwebel of technical personnel wears the Luftwaffe Fliegerschwert, or flier's sword. Note the close similarity in design with that of the first-pattern dagger. (*Jaques Calero*)

mirrored those of the dagger. The sword had silvered metal fittings to the throat and to the chape. The throat fitting featured a metal ring either side for attaching to the blue leather hanger. Unlike its counterpart dagger, which was subsequently replaced by a more modern design, the Fliegerschwert remained in use until the general prohibition on the wearing of edged weapons as sidearms in December 1944.

Generals carried far more elaborate swords than other officers. The first pattern, introduced in 1935 was a Degen, or court sword, with long, straight, narrow blade. It featured a ball pommel, D-shaped knuckle-bow and shellguard all decorated with foliage. The handle was completely wrapped

in silver wire and had a small Luftwaffe eagle affixed. The black-leather-covered scabbard had gilded throat and chape fittings.

The second, far more attractive pattern of Luftwaffe General's sword appeared in 1937. It was also a court sword with long, straight blade and generally similar in appearance to its predecessor. The handle, however, was in white celluloid with a spiralled groove carrying a twisted-wire wrap. The ball pommel and knucklebow were similar to the earlier sword but a much larger shell guard was featured, on which was carried a large, Luftwaffe-style eagle with swastika. Once again, the scabbard was covered in black leather with gilded metal throat and chape fittings.

CHAPTER SIXTEEN

AWARDS AND DECORATIONS

The Luftwaffe, in common with the other branches of the Wehrmacht, had its own series of awards and decorations. These fall into two broad categories: qualification badges and combat awards.

QUALIFICATION BADGES

These were all introduced before the war and generally consist of a highly stylised eagle, usually grasping a swastika in its talons, combined with a wreath of oakleaves. Luftwaffe badges were generally issued in a small, square, blue leatherette-covered box with the title of the award printed in gilt Gothic letters on the lid. The lid interior was generally dark blue satin and the base covered in dark blue velvet or flock. All these awards were presented along with an award document (or Besitzzeugnis, literally a certificate of possession).

These badges were to be worn on the left breast pocket or similar position on pocket-less jackets and usually had a hinged pin fitting on the reverse, though screw-back fittings were available for those who wished to purchase them at their own expense.

Those produced were as follows:

Pilot Badge (Flugzeugführerabzeichen). Introduced in March 1936, it consisted of a matt-silvered, vertical oval wreath of oak-leaves with burnished highlights, on to which was affixed an eagle with swastika, facing forward, the eagle fitting being chemically darkened.

Observer Badge (Beobachterabzeichen). Also introduced in March 1936, this badge was worn by observers, navigators and bomb-

The Luftwaffe pilot's qualification badge, worn on the left breast by all qualified pilots. To avoid snagging of the metal badge on various straps, many elected to wear a cloth, embroidered version of the badge, permanently stitched to the uniform.

aimers. It consisted of a matt-silvered, vertical oval wreath of oakleaves with burnished highlights, on to which was affixed an eagle with swastika, facing to the right, the eagle being chemically darkened. Either two months' service in the required role, or five operational sorties, were required for its award.

Pilot/Observer Badge (Gemeinsame Flugzeugführer und Beobachterabzeichen). As for the pilot badge but a matt-gold wreath with burnished highlights and silver eagle. Introduced at the same time as the pilot and observer badge. To receive this badge the flier had to have had both pilot and observer licences for a minimum of one year.

Radio Operator/Air Gunner (Bordfunkerabzeichen). A matt-silvered, vertical wreath of oakleaves with burnished highlights and with

swastika at its base, on to which was affixed an eagle, facing left with a bundle of lightning bolts in its talons. The eagle is chemically darkened. Introduced in March 1936. To qualify, an airman had to have completed two months' operational flying or, during wartime, five operational sorties.

Qualified Air Gunner/Flight Engineer (Fliegerschützenabzeichen). As for radio operator, but with the lightning bolts removed from the eagle's talons. Introduced in June 1942.

Unqualified Air Gunner (Fliegerschützenabzeichen mit Schwarzem Krauz). As above but with the colours reversed, i.e. a darkened wreath with a silvered eagle. Ten operational sorties were required to qualify for this badge, introduced in April 1944.

The Luftwaffe Paratrooper Badge. This was not a combat badge, but was earned by completing the requisite jump training to qualify as a paratrooper.

Leutnant Gerhard Hoffmann of Jagdgeschwader 52 wears the Front Flight Clasp for fighter pilots in gold, with the special numbered pendant indicating his participation in 200 missions. (*François Saez*)

Glider Pilot (Segelflugzeugführerabzeichen). A silvered vertical wreath of oakleaves, with swastika at its base, on to which was affixed a soaring eagle, facing right. The eagle is chemically darkened. Introduced in December 1940, it was awarded to qualified glider pilots.

Retired Pilot (Fliegererinnerungsabzeichen). A silvered vertical wreath of oakleaves, encompassing an eagle perched on a rock with wings folded, the wreath with swastika at its base. Introduced in March 1936. It was intended for wear by those who had been honourably retired after fifteen years' service (four years for those who had served in the First World War), though the qualification period could be reduced for those injured in the line of duty. It was also available to paratroopers, who were classed as aircrew. This badge was not bestowed after the outbreak of war.

Paratrooper Badge (Fallschirmschützenabzeichen). A chemically darkened wreath of oakleaves on to which was affixed a diving eagle grasping a swastika in its talons. The eagle is gilded. Introduced November 1936 for all those who had successfully completed the paratrooper jump course.

All of the above pieces were qualification badges only and not earned in combat. Most types were also manufactured in embroidered form, in machine-embroidered yarn for lower ranks and hand-embroidered bullion wire for officers.

COMBAT AWARDS

In January 1941, a range of so-called 'Flight Clasps' (Frontflugspangen) was introduced. These were all of similar design, comprising a central circular wreath of laurel with a swastika at its base, from either side of which emerged a spray of oakleaves. In the central wreath was an emblem appropriate to the type of squadron, as noted below. These clasps were to be worn above the left breast pocket, or in a similar position on pocketless garments.

The clasps were initially introduced in bronze-, silver- and gold-coloured metal, for 20, 60 and 110 combat flights respectively. Subsequently, small pendants were added to the base of the central wreath to indicate

Major Johannes Wiese of 2./Jagdgeschwader 52 wears the Front Flight Clasp for fighter pilots, with winged-arrow central motif.

Leutnant Jakob Jenster of 6./Sturzkampfgeschwader 2 wears the Front Flight Clasp for bombers' crews in gold, with the pendant indicating participation in at least 300 missions.

even higher numbers of flights. Initially this consisted of a small sunburst star flanked by three laurel leaves each side. However, this pendant indicated a different number of missions for each type of clasp, e.g. for bombers it indicated 400 missions, and for fighters 300. To avoid confusion, the pendants were altered to show actual numbers in increments of 100 from 200 to 2,000, the latter being awarded only once, to Stuka ace Hans-Ulrich Rudel.

The unique version of the Ground Assault Clasp produced for Oberst Hans-Ulrich Rudel was made from precious metal and had the wreath surrounding the central motif and a small pendant with the number of missions flown (2,000), set with diamonds.

The central motif was as follows:

Short-range day-fighters	Winged arrow pointing upwards. Introduced January 1941. Originally also worn by personnel from long-range day-fighters, and air-to-ground support.
Long-range day-fighters	Winged arrow pointing downwards. Introduced May 1942.
Short-range night-fighters	Winged arrow pointing upwards, surrounding wreath black. Introduced October 1942.
Long-range night-fighters	Winged arrow pointing downwards, surrounding wreath black. Introduced October 1942.
Reconnaissance units	Eagle's head facing left. Introduced January 1941.
Transport units	Flying eagle with swastika facing right. Introduced November 1941.
Bombers	Winged bomb pointing downwards. Introduced January 1941. Originally also used by transport and glider squadrons.
Ground-attack units	Crossed swords. Introduced April 1944.

The following badges were also created for non-flying units:

Ground Combat Badge (Erdkampfabzeichen der Luftwaffe). An oval wreath of oakleaves crowned by a Luftwaffe eagle with swastika. In the centre is a mass of clouds, from which a lightning bolt emerges to strike the ground below. Instituted on 31 March 1942 and awarded to ground troops after three engagements with the enemy.

Flak War Badge (Flakkampfabzeichen der Luftwaffe). An oval wreath of oakleaves crowned by a Luftwaffe eagle with swastika. In the centre is an anti-aircraft gun, its barrel pointing to top right. Instituted on 10 January 1941 and awarded on a points basis for shooting down the requisite number of enemy aircraft.

Oberleutnant Gerhard Krems wears the Front Flight Clasp for bomber crews with the winged-bomb central motif.

The Luftwaffe Ground Combat Badge. The example at left is the standard badge, awarded after the recipient had completed three separate engagements with the enemy. In 1944, additional versions were introduced showing the number of assaults in which the recipient had participated – 25, 50, 75 or 100. It is not believed that any of these numbered awards were ever issued.

The Luftwaffe Flak War Badge. This badge was awarded on a points basis to the entire crew of a flak gun, the points being awarded for either shooting down or contributing to the shooting-down of an enemy aircraft.

The Luftwaffe's version of the Panzer Assault Badge. It was introduced very late in the war, and it is not believed that any examples of this badge were ever awarded, Luftwaffe personnel receiving instead the standard Army version.

Tank Battle Badge (Panzerkampfabzeichen der Luftwaffe). The usual oval wreath of oakleaves crowned by a Luftwaffe eagle with swastika. In the centre sits a tank, facing to the right. Instituted in silver (for armoured-vehicle crews) and black (for Panzer-grenadiers) on 3 November 1944. No records exist of awards of the actual physical badge, though awards were definitely made on paper and in individual soldiers' records. Badges were manufactured in limited numbers but may never have left the manufacturers' factories for distribution.

Sea Battle Badge (Seekampfabzeichen der Luftwaffe). An oval wreath of oakleaves crowned by a Luftwaffe eagle with swastika. In the centre is a bow view of a ship, heeled over to port. Other than a few manufacturers' test shots, it is not believed that this award ever entered volume production. The badge, instituted on 27 November 1944, would have been awarded to those who had taken part in at least three actions at sea, and would have included personnel such as those Luftwaffe crews who served on board vessels such as air-sea rescue launches, meteorological survey vessels, etc.

Close Combat Clasp (Nahkampfspange der Luftwaffe). Introduced on 3 November 1944, this award was analogous to the pre-existing Close Combat Clasp of the Army. It was to have been bestowed upon Luftwaffe personnel who had completed the requisite number of days' close-combat fighting. It was to be awarded in three grades: bronze,

silver and gold, for 15 days', 30 days' and 50 days' combat respectively. Its design followed closely that of the Front Front Flight Clasps, but without the small swastika at the base of the central circular wreath of laurel. The central motif consisted of a Luftwaffe-style eagle and swastika over a crossed bayonet and grenade. Although awards of this decoration were certainly made on paper, it is not believed that any physical examples of the award were ever bestowed, the recipients instead being handed the regular Army-pattern clasp.

Both the ground assault badge and tank assault badge of the Luftwaffe were intended to have been worn with a small, numbered box (Einsatzzahl) at the base, indicating the number of actions (25, 50, 75 or 100) in which the wearer had participated, directly equivalent to the numbered general assault and tank assault badges of the Army. However, there is no period photographic evidence showing any of these numbered badges being worn and it is likely that only a small quantity of sample strikings of each may have been manufactured.

The following additional Luftwaffe awards were also created:

The Goblet of Honour (Ehrenpokal). This award, introduced in February 1940, was given for distinguished success in the air war, and consisted of a large, 20cm-tall, handsome silver (real silver, or later a silver alloy known as 'Alpaka') goblet with a beaten finish. One side displayed the Iron Cross First Class, and the other, two eagles fighting. Around the base of the goblet stem was engraved the recipient's name and rank and the date of award. The base itself featured the inscription 'Für beseondere Leistung im Luftkrieg', or 'For Outstanding Achievements in the Air War'. This award was modelled closely on an Honour Goblet issued to fliers during the First World War.

The Salver of Honour (Ehrenschale). Analogous to the goblet, the salver was awarded to ground troops as opposed to fliers. Instituted on 15 June 1942, it consisted of a large silver salver or plate (again, real silver or Alpaka) some 28cm in diameter, in the centre of which was the personal 'Reichsmarschall' emblem of Hermann Göring, surrounded by scrolls on which were engraved the recipient's details. Around the outer edge of the salver were embossed laurel and oakleaves. Awards of the salver

ceased in December 1944, after which time it was replaced by the Honour Roll Clasp.

The Honour Roll Clasp (Ehrenblattspange der Luftwaffe). One of a series of three such clasps (the Army and Navy also had their own versions) which were worn on the ribbon of the Iron Cross. It consisted of a small (just 25mm diameter), circular wreath of oakleaves, in the centre of which was the Luftwaffe eagle and swastika. Introduced in July 1944, only a small number were actually issued and photographic evidence of its wearing is rare indeed.

The Pilot/Observer Badge with Diamonds (Gemeinsame Flugzeugführer und Beobachterabzeichen mit Brillanten). First awarded in November 1935, this honour was in the personal gift of Hermann Göring to bestow. Similar in design to the basic pilot/observer badge but far more elaborate in its execution, it featured a real gold wreath and had the eagle and swastika made from platinum and set with a total of 104 real diamonds. As well as being awarded to a number of the most successful fighter aces, it was also bestowed by Göring as a personal gift to both German and foreign dignitaries (recipients included the Reichsführer-SS, Heinrich Himmler).

Non-portable awards. A large series of non-portable awards, generally in the shape of a rectangular metal plaque, usually in bronze or steel, were also produced for award on a local level by the various Luftgaue.

THE TOP ACES

DAY-FIGHTERS

Name	Victories
Major Erich Hartmann	352
Major Gerd Barkhorn	301
Major Günther Rall	275
Oberleutnant Otto Kittel	267
Major Walter Nowotny	258
Major Wilhelm Batz	237
Major Erich Rudorffer	222
Major Heinz Baer	220
Oberst Hermann Graf	212
Major Heinrich Ehrler	209

NIGHT-FIGHTERS

Name	Victories
Major Heinz Wolfgang Schnaufer	121
Oberst Helmut Lent	110
Hauptmann Heinrich Prinz zu Sayn-Wittgenstein	83
Major Wilhelm Herget	72
Oberst Werner Streib	66
Hauptmann Manfred Meurer	65
Oberst Günther Radusch	65
Major Rudolf Schönert	64
Hauptmann Heinz Rökker	64
Major Paul Zorner	59

Gerhard 'Gerd' Barkhorn, Gruppenkommandeur of II./Jagdgeschwader 52, one of only two fighter aces to exceed a score of 300 kills. Barkhorn, an Me 109 'expert', was Germany's second-highest-scoring ace, with 301 recorded kills. He is seen here wearing the Knight's Cross with the Oakleaves and Swords clasp awarded to him on 2 March 1944 after his 250th victory. Barkhorn survived the war. (*Josef Charita*)

Jet Fighters

Name	Jet Victories
Major Heinz Baer	16
Hauptmann Franz Schall	14
Oberst Hermann Buchner	12
Major Georg-Peter Eder	12
Major Erich Rudorffer	12
Leutnant Karl Schnorrer	11

Tank Killer Aces

Name	Victories
Oberst Hans-Ulrich Rudel	519
Oberfeldwebel Anton Hubsch	120
Hauptmann Gotz Stüdemann	117
Oberfeldwebel Alois Wosnitza	104
Leutnant Jakob Jenster	100
Hauptmann Hendrock Stahl	100

Stuka Aces

Name	Missions
Oberst Hans-Ulrich Rudel	2,530
Oberfeldwebel Erwin Hentschel	1,400
Major Theodor Nordmann	1,300
Leutnant Kurt Plenzat	1,217
Oberleutnant Gustav Schubert	1,200
Hauptmann Hendrick Stahl	1,200

Zerstörer Aces

Name	Victories
Major Eduard Tratt	38
Hauptmann Werner Thierfelder	27
Hauptmann Egon Albrecht	25
Hauptmann Rolf Kaldrack	24
Major Theodor Weissenberger	23
Major Helmut Viedebantt	23

GLOSSARY OF GERMAN TERMS

Abschuss	An aerial victory.
Adjutant	Adjutant or ADC.
Alarmstart	Scramble.
Aufklärung	Reconnaissance.
Blitzkrieg	'Lightning war'. The term was coined by the Western press to describe Germany's tactics of speed. During the Polish campaign Hitler is said to have detested the term.
dicke Autos	Slang term for heavy bombers, literally 'fat cars'.
Einsatz	Mission.
Ergänzungsgruppe	Advanced training group.
Erprobungsgruppe	Operational test group.
Experte	An 'ace' pilot.
Flak	Anti-aircraft gun (**Fl**ieger **A**bwehr **K**anone).
Fliegerdivision	Air division – a higher command containing several types of flying units.
Fliegerführer	Aircraft command/control unit or its commander. In the case of isolated theatres, the theatre air commander.
Fliegerkorps	Air corps – a higher command, containing several Fliegerdivisionen.
Flugzeug	Aircraft.
Flugzeugführer	Pilot.
Freie Jagd	A fighter sweep without ground control, literally 'free hunt'.
General der Jagdflieger	General of the Fighter Arms – a staff position in the RLM. Werner Mölders and Adolf Galland were the most prominent holders of this position.
Geschwader	The largest mobile, homogeneous Luftwaffe flying unit.
Geschwaderkommodore	Wing commodore, usually a Major, Oberstleutnant, or Oberst in rank.
Gruppe	Basic Luftwaffe combat unit.
Gruppenkommandeur	Group commander, usually a Hauptmann, Major or Oberstleutnant in rank.
Herausschuss	To inflict sufficient damage on an enemy bomber to force it to break formation, literally 'shoot out'.

Himmelfahrtskommando	Suicide mission, literally 'mission to heaven'.
'Horrido!'	Hunter's call used by fighter pilots, equivalent to 'Tally Ho!'
Jabos	Fighter-bombers (**Jagdbo**mber).
Jagdflieger	Fighter pilot.
Jagdfliegerführer	Fighter command and control unit.
Jagdgeschwader (JG)	Fighter wing, commanding three or four Gruppen.
Jagdgruppe	Fighter group, containing a number of Staffeln.
Jagdkorps	Fighter corps.
Jagdstaffel	Fighter squadron, usually of three Schwärme.
Jagdverband	The term was only used for JV44, the Gruppe of jet fighters commanded by General Adolf Galland in 1945.
Jagdwaffe	Fighter arm or fighter force.
Kampfgeschwader	Bomber wing.
Kette	Flight of three aircraft.
Kfz	Kraftfahrzeuge – Motor Transport Vehicle.
Kommandeur	'Commander' – a Gruppe command position rather than a rank.
Kommodore	'Commodore' – a Geschwader command position rather than a rank.
Lehrgeschwader	Training wing.
Luftflotte	'Air fleet' – corresponded to a numbered American air force.
Luftwaffe	'Air force' – refers to German Air Force.
Luftwaffenkommando	Air command – a small or downgraded Luftflotte.
Oberbefehlshaber der Luftwaffe	C-in-C Air Force.
Oberkommando des Luftwaffe	Air Force High Command.
Reichsluftfahrtministerium (RLM)	German Air Ministry.
Reichsverteidigung	Organisation responsible for the air defence of Germany.
Rotte	Tactical element of two aircraft.
Rottenführer	Leader of an element of two aircraft.
Schnellkampfgeschwader	Fast-bomber wing.
Schwarm	Flight of four aircraft (pl. Schwärme).
Stab	Staff.
Stabsschwarm	Staff flight.
Staffel	Squadron.
Staffelführer	Squadron leader (temporary or probationary).
Staffelkapitän	Squadron leader – usually a Leutnant, Oberleutnant or Hauptmann.
Stukageschwader	Dive-bomber wing.
Sturzkampfflugzeng	Dive bomber (Stuka).
Zerstörer	'Destroyer' (heavy fighter) – Bf 110 or Me 410 twin-engined fighter.
Zerstörergeschwader (ZG)	Heavy-fighter wing.

BIBLIOGRAPHY

Angolia, J.R. and Schlicht, Adolf. *Uniforms and Traditions of the Luftwaffe*, vol. 1, San Josc, USA, R. James Bender Publishing, 1996

——. *Uniforms and Traditions of the Luftwaffe*, vol. 2, San Jose, USA, R. James Bender Publishing, 1997

——. *Uniforms and Traditions of the Luftwaffe*, vol. 3, San Jose, USA, R. James Bender Publishing, 1999

Angolia, John R. *For Führer & Fatherland: Military Awards of the Third Reich*, San Jose, USA, James Bender Publishing, 1979

Brütting, Georg. *Das waren die deutschen Kampfflieger Asse 1939–1945*, Stuttgart, Motorbuch Verlag, 1986

Dabrowski, H.-P. *Focke Wulf Fw200 Condor*, Friedberg, Podzun Pallas Verlag, 1991

David, Brian L. *Uniforms and Insignia of the Luftwaffe*, vol. 1, London, Arms & Armour Press, 1991

——. *Uniforms and Insignia of the Luftwaffe*, vol. 2, London, Arms & Armour Press, 1995

Dierich, Wolfgang. *Die Verbände der Luftwaffe*, Zweibrücken, Verlag Heinz Nickel, 1993

Elbied, Anis and Jouineau, Andre. *Messerschmitt Me109*, vol. 1, 1936–1942, Paris, Histoire & Collections, 2001

——. *Messerschmitt Me109*, vol. 2, 1942–1945, Paris, Histoire & Collections, 2002

Feuerstein, Erwin. *Mit und ohne Ritterkreuz*, Stuttgart, Motorbuch Verlag, 1974

Leonard, Herbert and Jouineau, Andre. *Junkers Ju87 From 1936 to 1945*, Paris, Histoire & Collections, 2003

Michulec, Robert and Caldwell, Donald. *Adolf Galland*, Sandomierz, Stratus, 2003

Murray, Williamson. *The Luftwaffe 1933–1945*, Royston, Eagle Editions, 2003

Regnat, Karl-Heinz. *Heinkel He111*, Bonn, Bernard & Graefe Verlag, 2000

Roba, Jean-Louis and Pegg, Martin. *Jagdwaffe – The Mediterranean 1942–1943*, Surrey, Classic Publications, 2003

Scutts, Jerry. *Bf109 Aces of North Africa and the Mediterranean*, Oxford, Osprey Publishing, 1994

Toliver, Raymond F. and Constable, Trevor J. *Fighter Aces of the Luftwaffe*, Altglen, Schiffer Publishing, 1996

Williamson, Gordon. *Aces of the Reich*, London, Arms & Armour Press, 1989

——. *World War II German Women's Auxiliary Services*, Oxford, Osprey Publishing, 2003

Wittmann, Thomas T. *Exploring the Dress Daggers of the German Luftwaffe*, Pennsylvania, Alcom Printing Group, 1997

INDEX